For Robert

Contents

Acknowledgments

THOMAS JEFFERSON ONCE said that "Nothing can stop the man with the right mental attitude from achieving his goal; nothing on earth can help the man with the wrong mental attitude." Special thanks are in order to Peter Miller for helping me attain this goal and whose boundless energy and consistently positive attitude are contagious.

Many thanks to Linda Gray and Dawn Barker at NTC/Contemporary Publishing for their focus and dedication to this project and to Carmen Motes in Dallas for a notable measure of patience during the reviewing process.

Thank you to my families, both old and new, for the unconditional love, support, and good humor that make each day brighter than the one before.

Introduction

THE PSYCHIC WAS right. Skeptic that I was, I tugged at my mother's arm and persuaded her to sit down in the grass while the psychic predicted my future. I was fifteen and we were vacationing in California when we decided to take a stroll down Venice Beach one brilliant afternoon. We sat with the woman in the long batik dress, and she clasped my hands in hers as she closed her eyes in deep concentration. After a minute or so her eyes opened abruptly, her face illuminated with an expression of wonder, as if something very important had come to her quite suddenly. "I see you have brothers, one who is a troublemaker like you and one who is quiet, more even-tempered." I scoffed at the ridiculous observation and rolled my eyes, for I knew that I was an only child! Fifteen years later, I learned that the psychic had been correct all along.

This book is for the thousands whose lives remain incomplete without the knowledge of their beginnings. If you are searching for a parent, sibling, or other family member, this book will encourage you to take the steps necessary to gain the information you need to complete this part of your life. You are now one step closer to solving the mystery. If you are someone carrying the burden of a family secret, perhaps you will realize the importance of revealing it and how doing so can positively affect someone's life.

My own search for my father opened up a whole new world and blessed me with an entire new family with which I have experienced major life events. My grandmother's funeral, the death of my siblings' mother whom I had grown to love as my own, and a reunion, on the coast of Maine, of a family I hadn't known existed for twenty-eight years—all of these things have changed me forever and created a life separated into two distinct halves: the life before I found them and the life that began the day I picked up the telephone and called the family I thought belonged to me.

Life has a way of doing what it wishes with each of us, dictated by chance and circumstance and, when we're lucky, our own desires. Since finding my own family, I have worked with others in their quests to find missing loved ones. I often hear the same stories over and over, the same emptiness and confusion and fear of the unknown. Most have the desire to find their missing family members, but they don't know where to begin. Consider this book the starting point, the catalyst that will allow you to open doors and discover a whole new world. Life is too short to hesitate.

CHAPTER ONE

The Search

I often wonder where you are,
I feel your presence from afar
Why can't she tell me? It's in her eyes,
Those silent thoughts, I do despise

When were you there, why did you leave?
These wandering thoughts I can't believe
How did you feel? What did you say?
What could make you go away?

ANYONE WHO KNOWS where he or she came from cannot imagine the *incompleteness* of not knowing. One out of every fifty Americans is adopted, and countless others come from broken homes as a result of divorce. For centuries adoptions, affairs, and unplanned pregnancies resulted in thousands of displaced children, and the displacement continues today, as evidenced by the alarming number of innocent souls lingering in our nation's foster-care system. The American Public Welfare Association estimates that more than five hundred thousand children each year will spend time in the system, existing in emotional purgatory while the courts decide their fates. A natural evolution of the fragmented development of society, foster care is just one component in the complex formula of familial separation. Our society has evolved into one of fragmented family relationships, with parents separated from their children and siblings pulled apart to grow up in different households. Family history for these children becomes whatever their parents have chosen to share with them.

Most of us will have to ponder for only a brief moment before we are able to draw a mental picture of those in our immediate social or work environments who have been divorced or suffered broken relationships where children were involved. Multiply the number of people you know by thousands, and you have a somewhat accurate representation of our world. This progression has created families within families, some who have happily adjusted and integrated, and others whose circumstances have led to the breakdown and loss of family ties.

Many children who are raised by just one biological parent are lacking information about the other. Ordinarily, this is due to an emotional insulation of sorts, whereby the existing parent subconsciously chooses to ignore the absence of the other parent in his or her life, insulating the child from the truth, whatever it may be, and himself or herself from a complicated conversation. The parent often assumes that if the child has not asked, the child is not interested, and the topic of the other parent remains submerged like a shark prowling the ocean's floor. This type of "issue isolation" is quite common in adoptive households, even when the adoptive parents have resolved to remain open regarding the child's birth parents. The child does not open the Pandora's box, and the parent does not either, so the issue of birth parents becomes isolated, a taboo subject that no one acknowledges as having any significance. If a child has had limited contact with an absentee parent or if that child knows nothing about his heritage, he is likely to harbor confusion about his own identity. The past is a window to the future, and, as fundamental as it seems, identity is the cornerstone by which we live and breathe, as crucial to human development as the molecular structure of the cells that make us human.

Discovering one's identity is a lifelong journey in which we travel through the phases of life like a nomadic explorer roaming the solar system. We are in orbit, similar to the planets themselves, and are continually picking up patterns of thought, impulses, and beliefs along the way. Although some people seem enveloped by their sense of being much sooner than others, none of us emerge from the embryonic state to a fully advanced, evolved person overnight. We tend to draw on internal and external experiences that help formulate our opinions and future actions. We compare ourselves to our peers and seek guidance from our predecessors. We may be totally oblivious to how our identity is shaping up until the day we come to the realization that this is who we are, and this is what we believe. With identity comes direction, a solid idea of where we want to go. This realization hits some people like a rocket propelled from the sky, jolting them out of bed in the middle of the night. For most, however, the realization is a slow progression.

I have a friend who literally woke up one day determined that her destiny was to be an interior decorator. Her current job was in medical sales, but she called me, excited and out of breath, with the news that she had promptly enrolled in a decorating class that very same day. I was supportive of her, for I couldn't decorate the inside of a box, and she possessed the uncanny skill of transforming even the smallest space into a warm, elegant chamber. Two weeks later she phoned me with the news that she had quit the class and was sending a videotape of herself to a television station in New York, with the goal of becoming a broadcaster. She envisioned herself as the next Barbara Walters, interviewing celebrities in a suit from a Chanel wardrobe. That career choice didn't pan out either, and she has since worked in multilevel marketing, drawn up papers to buy a business, and applied for law school; none of these goals were accomplished. She has no shortage of energy or enthusiasm, but she is lacking a solid identity, which permeates all other areas of her life. Her relationships, goals, and career choices are all affected because she has not yet found a sense of who she is. She is terminally insecure about her appearance, her actions, her effect on others, and how she will live the rest of her life.

Identity is more than just knowing what your personal goals and predispositions are. It is far more than the information contained within your leather-bound day planner or the daily activities that guide your life. Identity is not defined by our careers, or even by the relationships we treasure. Identity is the internal evolution of self consisting of many things: genetic makeup, personality traits, characteristics, emotions, and even our sexuality.

For some it just comes naturally, but for others identity is always just beyond a pane of glass. For children without a link to the past, identity becomes even harder to attain. There is no way to view the identities of those who came before them, no confirmation of self, and missing pieces of medical or family history. Much like a tree without roots, someone with no foundation cannot grow. These children are out there, lost souls searching for the knowledge that will solve the mystery of their lives. As adults with a need to reconcile the past, they yearn to find the family members they have been detached from, yet most will put off the search for years until the mystery of the unknown becomes too large to ignore.

It is difficult to understand but easy to see how family secrets remain entwined in our lives for years. Life is complex, and relationships even more so, and difficult issues become easier to ignore than to explain. Mothers conceal the truth about a child's father, afraid of the consequences of acknowledging an affair. Teenagers get pregnant and choose adoption. Husbands keep the secret of children they had long ago from the wives with whom they have built new lives.

The possibilities of family fragmentation are endless and occur every single day. There are an estimated five million adoptees in the United States, and a record number of children fall into the category of "other," meaning children who were the products of divorces or affairs or were separated from members of their biological families.

The issues facing these children can be difficult to discern by the parents raising them, but they often stay with the adopted children into adulthood. Although some may feel completely free of internal conflict, many struggle with issues surrounding a parent's absence. Post-adoption counselors who have worked with adult adoptees and adopted children report that the most common emotions adoptees experience are:

- Lack of identity

- Intense curiosity about their genetic makeup

- Weak self-esteem linked to feelings of abandonment

- The need to gain control of their life by gathering facts about their past

The depth of emotion an adoptee faces will vary, depending upon her individual situation. Feelings of uncertainty, fear of abandonment, and identity issues are likely to be far more prevalent in adults who have no facts at all about their parentage or family history. If an adult adoptee has known since childhood that she was adopted, yet her adoptive parents did not openly communicate the reasons behind why she was given up for adoption, the questions can linger. An adopted child will usually begin the journey of exploration by asking questions of the parent, searching for answers that she may be too young to understand. Knowing this, the parent often delays the discussion, unable to articulate the situation in terms that the child will comprehend. When understanding does not come, the child is forced to live silently with the questions regarding her birth, searching for answers from within instead of searching externally. Adoptees ask themselves the difficult questions, such as, where did I come from, or why did my mother leave me? They often arrive at the conclusion that they were unwanted or abandoned, which is usually not the case at all.

In times past, adoption was a subject not openly discussed, much like abortion, sex, and other controversial topics that everyone seems to have an opinion on today. Extreme measures were taken to protect the mother from shame and embarrassment, and adoptions were conducted quickly and discreetly. It was not uncommon for the adopted child's birth date to be altered by a day or two to prevent future identification of the child's actual identity and in turn to prevent the child from learning the identity of his or her birth mother. Similar steps were also taken on behalf of the adoptive parents, and records were altered and names changed to protect them from future intrusion by a birth mother. Sound like a prehistoric process? Many of these same tactics are utilized today in private adoptions.

This would explain the difficult process in obtaining accurate birth records and the negative perceptions that continue to infiltrate many adoption agencies and hospitals throughout the country. Some of these institutions have been around for years and still employ the same procedures and "tell nothing" philosophies. In the sixties, a pregnant teenager commonly would be sent away to a home for unwed mothers before the first signs of her pregnancy began to show. Away from the support of her family and friends, the girl would be left with strangers until her child was delivered and placed for adoption. Many of these mothers report feeling as if they had no choice but to adopt out their babies, and most were far too young to make a decision of that magnitude.

Although adoption is widely accepted and talked about today, the shame in the adoption process is still present for many who are involved. Though it may be subtle, the shame can begin with conception and continue throughout the adopted child's life. Like a microscopic tumor that goes undetected for years, shame is often the invisible thread that ties the biological parent and child together, forever. The mother lives with an unplanned pregnancy for nine months until the pregnancy is behind her. If she has become pregnant by a man with whom she has no future, or is a child herself, her feelings of shame can be even worse. In addition, a biological mother may feel guilt because of the decision to place the child for adoption or because of her inability to care for the child herself. Furthermore, as the infant develops and grows into a feeling, thinking adult, the shame that plagued the mother may also stay with the child. Issues of shame that are not recognized in adulthood will remain within the individual. The best gift that parents, adoptive or otherwise, can give to their children is the gift of truth, which is paramount to unleashing the confusion.

Laura, a fifteen-year-old adoptee, was an above-average student and a happy child by all outward appearances. Her adoptive parents had given her everything she asked for and more, yet inwardly, Laura suffered from intense feelings of being unwanted and unloved. She expressed these feelings by living a sexually promiscuous lifestyle, in her own way yearning for acceptance. When she became pregnant unexpectedly, her parents placed her in counseling, where she verbalized her feelings of abandonment associated with her adoption. No one had linked her behavior to being adopted, but the theme of isolation surfaced as Laura talked about her desires to know why her birth parents had not wanted her. She had never expressed this sense of isolation to her adoptive parents, and they may never have known. When they told her the truth—that her birth mother had been just thirteen when she got pregnant—Laura's self-esteem increased drastically. She could now rationalize the events behind her adoption and put it to rest.

This scenario is repeated over and over due to the lack of communication about family separation. Absence of understanding creates conflicting emotions within the adopted child, who may even have been subjected to negative circumstances prior to the adoption. Many times children who have been adopted after infancy have been in the foster-care system for years prior to adoption, awaiting a set of parents to love and care for them. Although foster care is a necessary and beneficial solution for many children, countless others have been moved from home to home or placed back in the care of the birth parents, only to be removed from the household again. Seventy percent of foster children enter the system as a result of neglect or abuse stemming from a parent's drug addiction, criminal activity, or just plain bad parenting. These children learn at an early age to adapt to change—change that is not always positive and not always to their advantage.

Currently, the system protects the rights of the biological parent, and the adopted child's rights seem secondary. For a system that strives to pursue the best interests of the child, there continue to be deficiencies. A mother whose child has been placed in the care of a foster parent due to substance abuse is often required to undergo drug-abuse counseling before she can regain custody of her child. While this solution gives the mother the chance to recover and regain her life, the cycle may have been repeated time and again, resulting in the child being given back, then taken away again, then placed once more back into the care of the birth mother. The child is the object of a system tug-of-war, pulled back and forth and frayed in the process.

Statistics show that the number of children in state-run systems is increasing thirty-three times faster than the entire United States population of children as a whole. Sadly, one in ten children in foster care will remain without a real home on average longer than seven years. The odds of a child's being drastically affected by living in this state of limbo are great, and legions end up as adults on welfare, with limited professional work skills. The American Civil Liberties Union confirms that approximately 40 percent of all foster children turn to welfare upon departing the state-run foster-care system.

A child is dependent upon the adults around him for his existence, yet when that child reaches the age of maturity he is classified as an adult, free to go as he pleases, to make the decisions concerning his life that have heretofore been made for him. Imagine being a baby bird raised from infancy in a cage, hand-fed by different faces who come and go each day. The cage is the only thing the bird knows until one day the cage door opens and the bird is set free to fly away, into the wild. Is the bird happy to be set free, or does it stay huddled inside the cage, afraid to spread its wings? Perhaps both. The bird, like the adult adopted child, faces a myriad of questions, such as, where do I go? Who will guide me? What comes next? And, eventually, what about my past?

Those who are in search of the past are far, and near. They are the educated, uneducated, conservative, and liberal alike. They are all races and religions and are your neighbors, friends, teachers, and mentors. Some who search have lived carefree lives and start looking into their past for no reason other than curiosity. Others search specifically for medical information or to confront any issues surrounding the separation that knowledge of the past could help solve. You could be searching because of any one of these reasons or a combination of all of them. Those who are searching are reaching for hope—the hope that they might feel connected again or the hope that they will find the answers to ingrained questions about their past. Who searches for a family? A searcher may have led a charmed and wealthy life, a fulfilling life, or a life filled with abuse and neglect. There is no singular portrait of the searcher; there is instead a collage of individuals searching the world over for someone they knew or wish to know, in order to know themselves.

The adoption search effort is undisputedly the most organized search, due to the studies and recent exchange of information between adult adoptees, their adoptive parents, and birth parents across the nation. Adult adoptees who have searched for their parents have often wondered about them since childhood. Even if these adoptees were raised in loving homes, their need existed to know more about their biological parents, especially if they knew nothing at all.

The range of emotions that adopted children face include feelings of anger, bouts of depression, and the feeling of being forgotten by the birth parent or discarded completely. In addition, an adopted child may harbor an unusual lack of trust, unable to trust anyone who enters her life.

A child who acts out of anger, responding irrationally to minor situations, may be doing so because of underlying struggles. Rebelling can be a reaction to what the child perceives to be rejection, especially if the child has been denied something. Although many parents will identify this type of behavior in their child, it is the consistently inappropriate behaviors that could be characteristic of a child dealing with unresolved issues. Even so, we must be cautious not to overanalyze, because every one of us expresses emotions of anger, sadness, and rejection. The key to understanding is awareness and communication regarding the issues specific to the adopted child.

Attend an adult adoption support group and two pervasive emotions will reveal themselves: rejection and the feeling of being forgotten. Both are commonalities felt within children who have no knowledge of one or more birth parent. The feelings become apparent in a variety of ways, manifesting in the actions of the adopted child or in his or her adult relationships. The adopted child may develop into an overachieving adult, a perfectionist striving to keep everyone happy. By doing this, the adoptee attempts to avoid abandonment again. Even more common is the adult adoptee who withdraws from personal relationships at the first signs of trouble, unable to focus on working through the problem. The desire to leave is linked to the fear of being left first. Emotional barriers are constructed to prevent the intrusion of hurt and negative emotion. If feelings of abandonment remain below the surface, they become a lifelong companion to the adult, like a parasite that subsists in the skin of an animal.

Studies canvassing family separation and adoption issues have led psychologists to document life and personality traits shared by those who have searched for family members. You may or may not see yourself in some of them.

- A portrayal of confidence but inner feelings of insecurity, especially when it comes to relationships

- A tendency to cling to the object of your affections, afraid that he or she will leave

- A tendency to leave a relationship at the first sign of things going wrong, before you are left or abandoned by the other person

- The inability to maintain intimate relationships for any length of time

- Aggression; rage; escaping with drugs or alcohol

- Uneasiness about your medical history; curiosity about family diseases and genetic makeup

- Feelings of isolation and loneliness, like you don't fit in with the rest of your family

- Black-and-white thinking—no gray area and no room for deviation. Something either is or isn't. This is particularly applicable in the areas of truth, trust, and honesty

- Ambivalence toward parents

- Feelings of shame and guilt related to the feeling of being someone who was given away

- Feelings of anger toward birth parents or adoptive parents, then subsequent guilt about the anger

- Feeling out of control and displaying combative behavior

- Learning disabilities or difficulty remaining focused on one thing for long periods of time

An adult can experience one or more of these things without realizing their root cause, an awareness that may come only after a search for family has been completed. Fortunately, we live in a nation that welcomes the analysis of ourselves, and we are far more advanced in many ways than our ancestors. Seeking assistance for the things that ail us is not an anomaly, and both public and private assistance exists for those with family separation issues.

Carol Demuth, an adult adoptee and the author of *Courageous Blessing*, a book for adoptive parents, recognizes that adoptees have special issues that need to be addressed, but she feels that they should not be made to think that they are victims of their circumstance. "Sure, we have issues like low self-esteem, but so does everyone else in life," she explains. Carol became a social worker as a result of her interest in the dynamics of adoption, and she has worked with several adult adoptees who have even experienced marital difficulties linked to their feelings about themselves. If an adoptee has not found his or her identity, problems can arise. "When they do, they relate differently to the other person. I've seen many marriages dissolve because of it. Some people write off searching as just curiosity, but there is so much more than that; the depths of desire for connection are stronger than most people realize because as an adoptee, you feel totally removed from the chain of life, and disconnected in many ways."

This disconnection is quite frequently experienced by adoptees who have no explanation for the differences in appearance between themselves and their adoptive families. Though physical attributes may seem like a minor part of who we are, the need to have them mirrored by those around you can affect the development of self-esteem. Questions regarding ourselves can lead to insecurities, even if they are minor. Consider the statement we've all heard before: *we are our own worst critics.* A beautiful model can agonize over an insignificant imperfection—a mole, prominent lips, a feature that everyone else sees as beautiful. We all look in the mirror and see things every morning that no one else notices. Think of your weakest feature. A large nose, a ruddy complexion, or a fading hairline is something that causes many to pursue methods to conceal or repair what they perceive to be a physical flaw. Imagine having this so-called imperfection while no one else around you does. Imagine questioning yourself, your appearance, and your actions continually, because they do not mirror those around you.

Communication about an adopted child's birth, family history, and biological parents can clear the way, helping to establish the foundation that is missing for the child or adult. The realization that adoptees were not unwanted, discarded, or forgotten is sometimes all it takes. Sorting through this particular issue is extremely important in developing a healthy sense of self-esteem, which may have been eroded subconsciously.

Several adoption centers now include mandatory adoption counseling as a prerequisite for adoptive parents wishing to adopt a child. Counseling includes discussion on communication and the questions they will be challenged with as their adopted child becomes more curious. Progressive adoption centers even provide triad seminars whereby prospective adoptive parents can interact with birth parents, adoptive parents, and adult adoptees. This interaction promotes a freely flowing river of communication.

Some adoptive parents have very open relationships with their child's birth parents and keep history files which include letters, photographs, and genetic information that can be shared with the child after he or she reaches maturity. Remarkably, some adoptive parents today interact with a birth parent—usually the birth mother—on a regular basis, inviting the parent to dinner, birthday celebrations for the child, and other significant events. While this degree of openness is not comfortable or even practical for everyone, any glimpse into the past will help adopted children become more connected with their beginnings and, consequently, themselves.

"My wife and I are prepared for the day our child asks about his birth parents," explains John, an adoptive father from Long Island. "It was a private adoption, but we created a file that includes photographs, postcards, and letters from the birth mother, and even a family lineage that dates back to the Revolutionary War." John and his wife were fortunate enough to be present at the birth of their adopted child and to obtain knowledge about the birth mother that they will one day share with their adopted son. "We plan on being very open with him, when the time is right. Even now, when we pass the hospital where he was born, he knows that that's where he came from—that Mommy and Daddy went there to get him because Mommy had a broken tummy so another mommy had him in hers."

Adoption and family separation are not something that occurs one day, then goes away. When a child is separated from a biological parent, whether through adoption or divorce or by state intervention, the journey to find answers becomes a lifelong excursion for the child. Indeed, the number of people who are currently searching for a missing family member is astonishing. One national search firm reportedly receives fifteen thousand calls every week from those who are searching for missing loved ones. *Fifteen thousand*, and that's just one organization. That firm reports that the callers who phone in and leave messages are looking for friends, parents, siblings, and children, and most of them are connected to adoption in some shape or form. The search effort is massive, particularly when you consider that the majority of those searching for someone wait years before beginning. How many people are out there who haven't yet begun to search?

Those who are searching for a biological parent have struggled for an eternity with the mystery of unanswered questions. They have lived through successes and tragedies, graduations, marriages, and children, and they have experienced them all without every piece of their biological puzzle. Chances are they still have contact with someone who raised them, whether a foster parent, adoptive parent, or legal guardian, yet they still have a compelling need to search.

If the adult adoptee can successfully reconcile his past, issues such as lack of trust will slowly disappear. Trust is a common ingredient lacking in those who search, as it weaves its way into a child's heart, often causing attachment disorders that make it difficult for him to maintain long-lasting relationships. An adult who has never had a constant mentor or parent, for instance, may not know how to be one.

Someone who has always felt the desire to search for a biological parent has an infinite list of questions traveling through her mind. She lives each day with these questions, yet delays her search for years, not knowing where or how to begin. Oftentimes adoptees are adults when they learn the truth behind their beginnings, and the need to find their birth parents is immediate and consuming.

I recently met with someone who learned at the age of forty that the father who raised her is not really her biological father. While it might seem an unusual occurrence, since she first told me about it I've actually heard this same story repeated by others. The only indication that this woman ever had of this was many years ago, when she and her sister found an official-looking document that their mother immediately snatched out of their hands. Their mother scolded them and told them both to never mention it again. The mystery of that moment was unraveled when their mother died and they learned that the girls had different fathers. The girls are really only half-sisters, and one of them does not know who her biological father is. She suspects that the document was her original birth certificate, with her biological father's name imprinted on it. Now, in the middle of her life, she finds herself consumed with questions, yet she isn't quite sure what to do because the father who raised her is still alive and is unaware of the truth. He does not know that his daughter is really someone else's biological child.

This same situation could exist a million times over, without anyone ever being aware of it. The most common scenario of adults searching for their biological families is of adult adoptees searching for a father. Due to the high incidence of divorce and teen pregnancies, many children are raised from infancy without a father. The next most common search is an adult adoptee's search for a birth mother, followed by a search for a sibling. Some of those who search focus on finding lost loves in hopes of rekindling a romance. The search process itself is a voyage revolving around the heart and the search for a peace that can only come from within.

Regardless of what you are searching for, the basic principles and procedures are the same, as is the assortment of feelings behind the search. The element of the search that will have the most impact on how you handle your emotions throughout will be your ally, a friend or loved one who will support you through the flurry of emotions that comes with the search itself. If there is someone close to you who already knows about your situation, that person might be the one who will best understand it. If your ally is your spouse or significant other, remember that he or she can try to understand what you're going through, but it will be hard for someone else to truly understand everything. Unless they themselves have been in the same situation, it will be difficult for others to empathize completely. You'll be on your own most of the time as you pursue this very important goal, but your ally will be someone with whom you can share your successes and, most important, your frustrations.

A surprisingly large number of people begin searching without an ally, keeping their search a secret from spouses and friends. This is how they have been conditioned to handle this subject in their life, and this secrecy creates a barrier that will protect them from further shame if they are rejected by their birth family. A searcher may be ashamed to admit she is in need of this information to move forward with her life, or she may be afraid of the opinions of others. Without an ally, searchers have no one to share things with, and their perceptions of the events that occur can be skewed.

Like many who keep their most personal emotions to themselves, I, too, kept everything inside as I wondered silently about my father, whom I had never known. I kept my desire to search inside as a child, after encountering resistance to my questions about him, and I continued keeping it inside as I grew. When I was ten or so, I began to define my feelings on paper, which I kept confined to a small leather-bound writing journal that I hid in my room. It was not until fifteen years later, after my search was over, that I discovered my best friend had read it and, of course, not wanting to reveal herself, had kept quiet about it. When I called to tell her that I had found my family, she was ecstatic, and the following week I received this letter.

9/22 12 A.M.

Tammy Lynn,

It has been a while since I have written you. I am so compelled now by the story you have told me, it has left me mentally giddy. I cannot sleep at this moment. I just completed a search for the poem you wrote.

I remember the first time that I ever read it, I was on my way to Tallahassee from Miami and had pre-arranged to stay in your apartment in Gainesville for the night. When I arrived I was tired and looking for something to read. I found some of your poems. Many were comical, however this one moved me to tears. As your best friend, reading this poem was the first glimpse I had of your need to reconcile the past. I am copying this over because the original is hardly legible.

Tam, I do not know when you wrote this, but I read it in 1986. Shortly after, I was inspired to write a poem from my perspective, which I am xeroxing and sending you. I am happy your soul is finally at rest.

All my love and best wishes,
Denise

The following is an excerpt of the poem she wrote from her perspective as an outsider who understood and supported my need to know.

Beautiful Child, how have you come to be?
Surely a mother and father gave you to me.
What can they be like to provide such a friend?
Your genes must be royal from
beginning to end.

It's important to have a close network of friends or even just one supportive person throughout the seek-and-find process. Mine came in the form of many supportive confidants, but only after my search had already been completed. I chose to go it alone, as I had been taught to do all my life, and I did not tell anyone about the search until it was over. I simply did not want to answer questions from others when I had enough of my own that remained unanswered.

Others who have searched for someone have had support from the very beginning. I've even talked with adoptive parents who have helped their adopted child instigate the search process. Everyone's situation will differ, yet the desired outcome is the same. The goal of finding a missing family member is meaningful to anyone who desires it, and a significant life event to those who achieve it.

A search that requires more than just your own individual resources and perseverance is a search for someone missing due to suspicious circumstances. If you are searching for a missing child or for an adult who has disappeared suddenly, there are very specific legal avenues for you to take to increase your chances of finding him or her. A missing person differs greatly from someone who is being sought truly for the purpose of making a biological or emotional connection. The person searching for a birth mother, father, sibling, or child is searching for someone who is not really missing; they are just lost to the searcher. Those being sought after are actually interacting with others, somewhere in the world, unless they have died.

A missing adult or child who has disappeared can be traced legally and entered into the FBI criminal database. Contact your local law-enforcement authorities as soon as possible for more details. Abduction of children and adults is a sad and, unfortunately, common occurrence in every part of the United States. A network of professionals armed with information and techniques in locating missing children is available.

Those in search of a biological connection are generally seeking connection with someone in the immediate birth circle, perhaps someone with whom they will have an ongoing intimate bond. If you are searching for a parent, a child, or siblings and do not know the circumstances surrounding your separation from them, chances are you have lived with a surge of different emotions that can be linked back to this one unknown. If you have bits of trivia about the circumstances that led to your separation, you are undoubtedly anxious to fill in the blanks.

Traditionally, it was thought that only the child experienced issues of separation and abandonment. However, we now know that the biological parents also experience strong emotions that can stay with them for a lifetime. In the adoption circle, where studies have allowed for the compilation of statistical data on the psychological effects of adoption, it has been validated time and again that each of the three members of the adoption triangle experiences similar outcomes and emotions that stem from the adoption experience. These emotions are very real, and understanding them is important before launching a search.

The adoption triad is composed of the three parties involved in any adoption: the birth parents (B parents), adoptive parents (A parents), and adoptive child. Every member of the triad is like an individual branch of one tree, seemingly independent of each other, yet reliant on the roots that bind them together. Those in adoption circles refer to the triad as one entity, although each of the three parties has independent issues associated with the adoption enterprise. Even birth parents have specific commonalties and feelings after they have relinquished a child, and what birth mothers feel will vary from what birth fathers experience. A birth mother often feels an immediate loss, a loss that results when the infant she has carried in her womb for nine months is taken away. Other birth mothers may not feel the loss until years later, when memories are triggered by something such as the child's birth date or the date of its relinquishment. These dates can become mile markers, each one marking another year on the highway of the life of the child. It is also common for a biological mother to worry that her child has died or that it has not been taken care of properly—all things that are beyond her control. For some, feelings of guilt arrive years after the decision was made to give the child away, and they may try to overcompensate for this loss by becoming a mother again. A birth mother might raise numerous children or go to the other end of the spectrum and have none at all. Oftentimes a biological mother will ignore that the birth of her child ever happened, in an attempt to keep the past at bay. For this reason she may naturally reject anyone who reminds her of it, including the child who has searched for her.

Although the birth father's role in adoption has traditionally been secondary, the emotions he faces are unique and just as deep. A father may not be present at all during the child's relinquishment, because he may think he does not have a choice in the process. This scenario is reported frequently by older men who had given up a child in their youth.

The birth mother's parents were quite often the ones making the decision to adopt the child out, causing the biological father to feel insignificant and sometimes cutting him out of the process completely. Just as important to note, however, is that some fathers and mothers alike simply do not want the responsibility of raising a child. The reality is that there are birth fathers who will not acknowledge their parentage, refusing any involvement in the adopted child's life. Many of them will recall only blurry, unclear memories about the period around which the child was born.

As adoptive parents become educated on the special needs of their adopted child, it becomes easier to address these needs. The adoptive parent can turn to pre-adoption counseling seminars, as well as post-adoption counseling that will assist both parent and child long after placement. Seminars are conducted by birth parents, adoptees, and adoptive parents in virtually every part of the nation, with the goal of educating everyone who has a vested interest in adoption on the issues involved.

In open adoptions, honesty is encouraged, setting the groundwork for a healthy relationship between parent and child. Unfortunately, it is less likely that the other categories of those in search—adults who were products of teenage pregnancies, unwed unions, or divorce and familial separation—will have access to as much information as an adoptee. In adoption circles it is often said that adoptees suffer a primal wound, the explanation being that the emotion behind adoption is worse than suffering a death or divorce because it is a wound of loss, abandonment, and rejection that is not recognized by society in general. Many adoptees were told that they were chosen and therefore should feel lucky, because some babies were not chosen. The adopted child was made to feel as if he should count his blessings, not seek answers. Some adoptees are still told this their entire lives in one way or another and are made to feel as if their emotions of loss and confusion are invalid.

If an adoptee suffers a primal wound, the illegitimate child could be said to have suffered a fatal wound. The issues for both children are parallel, and their births are usually rooted in shame and secrecy; however, the stigma attached to illegitimacy is present. There is no clear-cut definition for illegitimate children, and the circumstances surrounding their births are often distorted as their mothers move on in an attempt to forget the past. Adoptees are searching for answers, but they know one thing for sure: they were placed for adoption and given to parents who wanted them. Illegitimate children may not even have this much information about their beginnings.

There are many more illegitimate children in the world than there are adoptees, and thousands are searching for a parent or family member from whom they were separated. The word *illegitimate* means many things but has generally been thought to have a negative connotation to it. When something is illegitimate, it is perceived as meaningless and unrecognized. This perception follows illegitimate children for a lifetime, though it may never actually be spoken of. Illegitimate adults know exactly what the term means, and are often hesitant to mention the details of their birth to strangers. Some religions openly associate the illegitimate child with shamefulness or sin, and it is this type of thinking that causes an individual to conceal his past, delaying the search and the healing process even further.

The rainbow on the horizon is that the stigma of illegitimacy is fading away. While archaic attitudes will always exist in a society of millions of individuals with differing beliefs, society as a whole is more open-minded. Some are educated by personal experience or by the experiences of their friends and relatives who are single mothers and fathers. Some who have been branded illegitimate have come to the realization that they are not alone, as well-known people and even religious figures stand up and proclaim that they, too, were the product of unwed parents.

The evolution of our society has taken many turns, each affecting the makeup of our general population. Women are a norm in the business world and now hold high-level executive positions in the workplace. This was not the case with past generations, where the norm was the woman as matriarch of the household. The dynamics between men and women have changed, and at times their roles have reversed. Women are making choices that would have been unthinkable in the past—decisions such as bearing a child without a husband in the household and raising it alone (technically, an illegitimate child) or waiting until later in life to get pregnant. Both men and women are now adopting children as singles, fulfilling their desire to parent before they find a suitable mate.

With adoption, there is an organized movement of reform to which the adoptee in search can turn for answers. Adults who were not adopted but wish to search may not realize that this information could assist them in finding their loved ones and help them to begin the process of coming full circle. On the Internet, a web page exists with the title Bastard Nation, a tongue-in-cheek effort by those who have lived with the issue of illegitimacy. A creative outlet to address the issues and societal attitudes facing these adults who were illegitimate children, this site also features links to resources and search options. Its authors even offer bumper stickers and buttons with sayings that humorize the issue. Although it may be more overt than some people would prefer, the site is a wonderful example of how openness leads to acceptance and healing, simply by communicating with others in similar situations.

The key to raising a healthy child is truthful communication about her birth experience, even if the truth is difficult to convey or accept—not just communication in the form of a sit-down, once-in-a-lifetime conversation, but communication that is continual, descriptive, and consistent throughout the child's development. This way, if the child does not remember early attempts at communication, the ongoing process will ensure that she understands the reason her birth situation and childhood were different from those of people around her. Even if the child is unaware that she was raised by parents other than her biological ones, communication is necessary at some point in her life to help her understand the truth when it is presented. This view is argued by many, but some adoptive parents still choose to keep the adoption and details of the birth and birth parents a secret. When the secret is eventually released, it is up to the adult adoptee to come to terms with it. Some adoptees are certain to feel betrayed by this truth, seeking to comprehend the reasons behind why they were denied it.

Actress Jamie Lee Curtis, an adoptive mother, authored a recently published children's book for the adopted child. *Tell Me Again About the Night I Was Born* is a colorfully illustrated account of the adoption process. Written from the child's point of view, the story follows the adoption process from its inception, even before the adoptive parents bring their newborn infant home from the hospital. Besides conveying the love and excitement an adoptive parent feels before the child is theirs, the book helps the adopted child understand adoption in simplified terms.

Another recent development in the area of communication is the birth mother book, a journal specifically devoted to the thoughts of the birth mother. The journal is a keepsake that the adopted child can refer to later in life, a book containing the birth mother's thoughts during pregnancy or even after her child was relinquished. Modern adoption facilities encourage birth mothers to record their feelings about the upcoming adoption, and the birth mother book is just one more way to express their feelings for the child.

Reading is one method of communication available; however, there are also videos on adoption, audiotapes, and group seminars devoted exclusively to talking with a child about adoption. Celebrity adoptees worldwide are helping to bring adoption reform issues out into the public eye. Melissa Gilbert, best known for her role as the television character Laura on *Little House on the Prairie,* is an adoptee who was reunited with her birth parents after a successful search. Melissa has spoken out on the subject of adoption and shared her personal story with millions. Others who were raised without one or more biological parent include President Clinton, Newt Gingrich, and Marilyn Monroe. Several famous adoptive parents also exist among the ranks of the adoption triangle, including Willie Mays, Michelle Pfeiffer, George Burns, and Ronald Reagan.

Whether you're a celebrity or just one of the thousands in search of a family member, getting past the obstacle of whether or not to search is the biggest hurdle to unlocking the door to your past. If you are already there, then you've climbed the mountain of pre-search issues and are standing at the top, ready to embark upon your journey. You've reached the plateau. If you are someone who has known all along that this is a goal you would pursue one day, congratulations! You're one step ahead! For most, the decision to search is fraught with a series of complications and concerns that delay the process even longer.

If you have waited to address this very important part of your life, let me assure you that you are not alone. People are commonly held back by feelings of fear and resentment or simply not knowing what they will find. All of these things are to be expected and are thoughts that someone else in another part of the world has already experienced. There are thousands of adoptees across the globe, a multitude of people separated from their families, and many of them are involved in the search process. The desire to search is not limited by geography, for there are those who are searching in Paris, Peru, and Peoria. All are inextricably linked by the equation of the unknown. If it were a mathematical equation, the equation of the unknown would look something like this: $X + Y + Z = ?$ (X being the birth parents, Y being the parents by whom the child was raised, and Z being the child himself). The entire equation always adds up to $?$ until the mystery of the unknown is solved. There is no other solution or answer to the equation until the search is concluded.

Sadly, the equation does remain unsolved for some people. To solve it, the desire to reconnect must be strong, and you must be armed with a potpourri of resources. Luck will play a part in your achieving success, but so will determination and drive. Whether it be for reconciliation or to satisfy a curious mind, the reconnection process can be a trying, yet rewarding, pilgrimage. It gets delayed when the seachers are hesitant to disrupt their own lives or the lives of the ones they are searching for. In addition, friends or relatives may caution against searching, advising to leave well enough alone. All of these forces play a part in one's decision to search, making the burden seem even larger than it really is. Another very common reason for procrastinating, as given by mothers who wish to search for a child, is the fact that oftentimes the mother has not told anyone about the child. Her husband may know, but her other children may not. All of this excess baggage escalates internally until it becomes a stressor, weighing on the mind of searchees, possibly even causing moodswings or depression, for no reason apparent to those closest to them.

The search is a very individual process, and only the one who is searching can govern it. Recently, a story was published in the national news media about a woman who found her biological mother after more than thirty years of separation. The mother was white, and the daughter, who was black, was a child conceived by a rape that had occurred when the woman was walking home one night. When the infant was born she was placed for adoption and raised in a white household. When she grew up and decided to search, she had children of her own and a warm, loving husband who was supportive of her desire to reconnect with her mother. Despite their racial differences, her newfound family accepted her immediately, and the daughter who had been given up for adoption many years before is now reconnected with her biological roots. Best of all, her newfound siblings report that their mother seems happier than they've ever seen her, as if an incredible burden has been lifted from her shoulders.

People change as time goes by, and the beliefs and attitudes they once honored can change as well. Someone who gave up a child many years before may develop her own reasons for wanting to find the child later in life. As we grow, our priorities and needs shift, and the longing for a connection to family and the world around us develops. Have you ever been around elderly people who derive pleasure from recalling the same memories of the past, over and over? Preserving the past is important and comfortable to them, perhaps because the future is unknown.

I tell everyone what I firmly believe: that family history is a basic part of who you are and who you become. Family history is something that everyone is entitled to by virtue of being born into this world, and if it is something that you need for your own personal growth, then no person or organization should hinder you from learning about your heritage. The search is a very personal endeavor and, for me, was a catharsis that changed my life. Literally in one single moment, my life was forever altered and years of despair lifted from my heart. The day I discovered the identity of my biological father, my world became instantaneously clear, as if I had been blind one minute and cured the next. I only wished I had begun my search sooner because the mountain of questions tumbled down when I learned the truth behind my beginnings. The truth had set me free.

The decision to search for your family is a solitary one, and it's important to note that not everyone will understand or share the same desire to find their biological roots. Chances are that you fall into the "wanting to search" column, since you're reading this book, but everyone is different, and some people may never want to know. If you have decided to search in bits and pieces or are determined to enter into a full-blown search at this point in your life, the choice is yours.

If you've already made your choice but don't know why, consider this. Research of adult adoptees has shown that the decision to search is most often triggered by a major life event. A marriage, divorce, or the birth of a child can act as the catalyst that prompts one to begin the search. For many, the death of an adoptive parent invokes the curiosity to know more about one's own beginnings. The loss of love or a loved one creates a vacancy that needs to be filled, just as the birth of a child can bring longing for the answers behind your own birth. All of these feelings are normal for those who are in the process of searching for a family member. The catalyst to search can be as subtle as the result of a series of small events throughout the years, or as overt as a significant single life event. Talk to anyone who has gone through a search and you'll find that there are a lot of similarities, but no hard-and-fast rules.

My own catalyst emerged from the simple realization that life was getting shorter, and I was afraid that my birth father would pass on before I could find him. This realization came in many forms over a period of time, until the need to search became the most important priority in my life. It was all I could think of, and I added it to my list of goals and resolutions to achieve that year.

It was already August when a series of specific events caused me to pause and think about my life. The first event occurred on an airplane. I had been traveling for three days and was settling comfortably into a first-class seat on an American Airlines flight from Dallas to Tampa. Just when I was feeling grateful for the empty seat beside me and the solitude of the lengthy flight ahead, a tall, muscular young man boarded the aircraft and sat down in the seat next to me. Knowing from experience that flying has the strange effect of persuading otherwise normal people to converse for hours on end with total strangers, I kept to myself, my eyes carefully trained on an in-flight magazine. I had been through it all before, the invasive questions about my life, my work, my marital status—all of the things that come with traveling beside someone in a bullet-shaped vessel high above the clouds. I was in no mood for conversation and silently hoped that my seatmate wasn't either, for I had already prejudged his presence to be an invasion of my privacy.

Thirty minutes into the flight, I felt his eyes upon me. "Do you fly much?" he asked, not to be dissuaded by my coolness. "Yes," I replied, "I do." He paused for a moment while I went back to my reading. "Not me," he said, searching for a reply, a question, anything. "My father died," the young man said suddenly, his voice cracking and eyes filling with tears. "He was my best friend in the whole world, and he died in a small plane crash this weekend. Now he's gone . . . I just came back from his funeral." He was sobbing openly now, the tears streaming down his face. His pain was fresh and deep, and I instantly felt it. I leaned toward him and focused everything I had on this stranger who was obviously in need of a friend.

Powerless to do anything to ease his suffering, I listened as he told me the story of his father, whom he called Big Large. The father was given the nickname somewhere along the way because of his burly physical presence. I envisioned him a strong, jovial man with a heart just as big as his body. His son was the most important thing in the world to him and, even more importantly, his son knew it. I listened as my seatmate told me story after story of the things they had done and the trips they had taken together, just the two of them. I was drawn into their lives, feeling the overwhelming legacy of love the father left behind. Big Large was a successful developer, and flying was one of the things he loved the most. He died unexpectedly while flying his plane, and his child was devastated, more alone than he had ever been before.

My heart and eyes were opened that day as I learned more than one valuable lesson. I had prejudged the situation and forgotten the one thing I swore I would always live by. I read it long ago and found wisdom in just five words: *Be kind; everyone is suffering.* Secondly, and just as important, was the simple lesson that life, though truly a miracle, is entirely too short. I thought about the son and Big Large even after my feet were firmly planted on the ground, and I tossed their story about in my mind.

I thought about them a week later when something reminded me of the young man and that flight we had shared. I eventually realized that although his father's untimely death was tragic, the son was left with a precious gift, the gift of love. He would continue to remember and love his father, who had been his guiding light, his mentor, his idol. He had experienced something genuine and rare that would stay with him for the rest of his life.

I envied the bond the two of them shared, and as the days and weeks went by I realized that I didn't even *know* my father. Though this realization had always been kept underneath the surface, it now came bubbling to the top. I missed him more and longed for the special relationship the young man on the plane had shared with his dad. To me, this boy was an angel sent from heaven to wake me up. The alarm clock was blaring, but I had been hitting the snooze button over and over, ignoring this great need that was welling up inside of me. That event had a profound effect on my desire to search, but there were other events as well. They eventually snowballed until I had no choice. The desire to search became overpowering.

Although you don't need a reason to search other than your right to know who you are, the reasons people give for wanting to search vary and range from questions regarding genetics to basic curiosity. A routine visit to the doctor's office can bring uncomfortable feelings to the forefront, as the realization once again sets in that essential medical information is missing.

"All I really want is to know what my father looks like," says one adoptee, a beautiful young woman from Chicago. "I know that once I see him, everything will fall into place." Indeed, the desire to know what a birth parent looks or acts like can be intense and a significant factor that drives one's desire to search. Another driver is the need to find comfort and stability that adult adoptees may think can only be discovered in their newfound family. Sometimes comfort is found when they witness similar traits, physical characteristics, and interests.

The desire to search and the reasons behind doing so may have come recently. You may have denied that you ever wished to search but now feel the need for your own personal reasons, or for medical reasons that could affect your own offspring. An encounter that still sticks in my mind is one in which a man told me about his sister, who had died from leukemia in her last year of college. They had different fathers, and his was the father who raised them both, yet he recalled how, as a teenager, his sister often said that she had no desire to know her birth father. I could not help but wonder if knowing him would have saved her, but I also wonder if she would ever have changed her mind, or if those were really her true feelings.

We can never know what truly lies in the hearts of others—we can only try to discern what lies within our own. Sorting through the twisted web of emotions that lies within us is a task daunting enough, and large enough, to take a lifetime. That's certainly how it is meant to be, for if it weren't, the answers would come swiftly and easily and life would be a clear blue sky. A sky without thunderheads, clouds, or lightning bolts to interrupt it, and a world without seasons that change. Life is not simplistic, and we do not arrive as babies gripping instruction manuals in our little fists, manuals that contain the answers to our questions.

The questions will always be there, and it is up to us as life's warriors to find the answers on our own, with help from our fellow soldiers. Whether you have just one reason or several reasons for embarking upon your search, the time to begin it is now. Whether you have just one question or a multitude of them, there is no better time to begin the search that could change your life.

CHAPTER TWO

Unlocking the Door

I try so hard to imagine your face,
The questions are there they won't erase
If you were here, I'd want you to know
How much your child could love you so

IT MAY SOUND simplistic, but making the decision to search for your family is the first step toward finding them. Chances are that you made the choice long ago subconsciously but haven't given it the effort it deserves, and it's been pushed to the back burner while work and family obligations remain in the forefront. The need is there, the desire is there, it has affected your life in many small ways, but you haven't acted on it. Or perhaps you have already tried throughout the years but have only gained bits and pieces that still don't quite add up.

In today's accelerated world, it's easy to procrastinate and overlook the things that are important to us, the things that would still have meaning if we were stripped of all our material possessions and careers and left with nothing but our thoughts and dreams. We are inclined to put everything off until tomorrow, and before we know it tomorrow is gone.

Even more probable than sheer procrastination is the likelihood that you have delayed the search due to the paradoxical psychology that lies behind the desire to search. Because the issues are so diverse and the fears so subtle, you may not even realize that they are holding you back. A young woman who was adopted as an infant said of her desire to search for her birth parents, "I wanted to find them but at the same time was afraid of what would happen if I ever did. They had abandoned me once—who's to say they wouldn't turn their backs on me again?" Her desire to find her parents was very real, yet she was trapped by her fears.

I once read a fascinating article about a prominent psychologist in Dallas who developed a theory on such human behavior after he lost the use of his limbs, and life as he knew it, to a massive stroke. The man made his point using the analogy of a monkey trap, which captures the monkey when the animal reaches into it to grab the bait. The trap is designed so the monkey could free itself if it simply let go of the bait, but it never does. The stroke, said the psychologist, was a mechanism that actually freed him from the monkey traps that had previously controlled his life, giving him the power to do what he had always wanted: to think and to read and to write.

Most of us are monkeys at one time or another and find ourselves trapped even though all it would take is one step forward to set us free. It's truly easier envisioned than attained, but to unlock the door you must first have the will and the desire to be free. Margaret Lawrence, an adoptee, talked about this desire at the 1976 annual convention of the American Psychological Association in Washington, D.C. She concluded that "the search" comes from the need to seize the power of choice, to take control in a situation that is out of your control, and thus to become free. Sometimes even when we do feel the desire, we just don't know what to do about it. And the only thing we can do is remember that it takes far more courage to confront our demons than to ignore them.

The decision to search for your family is subconscious, but it takes a conscious effort to find them. This means confronting any unresolved feelings you have and making the conscious decision to embrace change in order to reconcile your past. Change, the most awesome of events, can be frightening. Yet the irony is that we are afraid of the disruption that change may bring to our lives, so we stay in our current state of "not knowing" forever, afraid of the unknown that change will bring. One is torturing us, but the other has the potential to torture us, so we are afraid of it.

Even if you are brave enough to confront your own fears involving the search, be prepared for the fears that others will transfer to you. Jessica, who had been the only child in a very bitter divorce, tried to confront her mother as to her father's whereabouts after the dust had settled. Though Jessica was nineteen, her mother made her feel ashamed for asking and refused to talk about her father. It wasn't until many years later, long after Jessica left the household, that she sat her mother down again in an attempt to explain her desire to know the man who fathered her. Jessica longed to have her own child know his grandfather and wanted to know him herself. Despite Jessica's pleas, her mother refused to tell her, and the two didn't speak for years because of it.

Managing Expectations

If you've made the decision to search and are ready to begin, the next step is to take stock of your expectations. Ask yourself the following questions: What do I think the outcome of my search will be? Do I want a relationship with my new family once I find them? What if they don't accept me? It's important to face the reality of all the things that can happen before you actually begin searching. Review all the options in your mind and remember that what you expect to happen may not. Be prepared for the unexpected.

The search outcome won't be black and white, for the possibilities are endless. It's a fact that most people consider only two outcomes: (1) they will accept me, or (2) they will reject me. In actuality there are many different feelings and events that can take place. Part of your new family may accept you, and part may feel skeptical, uneasy, or unwilling to open their hearts. Be strong and willing to accept whatever you are faced with. Be prepared emotionally if you are not received with open arms, and keep an open mind, because the one you are searching for may not be the person you have imagined him or her to be. This is especially true if you are searching for a parent you have never known, since children often create idealistic fantasies of the parent they are searching for.

If you are searching for a parent and already have preconceived notions about what he or she looks like, acts like, and sounds like, discard them. You'll probably be surprised. The same thing can be said for anything we assume. One man I worked with during his search effort was ready to give up before he even began, hesitant to search for his birth mother because he didn't think she would want him to find her. When he finally did locate her, he was shocked to learn that she had been searching for him for ten years and had only recently given up her search efforts!

Spend some time thinking about what you want to achieve when you find your missing family member. Put these thoughts on paper in your search file, so that when your search is complete, you can remind yourself of what your earliest expectations were. Expectations will differ from preconceived notions. A preconceived idea is something that you think or feel about the one you are searching for, while an expectation should be what you expect to achieve from the search. Do you want to know just the minimum about your family member and where you came from, or do you hope to develop a long-term relationship? Are you uncertain what you want at this point? Perhaps your mind is open and ready for anything. If you are prepared and ready to move forward even if the outcome isn't all that you hoped for, you are in the best state of mind to complete a search for a family member.

Always keep in mind that the search can be arduous and emotionally draining, and you may have to face uncomfortable issues, or even pain, with your current family. You might find something you hadn't bargained for, or you may discover that the person you are searching for has passed away. Pain is not something we ever wish to experience, but it could be unavoidable in order to reach a conclusion. Picture pain to be like a giant monster that you try to bury in your backyard. You dig a hole and bury it alive, covering it up with dirt until you cannot see it anymore, and you continue on through life ignoring it, avoiding it, becoming cold and immune to it. But the monster was alive when you buried it; you did not confront it, did not kill it. And so it stays with you, tormenting and taunting and eventually surfacing again until you acknowledge it, fight it, and move on. We must first feel the pain to free ourselves from it. Only then can we move forward.

Embarking upon your search is part of solving the puzzle of who you are and where you came from, but not everyone will agree with your decision to begin the search. The search issue is controversial, and there are those who will deny you information or argue the point of why you are searching at all, solely based on their beliefs and lack of understanding. Valuable information and documents may be difficult to obtain if you are faced with one of these human roadblocks, but keep your goal in sight and remember that there is nothing illegal about searching in any state or any country.

Stay focused, and handle each roadblock as it appears. If you encounter a negative reaction, choose another angle or pursue another route altogether for obtaining the information you need. Those who have been through a search for public records often advise withholding specific information regarding your adoption, or hiding your desire to find your birth parents, when dealing with government agencies, clerks, or adoption professionals. Genealogy is not a controversial subject; however, adoption is, and for this reason some adoptees use the premise of a genealogical search during their quest for information. Use your good judgment and be careful not to lie or misrepresent yourself at any point during your search.

It's important to stay true to yourself and your family while managing to be creative at the same time in order to achieve your goal. At this point in your life you have already achieved many things, so think of the search as just one more goal for you to accomplish successfully. Recall your previous wins in business, sports, relationships, or hobbies; exert the same energy into searching for your family, and you will be just as successful.

Overcoming Obstacles

Although most adoptions are legitimate, as with every business in this world fraud does exist, and illegal adoptions do take place. If you were the product of an illegal adoption, your search could be far more difficult or even impossible to complete. Most illegal adoptions are transactions that occur between a very small number of people who have an incentive to keep their activities confidential. They could be prosecuted if anyone ever discovered the truth! More often than not, an illegal adoption would be performed with false names on both sides and with absence of legally binding documentation.

Even in today's sophisticated adoption environment, innocent people can be drawn into an illegal adoption. Baby brokers have led childless couples on for months when there was actually no child at all, taking them for thousands of dollars and then disappearing from their lives. Babies are a valuable commodity in many parts of the world, and some criminally inclined people have taken advantage of this fact. In the 1920s it was commonplace and certainly not illegal for adoptions to be conducted by the delivering physician, who would create a false birth certificate for the child. The birth certificate would be the only documentation ever recorded. If you are in your seventies or older, obtaining an accurate record of birth with actual, legitimate names could be very difficult.

Luckily, the odds are against an adoption being performed fraudulently, and it's probable that a documentation trail has been formed. You just have to find it. Whether you were adopted or not, the person you are searching for has created millions of reams of paper throughout her lifetime, and finding that person is as easy as locating just one piece of paper along her trail. She's out there, and she may be missing to you, but each and every day she has contact with others, completing daily transactions just like you and me. Think of everything you did within the past two weeks. Open your wallet and pull out your Visa or American Express card, and remember the dinners you bought; the gasoline you put in your car; the dry cleaning, groceries, or any other purchases you may have made with plastic. Better yet, look at your driver's license, which is on record with the Department of Motor Vehicles and with any city or state in which you've gotten a traffic citation. If anyone ever wanted to find me, my driving record would reveal that the last two speeding tickets I received were very recent and in the same city, a sure sign that I've been driving there and, therefore, with a little searching, could probably be found there. Do you have your Social Security number committed to memory? So does your bank, credit card company, mortgage holder, and employer. The information is there, in many channels.

It's up to you to sift through the possibilities and clues that will lead you to your "missing" person. Use a variety of resources and tools to increase your odds of a successful search. After my own search, I went back and made a mental list of all the steps I took that led me to the one I had been searching for, my biological father. In doing so I realized that I used virtually an entire toolbox of resources throughout the search process. It wasn't one specific tool that led me to my family—it was a combination of them. I used everything from old-fashioned tools such as the phone book and library to the latest in technology: computer databases.

My re-created search path looks like this:

Step 1: I approached Mom for the name of my father. I learned his full name, the town in which he died, and the approximate year of his death. The news of his death was an unpleasant surprise.

Step 2: I used the telephone to call Information in that town. I asked information for the numbers of funeral homes and the public library.

Step 3: I called the funeral homes and found the home that handled my father's services. The director who handled his burial had long since retired; however, his son had taken over the business and agreed to research the records. He placed me on hold and came back with the exact year my father died and the cause of death.

Step 4: Armed with the exact year of death, I called the library in that town and asked for the obituary. A sweet old lady on the other end of the telephone line offered to research it for me, and I received a copy of my father's obituary in the mail within a week. The obituary was a wealth of information and gave me the names of my grandparents, aunts, uncles, and siblings, information my mother did not have.

Step 5: I immediately called Information again in that town and requested the numbers for the names of the relatives who appeared in the obituary as residing in that town.

Step 6: The first number I called was the wrong number, but the town was so small that the person who answered knew my grandparents and gave me a wealth of information about them.

Step 7: I continued the phone calls and finally reached an aunt, who knew about me. Her brother, my father, told her about me twenty years prior, just before he died. This aunt gave me more information on my family and told me the state in which one of my brothers lived. She did not feel comfortable giving me any details such as phone numbers or addresses.

Step 8: Using a computer database, I scrolled through a list of five hundred people with the same last name as my brother, and I narrowed the list down to those who lived in the state my aunt had mentioned. My brother was the first name I called, and I knew he would be, because my stomach was in knots as I dialed the phone number.

Step 9: I flew to meet my family the following day.

Although on paper it looks simple, my search wasn't as easy as it seems, and there were obstacles along the way. The first relative I found was hesitant to help me find the rest of my family and during our conversation even discouraged me from proceeding. I delayed my search for two more weeks based on that initial phone call and was overwhelmed with conflicting feelings. When I finally got the courage to place the second call, to my sibling, I learned that one of my brothers had actually searched for me and given up, long ago. Both of my brothers had known about me all along and were welcoming from the start.

From that point on it was a nonstop family reunion. It's been three years, and I have a wonderful new family and all of the information about myself and my heritage that I had been searching for. It wasn't until long after my search had been completed that I really had time to reflect on the enormity of it all. I took a step back and realized then that the search wasn't entirely about finding my father; it was about finding myself and my identity. This is something that I had never expressed to my family before searching, which only magnified their own feelings of confusion and alienation. As I began to spend time with my new family, this time was misinterpreted as discarding the family I grew up with.

Be prepared for similar reactions from family members. Their responses to your search can range from initial acceptance to rage, questions, fear, crying, and conflicting actions toward you as you embark upon your search. Most of the time these feelings are natural and are generated by fear or insecurity about what you are looking for. If you can, address them before your search. It might just make the road ahead a little smoother.

The adoption triangle normally involves three key characters: the adoptee, the birth parent, and the adoptive parent. However, there can be many variations. The triangle may include grandparents who acted as parents, or extended family, social workers, even friends who acted as legal guardians. Easing the uncertainty of the search process comes with understanding each unit of the triad and being sensitive to the issues each person faces.

Deborah, a fifty-three-year-old mother of an adopted child, remembers feeling a tremendous amount of dread when her seventeen-year-old daughter mentioned that she was interested in finding her birth mother. "She said it casually one Sunday afternoon, in passing almost, as if it was something that didn't really matter to her," Deborah reports. "She didn't officially mention it again, but I knew she was searching, because there were calls on the phone bill later that month to Information in Iowa, the state where she was born. I called one of the numbers she had called and it was the adoption agency. This black cloud hung over me from the moment she first mentioned it, and a feeling of profound sadness sunk in. It wasn't until months later, when we actually talked it over, that I understood how much she loved her father and me, and that she was just curious to know who her birth mother was."

Other adoptive parents have been less understanding and have even led the fight against open records laws. Some have elected to keep the details of their child's adoption a secret or have reacted angrily to their child's requests for information. Whatever situation you encounter, be strong and fight for what you believe in, even when it seems as if you are the only one who believes in your cause. Only you can make the decision to search and to embrace all the good and the bad that may come out of it. It's an investment in your future, so don't let the obstacles defeat you.

The search process can be a time-consuming and exhausting experience but ultimately one of the highlights of your life. If you are an adoptee searching for biological parents, it would help you to familiarize yourself with the adoption laws in the state in which your adoption took place. If you aren't sure how to sort through the laws, contact the National Adoption Information Clearinghouse, whose number appears in the resource section of this book, for a free copy of your state's laws. Assuming you have that piece of information, your search should take the course of pursuing the documentation that exists on your case. Start with your adoptive parents if possible, and get as much information from them as you can. Give them the benefit of the doubt, because you can bet it's crossed their minds at one time or another that you may one day have the desire to know your birth parents.

Becky Doolittle, the mother of two adopted children in Houston, Texas, remembers the feeling she had after she adopted her first child. "I remember thinking, I hope she never searches," she admits, "but then as the years passed, my feelings changed. Now I wouldn't hesitate to support her if she wanted to find her birth mother. I raised her, and I know I'm the one she thinks of as her mother. I'm even curious to know what [the birth mother] looks like, myself."

Although her adoption was performed privately and without any introductions between birth and adoptive parents, Becky's child is already one step ahead. If she ever wishes to search, she'll have a supportive mother behind her and a much easier task ahead of her. Adoptive parents like Becky Doolittle are part of the newest generation of educated adoptive parents, those who remain open-minded and seek post-adoption support throughout their adopted child's lifetime.

If you were adopted and have even a small amount of information, such as the state in which you were born, you've got a good place to start searching for your adoption records. Every state is different, with some more lenient than others about unsealed records. The adoption debate is ongoing and continues to be controversial, with one side lobbying for unsealed records laws to make it easier to find birth parents and the other advocating restrictions to discourage it.

Understanding the law and the process of adoption is important in recognizing the challenges you could experience as an adoptee searching for your birth parents. After an adoption is granted, it is incumbent upon the clerk in that county to file notification of the adoption with the Office of Vital Statistics in the State Department of Health Services. Once that has taken place, a new birth certificate will be issued bearing the names of the adoptive parents. The notification, or court report of adoption, and the original birth certificate are officially sealed and cannot be unsealed except by order of the court. Obtaining such an order is achieved by formally petitioning the court, whereby a judge is ordained to make the decision of whether to grant your request to unseal the adoption records. Several states have a "good cause" clause written into the adoption law, which means that a judge can determine that you have a valid reason, in his or her opinion, for needing access to the records. Over the course of history many different judges have made contrasting judgments concerning sealed records, with some granting access for no apparent reason and others denying it even in the most extreme cases involving the quest for medical information to help treat an illness. An adult adoptee's fate and future is in the hands of the state. Gayle Voiles was in her forties when she wrote to a judge in Florida requesting an order to unseal her adoption records. It surprised her when her request was granted immediately, and she received the details she needed to confirm the identity of her birth father and bring closure to this part of her life. If you can't find a sympathetic judge on your own, check with the state to see if it has an intermediary program which would provide for a third party, or intermediary, to work on the adoptee's behalf to secure information from the court. Either way, if your petition is successful and you obtain your court records, you will receive a variety of documents usually including the original birth certificate, final adoption decree, and any correspondence or reports filed by the agency or attorneys concerning the adoption transaction. Medical and biographical information may also be included.

Because of the nature of sealed records, national estimates concerning the number of adoptees who conduct a search for their biological parents are lower than actual figures. One study conducted by researchers Brodzinsky, Schechter, and Henig asserts that 100 percent of adoptees search in some fashion, if only in an "intrapsychic" search, which consists of fantasies and inner contemplation. This inner contemplation often leads to external contemplation and the crusade for answers. If you haven't yet sought assistance in finding your own answers, help is at your fingertips. Adoption has become such a visible issue that there are now countless resources specifically related to the subject. There are adoption centers, post-adoption centers for counseling, search services, adoption centers with religious affiliation, deaf adoption information services, interracial adoption services, international adoption services, and just about anything else you can think of. Finding the organization that's just right for you may take a little sleuthing, but aligning yourself with a search or support group in your area is sure to put you one step closer to finding the person you seek.

If you were not adopted, the resources available to adoptees are just as valuable to you, so don't overlook them. Take advantage of the huge reform movement going on with regard to access to sealed records, and use the tools that adoptees are using to find their families. Discard the adoption verbiage and filter through the rubbish to find your own treasures. There are thousands of people just like you, searching for the family members from whom they have been separated, dividing fact from fiction to unlock the door.

If you're doubting your ability to complete the search or questioning your competence with regard to finding someone, remember that you need not be an expert in a field to excel in it. Consider the story of Carolyn McCarthy, a homemaker in Long Island, who devoted her life to taking care of her family and household. Carolyn's husband and son were the focus of her life, a life which was drastically changed the day a gunman opened fire on the commuter train her son and husband were traveling on, killing her beloved husband and wounding her son, who witnessed his father's death. In one split second several lives were drastically altered, and Carolyn found herself thrust into the emotional fight against assault weapons. A lifelong Republican, Carolyn changed parties to run for political office against the incumbent Republican, who had voted against a ban on assault weapons. Carolyn McCarthy is now a full-time politician and holds a seat in the House of Representatives, where she can actively fight for her cause.

People with a passion or a cause can channel that energy toward making a difference in their future or in the futures of others. Sometimes the course of our lives carries us like debris caught up in a cyclone. As much as we scheme and strategize, fate steps in to alter our life plan in some way or another. Then there are those who follow their map every step of the way, and it seems that for them, there is never a dead end or detour. Unlocking the door to your past is a way of opening the passageway to your future dreams. Dreams are a series of goals and events that motivate each one of us to live and prosper, and everyone has at least one. If yours is to find your family, read on and watch as your dream unfolds and, with a bit of determination, becomes reality.

CHAPTER THREE

Street Smarts

I saw you today,
in her eyes.
Those untold secrets,
I still despise

I'm grown up now
and doing fine,
I think of you
from time to time

THERE IS NO standard formula for finding your missing family. It takes a series of small steps and a lot of street smarts to find the answers you are searching for. While the task can seem overwhelming, if you break it down into small steps it becomes much easier to overcome the obstacles. Envision the search process as a giant boulder blocking your path with absolutely no other way to get around it. The only options are to not take that path or to get rid of the obstacle. If you can chisel it down into small chunks, that boulder will crumble, allowing you to walk right over it.

Your search should be a series of small steps, rather than one giant venture. If you approach your search that way, you're much less likely to get discouraged when one step in the process doesn't pan out or when one lead turns out to be futile and you feel as if you've ended up back where you started. Remember that the most important underlying factors to a successful search will be utilization and motivation. The information you gain throughout your search will be worthless unless it's utilized, just as seven years of medical school would be worth very little to someone who never entered the medical field. Every step in the search process should lead you to the next, provoking you to move forward even when you feel frustrated by brick walls and a lack of information. Motivation is just as critical to a successful search, because motivation will drive your desire to continue. Frustration with the time that a search can take may make it difficult for you to persevere, but staying motivated is the key to keeping the momentum going and keeping your goal in the crosshairs.

Think of the search process as a round of golf. You never really know how it's going to end until you've reached the eighteenth green, and every hole along the course is sure to be challenging in a different way. Some holes will be frustrating, others rewarding, but ultimately the outcome will depend on a mixture of luck, skill, and the direction of the wind.

So Where Do I Begin?

Now that you are prepared to get off the starting block, there are four major components to beginning the search. Each component is meaningful to completing a successful search. The four components are:

1. Creating a personal profile

2. Developing an action plan

3. Completing an information tree

4. Pursuing legal documentation

The first step is to compile all the information you have gained thus far about the one you are searching for, to create a personal profile. The profile is a piece of paper that should contain all facts and information that you gather on your missing person, your family, or yourself. It should contain all facts and estimations about the one you are trying to find, including a physical description if known, former occupations, places of residence, and any clues you have uncovered. It should also contain specific information you may have on your own background, birth, and medical history. The profile sheet can be faxed or mailed to people who may have known the person you are searching for, and it will prevent you from having to restate the pertinent details about your case each time you contact someone.

To devise a profile, use a method that closely resembles your existing work style. If you have a distinct routine that you follow to organize your life, your business contacts, or personal goals, use the same method for planning your search. Anything will work, whether it's a three-ring binder, personal planner, file folder, or computer. Using whichever works best for you, write down everything you know about yourself and the object of your search.

If you are an adoptee searching for your birth parents, make a list of all pertinent details, such as the hospital you were born in, city, state, and county, and any physical or personal attributes that you have discovered about your birth parents. Your adoptive parents are the very best place for you to start gathering this information. Ask them the important questions about your birth, and record everything in the personal profile. Keep every piece of data no matter how insignificant it seems, and carry the information with you wherever you go. If you are searching for a sibling, start talking to your aunts and uncles or anyone who would have been around at the time the sibling was born.

The purpose of creating the profile is to assemble a snapshot of the circumstances surrounding your life or the life of the one you are searching for and to fill in the blanks whenever possible. Remember when creating and updating the profile that you can never be too thorough or have too much information. The things that are important will reveal themselves, and the things that aren't will be overlooked. You may have nothing at this point, so your profile sheet will be completed piece by piece as you engage in the search process. The profile will be referred to continually and updated as you learn more and more about your past, and it is the one thing you should keep with you at all times. It will remind you that you are conducting the search and will serve as a mechanism for storing the information you need to complete it.

If you decide to seek assistance with your search at any point in time, the personal profile will serve two purposes. It will provide critical information about the one you are searching for, and it will lessen the steps needed to complete the search.

Sample Profile

Name of missing person: _____

Date of birth: _____

Place of birth: City: _____ State: _____ County: _____

Date and place of death if deceased: _____

Last known address: _____

_____

_____

Any previous addresses: _____

_____

_____

Occupation(s): _____

Hobbies: _____

Distinguishing physical features (hair color, eye color, height, and

weight): _____

Descriptions of scars, moles, tattoos, physical markings: _____

_____

Accent: _____

Languages spoken: _____

Religious affiliation: _____

Military service: _____

Known magazine or literary subscriptions: _____

Financial status: _____

Criminal records/crimes: _____

Potential location: _____

Names of any known friends or relatives: _____

_____

Pertinent identifying information (Social Security number, driver's

license number, etc.): _____

Distinguishing life events (divorce, marriage) and places events

occurred: _____

_____

Your Personal Information

Full name: _____

Date of birth: _____

Place of birth: City: _____ State: _____ County: _____

Social Security number: _____

Age: _____

Name and location of adoption agency, if applicable: _____

_____

Name of adoptive parents: _____

Date and year of adoption: _____

Name of adoption staff or attorney: _____

Name of any foster parents: _____

Name and location of hospital where born: _____

_____

Names of doctors/staff working that year/day: _____

_____

Relationship to the person being sought: _____

Names and addresses of any known biological relatives: _____

_____

Step two is to utilize the information you have already gathered to create an action plan for finding your family. The action plan can be very brief or even quite involved, but either way it should contain specific action items that will help you reach the goal of finding your family. Approach it as you would a business proposal or school project, with the concentration and thought it requires. Develop a strategy and stick with it, clearly defining individual goals. Most important, don't delay! The action plan is a general, step-by-step guideline to keep you focused. The following is a sample of an action plan with specific and concise objectives:

Sample Search Action Plan

Goal: Find biological mother

1. Fill out profile sheet and create a search file
2. Call target list of relatives and family members for any information
3. Register with national search database
4. Get on the Internet to get more information on searches
5. Request original birth certificate from Office of Vital Statistics

The search action plan is your blueprint for finding your missing family. It will be a living document that you will continually refer to, and it should explore all avenues. Each step in the action plan may actually consist of much greater detail. For instance, contacting a list of relatives and family members for information on your missing loved one could translate into several hours of phone time. In addition, the action plan means preparation, getting yourself ready for that initial conversation, and knowing what you expect to achieve from it. Requesting a copy of your original birth certificate will require gathering documentation and facts about yourself that are necessary to obtaining the certificate. Set goals as you would with any important endeavor and think through the steps you need to take to reach those goals.

The more prepared you are, the more success you will have. If you're not convinced, think of how many times you've gone to a job interview totally unprepared. Probably not many, if ever. Most people take great care to prepare for a job interview, from choosing the suit they wear to researching the company's background. Searching for your family is at least as important as landing that job, so prepare for it as you would for that interview, and think about all the things you have to do to "get the job," or reach the goal, of finding your family.

Step three is the creation of a separate target list of all the people you will contact in your search. This list can be written in any format and should be thought of as an "information tree" of names of people who can provide you with information about yourself, your beginnings, and the one you are searching for. Imagine the information tree to be an extension of your family tree, except that it will include friends, family, acquaintances, and anyone who may have access to information about your past.

Your information tree can look like a corporate organizational chart with rectangular boxes filled in with the names of people, featuring at the top of the chart the person most likely to have information, and at the bottom the least likely to know anything. It could be a series of stick figures with their names drawn underneath them, or simply a basic list of names. Put the names in descending order with the people whom you suspect might have something to offer at the top. Contact them first and be prepared to tell them the reason for your call. Take copious notes during each and every conversation, and have a clear objective set in your mind prior to every call. After you've contacted someone on your information tree, cross off that person's name and move on to the next one.

Attached is a sample of the information tree I developed in my own search for family. It worked for me. Combining this information tree with the other methods I've described here, I was able to locate my family pretty quickly. It helped to organize my thoughts and strategies as I spoke with different people, and I have since used it to achieve other goals as well. For instance, if your goal is to land a job in broadcasting with a major news network, you would write that goal at the base of the tree and the names of the people who could help you attain it on the branches. This network of contacts may include your father's friend who works at a television station, an old friend who majored in television, or total strangers whom you have targeted to call for information about the broadcasting industry. During a search for family, the information tree will remind you that there are several branches and directions to take. When one fails you, cross it off and move on to another.

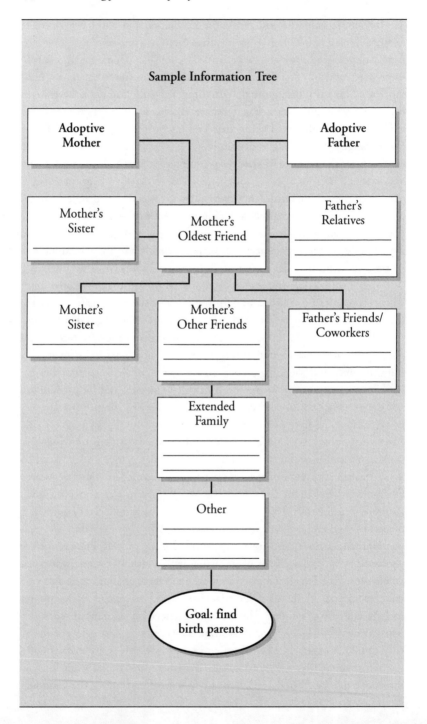

Sample Information Tree

Adoptive Mother

Adoptive Father

Mother's Sister
_____

Mother's Oldest Friend
_____

Father's Relatives
_____
_____
_____

Mother's Sister
_____

Mother's Other Friends
_____
_____
_____

Father's Friends/ Coworkers
_____
_____
_____

Extended Family
_____
_____
_____

Other
_____
_____
_____

Goal: find birth parents

Be careful not to leave anyone off your information tree. If you were adopted, your adoptive parents' closest friends should be on it, and so should relatives who are much older and may have been around to witness the events of years past. If you're not sure where to begin, spend some quiet time alone thinking of all the people you and your family have interacted with over the years. Go through your address book, Rolodex, or computer file, and don't be afraid to contact everyone you know.

Arranging to call or meet with people who may have the answers you need is taking a step in the right direction, but you must also be prepared for what will happen when you get them on the phone. To begin the task of gaining the facts you need by contacting those on your information tree, compose an opening sentence. Your opening sentence is the most significant part of the dialogue, because it sets the foundation for the conversation. Compose your opening sentence and write it down at the top of the page you plan to use to take notes, if it helps. You won't choke up and dance around the subject when you actually get somebody on the phone, and your opening sentence will open the door. If you know that you are always going to begin a call with, "Hello, Aunt Jane, this is your nephew, Peter, and I have something important to ask you," then you have already overcome one obstacle, which is the dilemma of how to approach the subject. People delay their search for years because of this one obstacle.

Each and every relative or friend has a unique relationship to you and your family, and a variety of questions may enter your mind before you feel comfortable approaching him or her. What if she tells my adoptive parents I am asking questions? What if the whole family finds out I am searching? What will my sister think? What if the person whom I am asking for information doesn't have time or asks why I want to know? These are all normal questions, just lurking in the back of your mind, and to best overcome them, keep yourself centered and concentrate on your objective. Put yourself and the issues you have been dealing with first, before anything else.

Human nature is on your side, because it is rare that anyone will keep a secret for a lifetime. There is a weak moment, a passing conversation with a neighbor, or a heartfelt talk with a friend, and the secret is no longer a secret. If a near or distant relative knows something, many times all you have to do to find out is ask. The big "secret" may only be information that you haven't asked the right people for, and it may not actually be a secret at all. Put yourself in their shoes and ask yourself how you would react if someone posed the same question to you. Would you want to help? You may have a distant relative who didn't believe in keeping the past from you but didn't want to get involved. One simple question may solve the mystery or give you another path to travel. It is very likely that someone out there has the information that could lead you to find your missing family, and you just need to find that person.

Don't ever assume anything, for the most insignificant detail could be the clue that leads you to your missing family member. When we assume, we tend to think inside of a box, keeping our mind closed when it should be open. If you are looking for your biological father, and your mother is deceased, don't assume that your living relatives are your only link to finding him. Your mother may have shared the circumstances behind your birth with others. She might have mentioned the circumstances to a teacher in your grade school, a doctor, a neighbor, or even her former spouse or boyfriend. Don't be afraid to seek out these people, even if you haven't spoken with them in years. One searcher, whose family gave him conflicting stories about his father, tracked down an aunt's old boyfriend. The boyfriend had been around thirty years before, when the searcher's father and mother were still together. The boyfriend was still living in the same town and was able to provide numerous details about the man's father.

If you were raised an only child, don't assume you *are* an only child. I was so focused on finding my father that the possibility of having siblings never entered my mind, yet here I am at thirty with siblings, aunts, uncles, and even new grandparents. There is always the possibility that there are siblings or other family members out there who know that you exist and are searching for you to complete their family.

If you are already beyond these steps, you're far ahead of most people who are looking for their family. Most have tiny bits of information, such as a first name, a memory, or another family member's recollection of the person they are searching for. Others may have nothing at all. Without a starting point, people put off their search for days or months and sometimes even years.

Step four is to pursue any legal documentation or public records that may exist. These documents include:

- Copy of your original or amended birth certificate

- Hospital records from birth

- Any nonidentifying information you can obtain (usually information about your birth parents, obtained from the adoption agency or attorney)

- The petition for your adoption (court records)

- Final decree of adoption (court records)

- Certificate of death, if you know one or both of your parents are deceased

- Certificate of divorce, if you know your parents are divorced

Obtaining your birth certificate is usually a fairly simple process that involves a written request, a small fee, and proof of identification, such as a photocopy of your driver's license. The birth certificate may be the only document listed above that you can easily obtain without first having a birth parent's name, Social Security number, or other vital information. More often than not, your adoption records will be sealed and off limits to you without a court order. Your birth certificate is accessible and can be obtained in a short time frame; however, the downside is that if you were adopted, you will receive the amended certificate containing your adoptive parents' names, not the original. Look in the phone book or contact Information for the telephone number of the Office of Vital Statistics in the state in which you were born, or refer to the resources section in the back of this book. You must first know where you were born to obtain a copy of your birth certificate.

Although the birth certificate you receive will in all probability be a modified copy of the original, it will contain other information that could be helpful in your search. The actual place of birth is not usually altered, even on the modified certificate. If you didn't already have this information, the birth certificate has provided you with one tiny clue that could assist you later on.

Most states also offer what is termed nonidentifying information concerning your adoptive parents. This information is generic in nature but provides a good base to search from as a rule. By paying a fee to the state agency and submitting a letter outlining your request for information, you can receive details such as the age of your biological parents, your time of birth, your place of birth, and sometimes even your parents' first names. The fee for this varies by state, as does the information that is provided. Some states actually have laws mandating your entitlement to your biological parents' first names; however, you may not receive that information if you do not specifically request it in your letter. As with everything else, be thorough and don't be afraid to ask everyone for everything. You are entitled to it.

The following are samples of letters to request information from libraries, government offices, or adoption agencies regarding adoption and birth records. The first is a general letter to request information. It should be in a business format like the professional correspondence the office normally receives and, obviously, should be free of punctuation and grammatical errors. Do your best to get your point across as briefly and definitively as possible.

This sample letter can be modified and used to request public records or information from private agencies or individuals. If possible, call ahead and get a contact name to address the letter to. A contact name for a specific person adds a touch of familiarity and immediately gives the addressee

---

Ms. Darcy Bathgate
Records Administrator
Department of Vital Statistics
XYZ Government Agency
IIII Everytown Street
My Town, ST 55505

Dear Ms. Bathgate,

This letter is to request birth records [or whatever records you are requesting] for myself, Timothy T. Raymond, Social Security number 555-12-9999.

I followed your agency's procedures and submitted a written request for these records on July 9, 1995, but have received no response. Please forward the original birth certificate and any other identifying information you may have directly to my address at:

125 Sunset Way
Palm Beach, FL 33444

Please contact me if you have any questions or need additional information. I may be reached via telephone or fax at the following numbers:

Phone: 407-579-9999
Fax: 407-579-9991

Enclosed is a copy of my photo identification, which was also enclosed with my original request.

Sincerely,
Timothy T. Raymond

---

a sense of responsibility. If a letter is addressed to "whom it may concern," no one in particular will feel a sense of ownership to your request.

Sending letters to request information can be done quickly, allowing you to immerse yourself in other aspects of the search.

If you were adopted, file a waiver of confidentiality with the state agency or adoption bureau, the hospital in which you were born, and your adoption agency, if you know these details. This waiver means that you are relinquishing your rights to confidentiality, and many states will then release information if a waiver has been signed and submitted by the adoptee and the birth parent(s). Some agencies will even conduct a search

Ms. Carla Baker
Research Assistant
Scottsdale Public Library
123 Sample Letter Lane
Scottsdale, AZ 85251

Dear Ms. Baker,

I am writing to request an obituary for Mr. Jim Steadman. Mr. Steadman was buried in the city of Scottsdale, Arizona, between the years of 1961 and 1964. I do not have the exact date or the place of burial.

I would gladly pay a fee for this search if required, and I would appreciate any information you can give me. There may also be newspaper articles on his death, which I believe occurred due to an automobile accident.

My preferred method of receiving this information would be via fax, at 212-530-1234. If you would prefer to mail it, my address and telephone number are as follows:

> Sharon Smith
> 101 East Meadow
> New York, NY 10023
> 212-555-1111

> Thank you,
> Sharon Smith

for you; however, this is rare, so you may want to gather information on the agency's specific policy before making a request. If you feel comfortable, go to the adoption agency in person and try to get the information you need. Be prepared for the bureaucratic response that the agency isn't allowed to divulge any of the information to you, but don't be afraid of stumbling blocks. You may gain some new information from the visit, or you may not, but either way it's worth the effort.

Don't forget the people in your life who may be able to help if only they are asked. They may not even realize that finding your missing person has been an issue for you. Search in your immediate circle first, your outer circle second. Imagine yourself standing alone on a wide-open beach, barefoot in the sand, with two imaginary circles drawn in the sand around you. One is small, and you are standing inside it. The other is a bit larger and encircles both you and the smaller circle. Now imagine that the edges of the first circle are lined with your immediate family members and the second, lined with friends and acquaintances. Exhaust all options within the first circle before moving to the next. Talk to the people who raised you and laughed with you, fought with you, and witnessed your struggles and life events. Reach out to each one for information. When you've tapped the resources in your inner circle, step out of it and move to the resources in the outer circle. Contact friends of the family, acquaintances, anyone who you think might know something.

The parents who raised you may already have the information you are searching for, or a fragment of it. If you can talk with your adoptive parents in person, that's ideal, but if distance prevents you from having a one-on-one conversation, or if the thought of a conversation intimidates you, a letter is another option for opening the door to your past. Preface the letter's arrival by telling your parents you have sent them something that's very important to you, and follow up with a phone call after they've received it. Your parents may feel comfortable talking with you directly or may respond by writing their own feelings down in the form of letters of their own. Every family is different and communicates in their own way. I've known entire families who solve their largest problems on paper, and others who yell and scream and vent their frustrations in person, still to be the best of friends afterward. However you choose to go about it, communication is the key. The following is a sample letter aimed at requesting information from a parent.

Dear Mom,

I've wanted to write this letter for the longest time but never found the courage to do it. I know I've mentioned my curiosities about my birth father from time to time, but we have never had any serious discussion about him. I didn't want to upset you, and I didn't want to disturb the wonderful life you created for me, either.

I'm now at the age where I know I will understand anything about my birth father and the circumstances surrounding my birth. It does not matter to me if you knew each other for years, a month, or a day, and it does not matter if he was a millionaire, a plumber, or a used car salesman. I'm not as concerned with finding him or in knowing him as a person as I am with finding my roots, my heritage, and the family history that I'm entitled to.

I'm simply curious as to who he was, where he lived, and anything else you can share with me. Mom, I love you and would never do anything to hurt you. I want you to know how hard it is to live with just one half of my genetic information and family background. The curiosities linger forever and never go away. I know that when I learn about my father, I will finally be at peace. The questions will have answers.

Please write if it's more comfortable for you, or call me and let's talk.

> I love you,
> Justin

The following letter also can be used as a guide.

Dear Mom and Dad,

There's something I've been meaning to talk with you about, but there never seems to be an opportune moment. I have asked you about my biological parents at times throughout my life, so you're probably aware that the curiosity is there. Now that I'm an adult, I feel the need to learn more about my roots. I'd like to conduct a search for my family history, and I want to make sure you understand why.

The only reason I desire to search is to know my full identity. You both raised me in a wonderful, loving environment, giving me all that any child could wish for. However, you also raised me to be a curious, thinking adult, one who examines all aspects of life in order to live it to its fullest!

Can you imagine for a moment that you don't know anything at all about your biological family? Everyone else knows where they came from, except me. I know I was raised by the two best parents in the world, but I know nothing about the people who sent me into this world. I don't know if my lineage is filled with farmers, or artists, or politicians. I don't know what they looked like, where they came from, what they accomplished, or how they died. I have no genetic history—information that may help me or my children in later years.

It is important for me to make certain you know that I am not searching to find a new family. I am searching to find the background of my life, my full identity. I know this may be hard for you to understand, because you've given me everything! Please know that I care for both of you more than words can say. No one will ever replace you as parents, because no one else raised me, and no one can know the relationship we have shared. Please understand my desire to know more about my beginnings, and trust me to move forward with this very important part of my life. I know it will help me see the past more clearly.

I love you both,
Morgan

There will be many other steps to take and places to explore; nearly all of them will involve dealing with people who have access to the information you need. You will encounter difficult ones, helpful ones, and those whose views differ from yours completely. There are thousands of intelligent professionals who do support the right to search, and hopefully you will encounter some of them along the way, too. If not, don't get discouraged. Believe in yourself and remember that through the course of history entire nations of people have opposed things that one man or woman believed in. It might seem ridiculous to us today, but in times past there were those who fought against a woman's right to exercise her opinion in a vote and others who lobbied to keep African-American athletes out of professional sports because of the color of their skin. One man, Hitler, convinced an entire nation to believe in his distorted views, leading to the murder of millions of innocent Jews. These issues were debated then, just as the adoption records issue is being debated today. Remember this, because although your cause—your right to know the details of your birth—probably seems like an obvious, fundamental right to you, there are others fighting against it.

Stay tied to your convictions and continue to fill in the blanks, gathering as much information as you can. Stay motivated, because the candle may be burning at both ends and there could very well be someone out there who is trying just as hard to find you.

Technology

Once you have exhausted the people possibilities and contacted everyone you can think of, it's time to turn to technology as a resource. There are literally thousands of trails to follow using the technology we have available to us today. Televisions, computers, and mass media have opened the door for global information sharing. Reuniting missing family members is a continual topic on all the daytime talk shows and has been featured on every major news network. Millions of Americans have witnessed family reunions right in their own living rooms through televised interviews, tabloid shows, and magazine articles.

Society as a whole is far more receptive to the discussion of issues that were once very personal and contained within the family. There are now hundreds of support groups, self-help meetings, newsletters, and books, and far more open communication transmitted by fax, phone, and the Internet, allowing strangers all over the globe to share information. In a world where consultants are thriving and everyone is an expert on something, information is the main ingredient of the future.

Technology is a tool that we can use as an infinite warehouse of information. Our ancestors did not have the luxury of technology in their searches, and the process was often cumbersome and time consuming. The technology we have available to us today can open new doors and provide valuable information to aid you in your search. Computers have made search data banks a successful tool to link adoptees and biological parents who have registered to find one another. These databases are offered by private companies, private investigators, search firms, or social agencies all over the world. Both parties must be registered for there to be a match, but it is worth registering to see if anyone has been searching for you. If you don't have a personal computer at home, you can easily gain access to one through your local library, print shop, or computer rental center. An abundance of books exists on the subject of computers and computer training, and you'll find a healthy listing of computer experts in the yellow pages of even the smallest of towns.

We are in the information age, and there is no better time for completing a successful search. Technology is advancing by leaps and bounds, and there are now databases that can search for a missing person using a first name or approximate date of birth. This makes it much easier to scan the names in the database to narrow the list to a few specific parameters.

You have several routes to take using the computer as a resource. A computer cannot find your person for you, but it can certainly act as a guide. Computer databases can also search for death records, which will provide you with the exact date of death and town in which the person died, Social Security records, or even driver's license information. You'll find your missing person through the process of elimination, so all of the possibilities should be explored. Computer data banks can be a fast and valuable tool to narrow down the leads you have. See the resource reference guide at the back of this book for a listing of many of them.

The Internet

The Internet as a search tool is so fascinating and monumental that it deserves an entire section devoted specifically to it. The Internet offers a world of possibilities with access to millions of subscribers on-line each day. Recent Nielsen survey data supports that thirty-seven million adults have access to the Internet, which can only increase the odds of finding the ones you are searching for or someone who knows them. Within the Internet lie missing-person pages, chat forums, and access to virtually any topic relating to adoption, divorce, and searches for missing persons. Getting on-line through an Internet provider would be the first step to exploring the options contained there.

If you have your own personal computer and would like to get on the Internet, look in the phone book under *Computers* to locate an Internet provider, contact one of the on-line services such as America Online or CompuServe, or visit your local computer store for advice on how to get on-line. If you don't have access to a computer and don't have a friend who does, call your local library to inquire about computer services or, again, try a local computer dealer. Cyber cafes, the newest trend in coffeehouses, provide customers with a setting in which they can access the Internet from a computer terminal while sipping a cappuccino. Getting to the Internet is absolutely critical in your quest to find your missing loved one. No matter what your age or comfort level with technology, the Internet can be tackled with ease.

As of this printing, there were countless pages on search-related topics to be found on the Internet. First and foremost, if you have the name of the person you are searching for, get on the Internet, go to a search page where you can enter that person's name, and forget about the rest of your search. You can usually locate someone just by entering the name and clicking on the search button. The computer system will give you the person's recent address and sometimes even a telephone number. There are several free search pages on the Internet today.

If you don't have a name, the Internet will still be important to you as a resource for your search. During a recent browse on the Net using just one search engine and the keyword *adoption,* twenty-five different web sites were displayed, each containing detailed information on adoptions and family searches. Using the term *genealogy*, more than one hundred thousand entries are displayed. You can also use the keywords *birth parent* or *missing*, and come up with other options to assist you with your search. Triad Resources is the name of an excellent web site that offers a surplus of adoptee resources. Whether you are actually an adoptee or not, this site is a groundswell of valuable information that should not be missed.

Once you have found a site on the Internet that offers information you think might be helpful, click on the various subtitles highlighted to view more detail and, if possible, print the data to keep in your search file for future reference. The Social Security Administration also has a home page on the Internet where you can conduct an immediate search for information by Social Security number. If you have a Social Security number, you can locate someone literally within minutes.

Other ways to utilize the Internet include reunion bulletin boards, where postings of those in search are listed for a fee or sometimes for free. The Internet-literate may elect to post a listing in what amounts to an electronic classified advertisement, and matches are made when the postings are viewed by the appropriate parties. One man located his birth mother by posting a classified with her name and state of domicile. The mother did not own a computer, but her neighbor did, and the neighbor immediately sent an e-mail response to the classified ad. Although this case is unusual, several people have been successfully reunited through the Internet. The power of computers is well beyond what we ever imagined it could be. Just recently, a convicted child molester was featured on a "most wanted" list of criminals on a popular television program. He was turned in by a small boy who recognized his picture from a page on the Internet, and the man was found evading authorities in South America. The boy lived in the middle of the jungle but had a desktop PC that linked him to civilization.

Specialized Computer Databases

Specialized computer databases can access very specific information on individuals who are still living. If you're a computer whiz and up to the heady task of researching, you may already be aware of what's available. Advanced computer databases can search for a person's Social Security number after you have entered identifying information such as a name or last known address. A query can be completed using the Social Security number as the data to search by.

There are also specific methods for searching college servers for e-mail addresses of college students by sending an electronic message to that server in the name of the one you are searching for. The same method can be employed for searching for a government or corporate worker's e-mail address; however, it will require some knowledge of computers and the network you are trying to reach. A private investigator who specializes in Internet or computer searches would be best suited to conduct this type of search for you.

The American Information Network offers an on-line database search that scans a number of proprietary databases to compile a report listing the five closest neighbors for a given address. If available, the report will provide the neighbors' names, telephone numbers, and addresses. To contact the company directly write to: American Information Network, 1258 Cleveland Avenue NW, Canton, Ohio 44703, and inquire about their "Nearest Neighbors Scan."

Airline Records

The power of airline databases is phenomenal. One major U.S. airline owns and utilizes the largest private database in the world. It is the backup system to the United States government in event of a national emergency and processes millions of transactions per second. The core of the computer system is highly secure, housed in an underground bunker in the midwestern United States, and the information contained within that database is so significant that extreme security measures are taken to protect it. Visitors to the facility undergo eye-retina scans and a multitude of security tests that even employees must endure each and every workday.

Airline databases contain personal profiles with travelers' addresses, telephone numbers, and next of kin in case of emergency. Each and every individual who has ever traveled by air will have a record stored in an airline reservation system somewhere. The computer system that one airline uses contains information on passengers booked on every other airline, including hundreds of car rental companies and thousands of hotels worldwide. If your missing person is a frequent flyer, chances are he's enrolled in a frequent flyer program and listed in the computer.

Travel agents have access to the computer systems but do not have the special security codes required to view all areas of the system which would include information on passengers other than those they themselves have booked. For instance, if a Mr. John Q. Traveler has contacted a travel agency and booked a round-trip flight on Continental Airlines to Denver, the travel agency could view his record; so could Continental, and so could any airline or computer-system employee linked to the computerized reservation system in which the record was booked and stored. If the passenger booked his flight directly with the airline, all of the same people with the exception of the travel agent could view the record.

Travel history is kept live in most airline reservation systems for forty-eight hours, so if you know that your person has traveled somewhere, you would have up to forty-eight hours to find him easily in the computer system. After that, the data is warehoused and stored on microfiche. It can be retrieved with a formal request and valid reason for needing the information, but it is much harder to get after it's been deleted from the system. Travel agencies frequently request this information through their local airline sales office when accounting errors are made or when a travel vendor charges the agency for something the agency feels is unwarranted.

Search Registries

Another resource to consider are reunion and search registries. Registries are operated by adoption agencies, search groups, and even state and government agencies. Each one will have its own regulations and fees, and some may even require an hour of counseling prior to registration. The objective of joining a registry is to expand your reach by providing your name in hopes that it will create a match in the registry with the one you are looking for. Search registries do not actually search but instead provide matches for those who are looking for family members. If the one you are searching for has already registered with the search bank you contact, a match would be made and your search would be over.

International Soundex Reunion Registry is the largest in the world and is free of charge. Its comprehensive database makes computer matches based on information provided by those in search. Other registries may charge for their services, and it is up to you to determine whether or not the fee charged is a worthwhile investment. BirthQuest is an on-line registry that will search by name and birth date. It was a free service until recently and has been successful in reuniting several families across the world. BirthQuest also has a medical emergency page for postings from people who have life-threatening illnesses. This page is only for someone needing a bone marrow transplant, donation, or other urgent medical need.

Another excellent on-line resource is called the People Finder search database. I personally tested it with a variety of names and received an 80 percent success rate. Not bad odds for finding someone in seconds. The Adoptee's Liberty Movement Association (ALMA) is one of the most prominent and massive adoption-related organizations and also offers a computerized cross-reference registry. Another useful service that ALMA offers is the aid of experienced search assistants, who will counsel and assist you as you progress with your search.

A list of some of the search registries available and their addresses is located in the reference section of this book.

Search and Support Groups

Search and adoption support groups exist in every state and can offer you guidance as well as contact with others in the same situation. If you are feeling alone in your search or are dealing with issues relating to the search process, joining a support group will furnish you with one more resource for knowledge and an instant support mechanism.

Even if you don't think of yourself as "the support-group type," a second look at the groups available might change your mind. Oftentimes a search support group will take the shape of an information-sharing session, benefiting everyone involved.

To find one close to you, contact a national adoption support organization such as ALMA, or go to your local library and research adoption. If you still don't find a suitable support group, scan the yellow pages under *Adoption* and contact a post-adoption counseling center in your city for details.

Telephone Directories

Telephone and city directories in particular are an excellent resource to turn to during a search. Switchboard, an on-line national telephone directory, is very useful if you have a name to search with. Switchboard offers business and residential listings in the United States. The Infospace search directory is another Internet-based service that provides residential listings in the United States and Canada, as well as e-mail, business, and government listings. Additional on-line directories include Big Yellow, which contains yellow page telephone listings for over sixteen million businesses; the French Phone Book; toll-free directories for finding 800 numbers; and an e-mail address directory.

For the technologically challenged, the local library contains local and national telephone directories that can be accessed from microfiche and city directories that provide even greater detail, such as a person's occupation, place of employment, and address. The criss-cross directory is a resource that provides street listings and the names, addresses, and telephone numbers of the person residing there. If you have a telephone number and nothing else, you can use a criss-cross directory to find the name of the person belonging to the phone number—almost like caller ID! Some cities provide this same service through the telephone, by letting you dial a number and provide the operator with the telephone number you are needing an address or name for. It's like contacting Information for a telephone number, only backwards. You already have the phone number but are requesting the name that goes with it.

Family History Centers

A Family History Center is an establishment dedicated to providing information on families for genealogy and the purpose of preserving history. The most notable, the Church of Jesus Christ of Latter-Day Saints in Salt Lake City, Utah, is the largest in the world and contains national and international archives on paper or CD-ROM, even providing computer workstations for those wishing to view records on-site. The Mormon Church is a wonderful resource for searchers, but bear in mind that it may frown on any reference to adoption due to the controversial nature of the issue. Consider it a useful reference source, but be aware that the church's main focus is the preservation of history.

Consult the reference section of this book for the locations of Family History Centers throughout the world.

Genealogists

Genealogy is a popular hobby for many Americans, even those who have a solid grasp of their heritage. The family tree has been used for centuries, as people struggle to re-create their family history and lineage, to discover those who carried the same name through life. For some people, the family tree becomes a treasure chest of memories, especially as they get older. My uncle Howard, a tough, cigar-smoking old man, began every visit to my house by repeating stories about his younger days in the boxing ring. Inevitably, the conversation would turn to the family tree he had worked so hard to re-create, and Howard's face would light up animatedly as he pulled out a cigar box filled with photographs and sketches of the tree. When he died, I thought back to his excitement and childlike enthusiasm for the link to his past, and I wished I had spent more time listening, asking, and enjoying.

Family Tree Maker is a product that offers a step-by-step guide for searching for family members and re-creating the family tree. It can be found in just about any genealogy store or catalog or on the Internet. Other products like it are available on the market, devoted to the reconstruction of the family bloodline.

The Bookstore

By now you should realize that you have literally hundreds of options available to assist you with your search. Your local bookseller is another wonderful resource, and while specific titles on searches may be hard to find, an employee should be able to research the topic in the bookstore's computer database to order a book for you. The sections on self-improvement, parenting, or family issues are the best places to start to find titles on adoption, and adoption organizations will also have access to a long list of books devoted to the subject.

Volunteers

In many states there are search volunteers who will help with all or part of your search in exchange for paid expenses only. There are obvious pros and cons to using a volunteer, ranging from the benefit of no fee for services to the lack of control that comes with having someone involved in your search. Volunteers have lives of their own, too, and priorities that could distract them from completing the search as expeditiously as you would prefer.

On the Internet, a page called the Volunteer Search Network allows you to complete a brief questionnaire that is electronically mailed to a volunteer in the city in which you want the search to take place. The volunteer will then respond to your request with an e-mail message outlining the details and methods used. The network is comprehensive and is composed of volunteers from all over the nation.

Volunteers may also be found through adoption support groups and at post-adoption centers. Search the yellow pages for a center near you, and call to inquire about volunteer services.

Paid Search Consultants

Many people employ a search consultant to help them find their missing loved one. If you don't feel like you have the time or desire to dedicate to the search endeavor, this route is an alternative you may wish to investigate. Fees for search consultants will vary by individual. Most consultants will provide you with a contract that outlines the cost and logistics of the services they provide, as well as the normal length of a successful search. Some fully licensed consultants have received credentials from a governing organization called Independent Search Consultants. ISC trains and certifies consultants to search and prides itself on providing consultants who have extensive experience conducting family searches. If you decide to hire one of them, be sure to obtain references and follow up to make sure the references are legitimate. The best consultants will probably have a personal interest in helping others and may even have been in the same situation at one time. If you can find a search consultant who has been through the process of searching for his own family member, you know you are getting assistance from an individual who can empathize with your desire to learn about your past.

Attorneys

Lawyers who specialize in adoption issues and obtaining unsealed records through court orders can be a significant resource in an adoptee's search for documentation. Oftentimes these legal professionals have had extensive experience lobbying for records and have been through the entire chain of events that makes a search successful. If you can find a lawyer who has had success in the search process, she may already have established contacts in the judicial system.

Although not everyone is enamored with the idea of hiring an attorney, knowledge of legal loopholes can be invaluable in negotiating the often obscure course of adoption jargon and procedures. When championing to open sealed records, an attorney is almost a necessity. Contact a local adoption support group or organization in your area to obtain the name of a good attorney, or start contacting law firms for an adoption specialist.

Investigative Organizations

A private investigator can be pricey, but if you have the money and not the time to initiate your search, hiring an investigator to do it for you could be the most viable alternative. Some private investigators specialize solely in adoption searches and will have the components in place to focus on a search for a family member. Be sure to ask for references, so you feel comfortable with the type of service and person you are hiring to conduct your search.

Like attorneys and other for-fee professionals, a good private investigator will offer you a contract in advance for his services, specifying exactly the type of services he will perform and outlining a fee structure. As with any other resource, you can ask the private investigator to conduct parts of the search or all of it. If the investigator can gain enough information to get you started, you may want to complete the rest of the search on your own. This will ensure that you, not a professional searcher, are the first point of contact with your new family member.

If you feel queasy about making contact yourself, a neutral person such as an investigator can do it for you. Think about how you would want to be approached if you were the one being searched for, and go with your instincts. The seek-and-find event is shocking enough in itself for the one being found; the added intrusion of a professional searcher may be a bit overwhelming. A common option is to allow the investigator to go through the entire process of locating your relatives, with the stipulation that you will be the one to contact them if and when they are found.

To peruse a list of investigators licensed by the National Association of Investigative Specialists, Inc., contact the organization directly by writing P.O. Box 33244, Austin, TX 78764, or phoning 512-719-3595. This organization has on record a list of screened and licensed investigators from within the United States and more than twenty countries worldwide. A listing can be provided by state, in its entirety, or even by area of specialization.

Public Records

In most states, marriage and divorce records are public and available upon request. If you have a last name, you can scan through decades of records for someone who matches the biographical profile (age, etc.) of the one you are searching for. Marriage records can provide you with a person's address at the time of marriage and a file-tracking number which will correspond with the marriage license on file. If you can then obtain a hard copy of the marriage license, additional detail about that person will be present on the certificate. Divorce records may be harder to obtain but can also supply you with priceless facts. If you are searching for a person whom you know was divorced, you should contact the appropriate agency in that state to request a divorce record. A list of agencies by state appears in the resource section of this book.

Public records are a wealth of information. I found out I had brothers by seeing their names in the obituary of the person I had been searching for (my biological father) and obtained a copy of my birth certificate by contacting the Office of Vital Statistics in the state where I was born. You may have difficulty obtaining specific public records, as many searchers have encountered clerks with antiquated views on the issue of family searches and access to public records. This can delay your entire process, not to mention dampen your spirits, so familiarize yourself with each agency's procedures for obtaining such records before actually attempting to get them. Make one phone call and ask for the procedures, fees, and any forms that could be mailed or faxed to you. The Freedom of Information Act was signed into law by President Lyndon Johnson in 1967 and offers Americans access to federal records with just cause. Fortunately, most public records are available by simply following the procedures the public office has established.

Nonpublic records consist of anything that is not readily available to the public. This type of record exists on each and every one of us. Utility bills, college records, and military, financial, and alumni records all exist and are filed in a database or in hard-copy files. Databases are sold every single day for profit, literally multiplying the existence of these records. Have you ever received unwanted phone or mail solicitations? Chances are your name and address have been sold to the organization soliciting you. Use your street smarts every step of the way and keep in mind that everyone leaves a transaction trail.

Census Bureau

The United States conducts a census every ten years to compile statistical data on the population. The census information includes figures on race, gender, age, and other specific data that is made available to the public after seventy years. Just like the old saying that it takes money to make money, you'll need to have some specific information about the person you are searching for to obtain the information contained within the appropriate census records. Any public library should have access to census data as provided by the National Archives.

The address for the census bureau itself is: The Bureau of the Census, Pittsburg, KS 66762. The census bureau will also provide you with a form for requesting someone's address if you have a legal and valid reason. Contact the bureau for details and current procedures on completing this form.

The census bureau is also accessible on-line, with an extensive web site offering various topics to drill down to. Their name-search page will tell you how many people exist in the world with the same name as the one you enter, though it won't actually search for a name or person for you. If you're looking for statistical data on subjects such as aging, the population, women-owned businesses, Hispanic households, or marriages and divorces, the census web site is the place for you.

Social Security

If you already know the Social Security number of the one you are looking for, your search could be minutes away from completion. Computer databases can find someone literally within seconds, just by entering the individual's Social Security number. More likely than not, a current address will be on file. Companies all over the world provide such services for a minimal fee. See the resource section for listings.

The Social Security Administration will not actually divulge information relating to a Social Security number, but it will forward a letter to the one you are searching for if you provide a humanitarian reason. This would require a written request to the agency including the person's full name and/or Social Security number, as well as the reason you would like the letter forwarded.

The Social Security Administration also manages the Social Security Death Benefit Index (SSDI), an electronic database containing the names of over fifty million people who died, yet remain on record as receiving Social Security benefits. If you are trying to find information on someone who passed away and he or his survivors received benefits, you can obtain records that will provide his birth and death date and zip code. This information can then lead you to the individual's death certificate, which would provide the actual cause and location of death. The Social Security Administration maintains information on earnings, former employers, and the employment location of the deceased. To access the SSDI database, order it on CD-ROM by calling 1-800-222-3766, or use it free of charge at Church of Latter-Day Saints Family History Centers. Most public libraries and genealogy centers will carry it as well.

Another way to utilize the Social Security number in a search is by using it to determine the state in which your number was issued. If you were adopted and are not entirely sure where you were born or resided, your Social Security number can tell you. Everyone has a Social Security number that is linked to a state, as identified by the first three digits. For instance, if your Social Security number begins with 261, you were born in Florida or your Social Security card was issued in Florida. If it begins with 000, you should really be curious, because no Social Security numbers were formally issued with that prefix. The Social Security Administration can fax you a current index of Social Security numbers that correspond with the state in which they were issued, or it may even be able to provide you with the information over the phone.

A private company called Task Force Software offers a Social Security number search database that will query for various facts about a specific number. After a number is entered into the database, which is available on the Internet, the date of issue, along with the state in which the number was issued, is instantly provided. This can validate the state the person was living in on a certain date. The database will also put up a red flag for any false numbers or any numbers that were issued to specific groups of individuals such as Korean refugees, for example. The software can be purchased by contacting the company toll-free at 1-800-397-3085.

Obituaries

If you have a surname, a very good resource is the state death index. This will provide you with a list of deaths and references to obituaries, which will allow you to research for more detail. To obtain the death index, go to your library or, for an obituary, go directly to the town in which the person you are searching for lived and possibly died. I located my father's obituary by calling an old library in a tiny town in upstate New York. Again, if you are comfortable on the computer, refer to the Internet first, as many newspapers and libraries have started to publish their periodicals on-line.

Hospital Records

In addition to the documents mentioned heretofore, hospital records, if you have your birth name, are filled with valuable information that can help you track down important medical history. Many hospitals archive records for a number of years, and some will provide them to anyone who makes a formal request. Others may not allow the records to be released. Again, every institution and individual will vary. If you run into a dead end with the hospital in which you were born, try contacting the company that acts as a warehouse for medical records. Be prepared to offer some creative explanations for needing the information. Sometimes, all you need to do is ask.

Another great resource, if you think you know the name of the doctor who delivered you, would be the American Medical Association's sourcebook of physicians. The *AMA Physician Select* has compiled data on more than 650,000 physicians nationwide. Published by the American Medical Association, this reference guide contains demographic and professional information on individual physicians in the United States. The intended use of this guide is for families or individuals searching for information on health professionals; however, the information within could lead you to a doctor or hospital that will be responsive to a phone call and sympathetic to your desire to know more about your biological family.

Property Records and Purchases

Property records are usually public information, available at the local county courthouse in the city where the property is located. Information brokers can provide reports on specific properties owned by an individual, usually for a reasonable fee. One such company, the American Information Network, offers a property-search database that runs a report from an address. The report comes back with the name of the owner, purchase date, parcel number, and assessed value. The American Information Network can be reached by calling 330-484-6272.

Religious Records

If you know your religion at birth, it may be valuable to pursue any records that exist on specific religious ceremonies that could have taken place. If the agency that placed you for adoption was affiliated with a religious organization, the church might still have records that could offer important information. Catholic agencies sometimes baptize infants after birth and often keep the baptismal certificates on file.

For more information, contact the church, adoption agency, temple, or other religious body that could have been involved with your birth.

Military Records

If the one you are searching for ever served in the military, you can try contacting the Veterans Administration to request information by calling 1-800-827-1000. There is also a form to request military records for every branch of the military, but you have to be next of kin to receive the information or have the form signed by next of kin. Either way, it is an option worth exploring. Contact the National Archives and Records Administration in Washington, D.C., for free information on how to request records of anyone who was born on a U.S. military base, or write to the General Services Administration, National Personnel Records Center, 9700 Page Boulevard, St. Louis, MO 83232.

Every country, city, and county will have a different method for disseminating this information. Canada's National Archives contains personnel files on more than five million former employees of the Canadian Armed Forces and the Federal Public Service. These records include the individual's employment history, military service, personal details, and pension data and are available by written request.

Also worth exploring are military alumni organizations, military publications, and military newsletters. Most branches of the service have reunions from time to time, and some military offices will forward a letter to a veteran for a nominal fee.

An address for each branch of the United States military locator service may be found in the resource section of this book.

Criminal Records

If you find during the search process that the person you are searching for has led a life of crime, it is very likely that you will locate him by way of the paper trail he's left behind with the criminal system. If he is currently incarcerated, it should be relatively easy to find him by contacting law enforcement authorities within the prison system itself. If he has been convicted of a crime or has previously served jail time, his name and current address may be listed in a justice system computer database. And yes, believe it or not, some prisons even have web sites on the Internet that list their entire inmate population. Like the roster of a hotel, the directory will list the names of every "guest" registered. If you know your missing person was convicted in a particular state, contact the prison officials within that state to inquire about an on-line directory or to ask that a hard copy be mailed to you.

Voter Registrations

Many Americans are registered voters in one state or another and actively participate in elections. Some states allow access to the voter registration database, and some do not. To determine if yours will provide you information (usually for a fee) on voters, contact the local elections office in the county or state in which you are searching. If available, voter registration information will provide a person's last known address and any other specific household information that was requested on the registration form. This data is usually available on hard copy or CD-ROM.

Law Enforcement Agencies

Don't discount human contact. In most successful searches, tips provided by another human being gave the key to the success. If your target has had a criminal history or died from criminal circumstances, the law enforcement agency in the town in which she lived or died could hold vital clues.

For missing children, TRAK (Technology to Recover Abducted Kids) is a privately owned system that enables law enforcement agencies to create, print, and electronically distribute information on missing children. The information consists of a high-quality color photograph which can be faxed to law enforcement agencies and various locations throughout a community within hours of a child's reported disappearance.

Backed by major corporations such as AT&T, Hewlett-Packard, and Chevron, TRAK is just one missing-persons tool that may be used to find those who are victims of abductions or criminal activity. If you are look-ing for a missing child or an adult who has vanished under these circum-stances or who has been abducted illegally by a parent or friend, contact your local law enforcement agency as soon as possible.

The United States Postal Service

The post office used to provide forwarding address information for a minor fee upon request. Now the only legal method of obtaining it is on-line, as the postal service strives to better manage this process. The postal service has outsourced this function to computer contractors who act as distribu-tors of information. These national change-of-address agents have purchased computer tapes containing change of address information to subsequently resell it to on-line providers such as Prodigy and America Online.

It is definitely worth a telephone call or a visit to the post office to determine that location's current modus operandi with regard to forward-ing address information. Another possibility is to send something to any address you already have for someone, to see if it is forwarded.

High Schools and Universities

If you have learned the name of the high school or university your target person attended, it may be worthwhile to make a trip there to investigate. Yearbooks and annuals of sororities, fraternities, and other organizations will provide listings of members and usually photographs. If your missing per-son was a member of the choir, football team, or student government, track-ing down the names of others who knew him could lead you to the one you are searching for.

Nursing Homes

Yes, even homes for the aged can be a valuable resource in your search, especially if the one you are searching for is from a very small town. One thing can lead to another, and there may be someone living there to whom you are related or who knew the one you are searching for. Janice, an adoptee, was fifty-three when she found her biological father in a nursing home in Florida. She had delayed the search for him for years, thinking he had abandoned her and her mother when she was just a child. When she finally discovered the truth—that her mother had been the one to leave, taking Janice away from him—Janice decided to begin a search. When she finally found her father it was too late, for he could not remember her and she could not tell him she loved him. He was frail and stricken with Alzheimer's, unable to speak or respond to anyone. Her father had been in the home for many years, and the nurses told Janice he often insisted he had a daughter who was one day coming to visit. On his eightieth birthday, he even asked to be dressed in his suit and shiny black shoes, as he was certain she was coming to see him that day. When no one showed, the nurses dismissed his behavior as the dementia of an elderly man.

Another woman, a nurse, found her father in the very same nursing home she worked in. Life is unpredictable and baffling at times, and even the most ironic or unusual scenario should not be ruled out. Consider the countless stories you hear or read about people who find that their parents work for the same company as themselves or that their long-lost sibling lives nearby. Virtually anything you can think of has happened once before.

Visit the retirement facilities and nursing homes and talk with the people there. If you don't find any information or a distant relative, at least you've brightened some elderly person's day.

Have You Exhausted All Options?

Review your profile and action plan again, and be sure that you haven't overlooked any viable option.

- Talk with neighbors, friends, teachers, and store owners.

- Place a personal ad in the classifieds in the area you think your missing person lives. Be creative. If you are searching for a birth parent, place the ad on or around your birthday or even the date you were adopted. Remember, many birth mothers have reported the feeling of loss around their relinquished child's birth date. Mother's Day is another important milestone reported by birth mothers, and a day that brings with it memories of their lost child. Put yourself in their shoes, and consider every alternative.

- Search for public documents at the library on microfiche.

- Find membership rosters for any organizations or clubs your target person had membership in. Americans have a variety of interests, and there aren't many who don't belong to some sort of club or organization. If you're doubtful that this is a road worth investigating, think back throughout your life and I bet you can come up with at least one organized group that you have been a part of. Whether it be the high school marching band or the American Association of Retired Persons, most everyone, at one time or another, has been a member of a group.

- Check with the Department of Motor Vehicles for a driving record report to obtain a recent address.

- Peruse old school yearbooks or fraternity or sorority membership rosters.

- Check with a genealogist for more search options.

- Contact a support group and think of it as another resource for you to use in your search. Oftentimes the people who attend have completed a search already or have access to valuable information that could put you a few steps ahead of where you are right now.

- Focus on your family for information first.

- If you feel comfortable, tell as many people as possible that you are searching for someone. Mention it briefly in a conversation, and you're opening the door for even more information on how to conduct a search. People are our most valuable resource, and someone you know may be able to put you in touch with someone who can help you. Talk, talk, talk. It's on your mind, so mention it whenever you can. I did, and I found a coworker who was searching for his mother, a manicurist longing to know her birth father, and others engaged in some form of the search process.

- At the courthouse or city hall, obtain tax or public property records with an address.

- Contact the courthouse for voter registration information on the person you are looking for.

- Contact an information broker who can enter the name of your missing person into a computer database.

- Contact any organization your person was affiliated with. Many have membership files on computer. Try real estate licensing organizations, the FAA (has licensed pilots on record), the American Institute of Certified Public Accountants, labor unions, model train collectors, etc.

- Don't forget the town gossip, the neighbors, the UPS man. Talk to as many people as you can. I know if someone wanted information on me and my life, the Federal Express man who delivers to my neighborhood could tell you that I send and receive several packages a week, work from home, often stay in my pajamas most of the day, and have a telephone permanently fixed to my ear.

- Search through trade manuals, Who's Who books, Chamber of Commerce membership lists, and the *Encyclopedia of Associations*. There are several such manuals listing organizations and their addresses.

- Search the church directory. Oftentimes, a church publishes telephone numbers and addresses of the entire membership. Even people with unlisted phone numbers can find themselves suddenly listed in the church directory. I was surprised to find the phone number and address of Ross Perot, billionaire and aspiring politician, listed in the printed directory his church mailed to me.

- If you have an address for the one you are searching for and access to a computer, get on the Internet and visit the Mapquest web site. It offers street listings and travel directions and will provide you with maps on a local and national level. Drive to the address you find, and investigate for yourself.

All of this information may seem overwhelming when you think of the time that searching could entail. In actuality, the time it takes to search could be anywhere from a day to a decade, depending on your situation and persistence. Every individual circumstance is different, and there are no givens. For the most part, searching for a biological mother could take a bit longer than a search for a biological father, due to the name changes that most women go through after marriages. Men almost never change names unless they have criminal intent or are avoiding apprehension.

Carving out time to engage in a search may prove to be complicated, but if it means temporarily eliminating something in your normal routine, perhaps it's something you should consider. Think of items that remain on your to-do list and keep getting pushed to the bottom of it. Our careers, families, and daily activities make it hard to achieve everything we would like to do, and the items that are not critical get overlooked quickly. Add researching your family history to the list, and it too becomes something that is delayed.

I'm one of those people who tend to have every second of my day filled with activity, never leaving myself enough time between meetings or personal engagements. Because of this, I reviewed my daily activities in an attempt to find a slot for searching. I couldn't, so I forced myself to cut back on a few things until my search was concluded. I completely gave up working out until my search was over. This was the hardest sacrifice of all, but the activity filled the hours I had available after work, and by the time I got home from working out, I was usually too exhausted to think about anything else.

Another place I freed up time was in my reading. I love reading, and when I made my decision to search, I was up to three newspapers a day, usually a local paper, the *Wall Street Journal,* and *USA Today.* I decided to eliminate the local paper during the search process and briefly scan one national publication. It gave me extra time in the day, and I didn't miss a thing. Not one person said, "You know, Tammy, you really should get up to speed on current events!" I also cut back on the books I was reading and shifted my habits. I used to reserve the time traveling between business meetings for reading, but I substituted paperwork and e-mail instead. These were the things I normally did after the end of a long workday, so the shift gave me those extra hours to focus on my search. Your job can certainly be time consuming, but you'd be amazed how much time the little things in your life take when added up—things such as reading, making personal phone calls, running errands, and socializing.

Don't compromise your existing relationships or sacrifice time with yourself. Reevaluate your typical day, take a closer look at your priorities, and cut out what you can. If completing the search is truly an important goal, you will make the necessary sacrifices to achieve it. Remember that the search process itself can be emotionally taxing, so don't give up anything that is a stress releaser for you, and try not to deprive yourself of the basics, such as meals, vitamins, and sleep. Exercise fits into the category of personal wellness, so it's best to maintain your normal workout routine if you can. Know yourself and set boundaries that you can live by.

A successful search can be conducted on weekends, nights, and every day, if even for a minute. Place a call from the office at lunchtime or from the car on the way in. Carry your search file with you at all times, even when you travel on business, sit in the waiting room for a doctor's appointment, or commute to work on the morning train. Wherever you find an idle moment, use it to prepare for the next step in the search.

Don't force yourself to do it; instead be guided by your heart and inner workings. Let the desire to search lead you, and trust your instincts to create your path. Rarely are we misguided when we follow our internal compass. As adults, we have the benefit of years of experience and wisdom to go on. We can become our own role models, we've crossed the line between child and adult, and most of the time can discern what is right and what is not.

I wish I could tell the children of the world that they have much to look forward to that they cannot yet imagine. When we are children we cannot understand why things have happened the way they have, why our friend has two parents and we have just one, or why we were given up by our parents. The headmistress of a children's school in the Deep South, where 90 percent of the school's children come from poverty and desperation, yet where 90 percent of them go on to college, said it best. "I tell all of these kids that they are responsible for only themselves," she said. "I tell them: you are not responsible for the actions of your parents, you are not to blame for your mother's alcoholism, your father's temper, your family's poverty—you are only to blame if you don't get your homework in on time."

Even as adults, it is easy to blame others for the predicaments we're in, but we can truly only blame ourselves. It is up to each one of us to create the best life possible, to choose the path of positive thinking and action, and to do the things necessary to bring ourselves full circle. If the search is something that will bring your life full circle, then do it, and do the best that you can to find what you're looking for. Use the methods described in this book, and if they aren't working for you, devise methods of your own. Don't take no to mean never, and keep thinking like a private investigator would. Exhaust all options using every feasible resource.

If you call the orphanage that handled your adoption transaction and are denied information, pursue another angle. Examine everything, and find someone who worked there years ago when you were born. This person may be separated from the organization and willing to share information. If that doesn't work, find the mail carrier who delivered there each day. He or she may have stopped in to see the children. The information channels are endless, and you are limited only by your imagination and persistence.

If you are looking for your birth mother and know that she was once a hairdresser, contact the salons in the town where she lived. Inquire at the ones that have been in business for years, for you may find someone who once worked with her or the daughter of someone who worked with her. Search through old telephone directories at the library to locate the addresses of beauty shops. Go and talk with the neighboring shopkeepers, because even if that particular salon is out of business, the businesses that were next-door may not be. You can't expect to walk up and find things unchanged after twenty years, but you can expect to find someone who knows something or someone who could point you in the right direction.

Every individual creates a paper trail spanning over years of simple and complex transactions. Uncovering just one detail could be the key to finding that person and solving the mystery of your life.

CHAPTER FOUR

Resolution

I wonder where your life has taken you,
I wonder how you feel . . .
I wonder if you think of me, as something that is real

ONE SEARCH ORGANIZATION offers for sale a bumper sticker with the saying, "Life can be puzzling when you're the missing piece!" It certainly rings true, and what some do not realize is that although the search itself can be a puzzling experience, the aftermath can leave behind a deluge of confusing feelings. If your search is successful and you locate even one member of your family, you will be open to a whole new world of information about your life, your birth, and the lives of your family members. They may have had very different backgrounds than yours, or they may have had other interests and aspirations or perhaps none at all. Your new family member could have a criminal history, political or religious beliefs unlike your own, or even a drug or alcohol addiction. Like the rest of us, your birth family won't be perfect; even if they are, there's no guarantee you're going to love them. Remain open-minded and be prepared to welcome your family and their viewpoints into your universe.

If you are reunited with a family that you were once a part of, it is probable that a systematic surge of repressed memories will flow to the surface as time goes by. Children who were separated from family members in their youth often report no recollection of what would seem to be significant events surrounding the separation. The memories are there but have been suppressed in some way and may eventually be triggered by inconsequential or major events. Something as simple as the smell of freshly cut grass, or the sound of a particular song, may bring back a memory associated with the childhood that preceded the break from the family. For most, these repressed memories reawaken only after a search has been completed, when the adult's mind is open to the analysis of the past.

Another common feeling that people face after being reunited is the desire to make up for lost time with their new family. Some do it by buying expensive gifts, while others seek to spend every moment possible with their newfound biological relatives. The families they have been raised by often interpret such behavior as abandonment, seeing their child pulling away, not toward them. Offer your parents or other family members reassurance that you will still be there after you've found what you're looking for. Make sure that they're aware of what you're thinking and feeling and that you still care for them. It's possible that they'll say they understand your actions, but people who have not lived with the mystery of their ancestry may not understand your desire to transfer emotions and love to someone whom you have just found. This is the time to share your feelings with your family, either verbally or in a letter.

On the other side of things, you might find that the one you have located does not share your desire to form a relationship or even to get to know you. In adoption circles this is referred to as the second rejection. The first rejection, in the mind of the adoptee, occurred at the time of the adoption, when the child was given away; the second, when he or she is rejected again by the birth parent or siblings. The second rejection can be immediate or prolonged. A biological relative may be curious and express interest in an initial reunion but back off after the novelty wears off. If a birth parent has other biological children, or a spouse who does not know about you, the parent may not be strong enough or mature enough to handle a reunion, or the reunion could take place and be followed by a change of heart or even total denial and lack of further contact.

Many who have been through the search event have experienced the initial stage of excitement and rush of adrenaline in rediscovering their roots. This phase is like a honeymoon where everything is positive and everyone is immersed in getting acquainted. It may last for a very long time, but eventually the honeymoon must end and the newness subsides. This can be particularly hard on the searcher who has entered an entire family. The family has had their own set of traditions and family gatherings, and even if the searcher has been welcomed into the fold, the others share traditions and memories that the new family member can never be a part of. A common occurrence for a searcher who enters a family of siblings is the creation of a bond with one or more siblings, which in turn creates a division or weakening of the relationship between the other siblings who have grown up together and experienced the conflicts that come with living together. Often when searchers find a sibling or other family member before locating a biological parent, they discover that one or more members of the family become a shield to the birth parent. This person may determine that it would not be healthy either emotionally or physically for the parent if the new family member entered their lives. Even when family members are welcoming, there is usually one or more who act as a filter, afraid of what someone else will think or feel about the newfound family member.

If the one you have searched for and found is welcoming, remember that you will be entering his life anew, without experiencing any of his previous imperfections. He might seem perfect, and your other family certainly will not, especially if they weren't supportive of your search efforts. Keep all of these things in mind and be sensitive to them as you proceed with your search. Of course, if you're a flexible person by nature, you'll have an easier time adapting to whatever you may find and to the events that transpire afterwards.

One thing that the reunion will not bring, no matter how joyful or perfect, is a change of self. Indeed, many who have searched have described changes within themselves, but not an entire change of *self*. Finding your family can change and even improve your feelings about yourself, but it will not transform you into someone else entirely. You're still going to be the same person post-search that you were before, if only a little more whole. The search may answer a lot of questions and clear up the uncertainties that weighed on your heart, but it will not solve your problems. If you are searching to escape the troubles that follow you, those troubles will probably still be there after the search is complete; if you had insecurities before the search, you'll have insecurities after the search. If you had low self-esteem and a poor self-image, the search won't take them away. You will still hold the same beliefs, mannerisms, and inherent emotions, but you're also likely to experience entirely new ones. You'll be the same person, only you will have grown, and, even better, you will experience resolution.

Resolution is simply the feeling that you've come full circle and filled the big, empty space that formerly occupied your heart. It's different for everyone, as are the reasons people search, and it can come in a variety of forms. Resolution is necessary to move on, but it may take some time for you to reach it, to get to the point where you feel like the circle is finally closed. The biggest obstacle to resolution is the fear of the unknown. It's worth reiterating because risk and fear, although sometimes subtle, can inhibit us from attaining our innermost desires.

Risk prevents people who dream of doing so from becoming entrepreneurs and keeps them confined to tiny office cubicles for the rest of their lives. Many people dream, but few actually take the risk. Risk prevents those who long for a child from having one, as they slowly convince themselves that their lives will be doomed when they do: they won't be able to travel anymore or have successful careers, and any fun they once had will cease to exist the very minute the child is born. Risk stems from fear and holds those back who never realize that in life there are no guarantees. Not one of us is born with a contract that says life will be easy and risk-free. Seasons change, people die, and pretty soon our safety nets are worn and tattered. We are not invincible, we will not all retire at forty as we predicted in our twenties, and we no longer take things for granted. To make things happen is to take some risk. To love and learn and discover what we are searching for is to embrace and accept risk into our lives. Eventually we come to realize that *risk* is the twin brother of *change*, and both remain with us forever as we travel through the lottery of life. The two are unavoidable and not to be reckoned with, never to be predicted, which is why life, in its unpredictability, is precious and valuable. You can't be certain that your mother, your father, your children, or even yourself will be here tomorrow. You can't guarantee that you'll read another book or see another day. There is some form of risk involved in anything that matters, and there is likely to be some semblance of risk involved in your search process.

Risk is something that everyone handles differently. If you are ever in Chicago's O'Hare International Airport and have a few minutes to spare, introduce yourself to someone who is truly an inspiration when it comes to risk and fearless abandon. This young man could be the poster boy for risk, and I found him one day in the bowels of O'Hare as I headed along the sterile corridor linking the bustling underground airport terminal to my hotel.

As I hurried by with the throngs of other travelers, I noticed the faint sound of a lively and soothing violin emanating from the walls. It grew louder as I neared the end of the corridor until it echoed through the hallway, the glorious sounds of the music rising and falling like waves on a moonlit sea. Imagine my surprise to find that it was originating not from a piped-in sound system but from a singular young man furiously playing at the end of the hall, entranced in his own world.

His leather violin case was open and scattered with no more than three or four dollar bills, and he continued to play even as I stopped, waited, and watched. He was immersed in his playing; when he finally finished we spoke for a while, and I listened as he told me his story. The young man's only goal in life is to gain admission into the prestigious Chicago Symphony Orchestra. With this in mind, he quit his former job in another state and moved to the Windy City, with the hope that by being closer to his dream, he could more easily pursue it. The young man arrived in the United States from his homeland of China, where he once taught music. Though he did not know English when he arrived, he earned his master's degree at Michigan State before fixing his sights on his dream.

It amazed me that he was here, standing in the basement of a Chicago airport, practicing, and playing his music. The man explained all of this by saying, "The risk is much better than remaining comfortable." He was one of those rare individuals with the vision to see that risk is inevitable and paramount to attaining your dreams. I have a feeling that even if he never gets into the Chicago Symphony Orchestra, this young man will find a way to make life meaningful, and will find for himself new goals to attain.

Evaluate the risk and what it means for you to achieve resolution in your life. If you find your family, and your search is successful, closure will be the ultimate reward. If you are not seeking closure but just want to find the one you are seeking, you have a practical approach and no emotional ties or risks either way. Some people who search are specifically seeking closure, and the smallest piece of information about their family history could satisfy their curiosity. Still others complete the search, learning all that they can about their genealogy and ancestors. There are no specific guidelines and no rights or wrongs as to what you should feel.

Ralph Shymanski was seventy and retired from a successful boat-building business when he discovered the answers he had been searching a lifetime for. He received an unexpected letter in the mail from a long-lost sister, living overseas. She had been adopted as an infant, and though he remembered little about his baby sister, he had always wanted to find her. After they were reunited, Ralph's whole attitude brightened, and he now sends her letters and photographs regularly. She is the last living relative in his family, and he is determined to remain close to her.

Although Ralph's story had a positive ending, not all family reunions will turn out that way. Statistics point to higher numbers of positive reunions than negative ones, but negative reunions do occur from time to time. Meagan, an adoptee, searched for her birth mother for five years with no success until a private investigator located her living in a town three hundred miles away. Meagan sent a letter and received a response in the mail just six days later. The letter was from her mother, who said that she wanted to meet right away. Meagan tried calling the telephone number that her mother provided in the letter, but it had been disconnected. Panicking at the thought of losing her again, Meagan drove to the town where she knew her mother lived, found the address in a run-down section of the city, and knocked on the door. The woman who answered looked uncannily like her, and Meagan knew it had to be her mother. When Meagan told her the reason for the visit, the woman became enraged and slammed the door in her face. Meagan left, shaken and devastated from the experience.

When family reunions are successful, it can be one of the most rewarding events to witness in the world. When they are not, it can be tragic. The longing to find a loved one is a very powerful thing, fraught with emotion. Shortly after an article was published about my own search for family, I received a call from a woman who was searching for the two children she had given up for adoption. This call came just one week before Mother's Day, and the message this woman left on my answering machine was desperate and somewhat unrealistic. She spoke in a halting voice, her words mixed with tears: *"Hello . . . my name is Mary, and I'm searching for the two boys I gave up for adoption as a young girl. I need to find them . . . before Mother's Day . . ."*

Mary probably didn't actually believe that she could find her missing children in just seven days, but the forthcoming Mother's Day holiday was the catalyst that prompted her call and her desire to search. There are thousands of Marys throughout the world who long to find children they have lost. They simply exist and continue about life after their child is gone. By the time they decide to search, they have already searched in their mind and arrived at conclusions about their child and the kind of life the child has led, much like children formulate fantasies about their biological parents. The mother may even have made a few phone calls throughout the years in an attempt to make contact, but the time to search has finally come.

If a birth mother has no desire to search, she may feel totally comfortable with her decision to give her child to a loving family and may have come to grips with it the moment the decision was made. If you are a child who is searching, you will never really know into which category your mother fell, until your search is complete. As a birth parent in search for a child, you will never know if your child will accept you until the search is over. The completion of the search itself will lead to a heightened level of understanding of the circumstances involved, eliminating the cobwebs in the process.

Just as you know it when you're really in love, you'll also know when resolution has come. You'll feel more settled than ever before, more balanced, and more complete. The feeling of resolution will clear your mind and free your senses, opening your eyes and spirit to even greater awareness. Resolution is not always the result of a happy event, but most often it leads to a feeling of awareness and the ability to move forward with life. People who have lost loved ones to war have said that the feelings they suffered while waiting months and years to hear the fate of their loved one were sometimes worse than the feelings suffered when the news actually arrived that their loved one was found dead. Resolution had come in the form of bad news, but it was resolution nonetheless.

Some who search for missing family members get within steps of finding them and decide against contact at the last minute. In one episode of the popular television series *Friends*, the character Phoebe searches for her father and successfully locates his address and telephone number. She calls to talk with him, but she hangs up when he answers. She drives to see him, but she gets only as far as his driveway before she chickens out and drives away, only to back out over his little dog. Phoebe has struggled internally with the dilemma of making contact and now has the problem of how to tell him she has injured his dog! Phoebe does not find resolution until much later, when she finally assembles the courage to confront her past.

More than a few have described the actual moment prior to the reunion as a terrifying mixture of emotions. One man said that he sat for hours with a bottle of wine and his search packet in front of him. He had the name and telephone number of his sister, and all he had to do was call, but he was literally paralyzed with uncertainty and fear. He wanted to make the call to her, he knew that much for sure, but he paced the floor, poured another glass of wine, and rehearsed the conversation over and over in his head. Finally, he picked up the telephone and dialed the number. When his sister finally answered, he got nervous and hung up on her! Luckily, she had caller ID and phoned him back, curious to know who the prank caller was.

I remember the day like no other—the day I drove along the water on a warm summer afternoon in Florida with my search file sitting in the passenger seat beside me. It was larger than life and so intimidating that it could have been the President sitting there on that seat in my car. It was just one manila folder, but within it was a computerized printout of names, and one of them, I knew, would lead me to my family. I pulled over to the side of the highway that day and opened the file with shaky hands, focusing my eye on one number that literally made my stomach twist and turn. As I picked up the cell phone and dialed the number, I was as nervous as if I were going to speak in front of an audience of five hundred. The phone rang and rang, and I counted more than ten rings before I hung up. There was no machine, no voice on the other end to tell me that, sorry, I had the wrong number. I drove another mile, pulled over, and tried again. The phone was answered on the first ring, and it was that phone call that changed my life.

In order to achieve resolution, you must actively seek it. The related words for resolution, as found in *Roget's Thesaurus,* are mastery over self, courage, perseverance, and to resolve, among others. All are applicable to the search event, for it takes courage, perseverance, and mastery over self to begin what eventually will lead to resolution. *Webster's* defines resolution as "the act or process of resolving something or breaking it up into its constituent parts or elements" and "a solving, as of a puzzle." The puzzle of family ties is magnified during the search and reunion process, more so than in any other aspect of the family relationship. Piecing the fragments of the puzzle together is a lifelong voyage and, like life itself, the puzzle of who we are has several ingredients.

The journey is not over after a reunion occurs; rather, there are several stages that a child or parent can travel through to reach the golden ring of resolution. Much like the stages of the grieving process, a person who has found her family can expect to experience one or all of the stages at some point.

The first stage, as reported by children, siblings, and birth parents alike, is the stage of excitement and denial. The one who has searched will experience a rush of excitement and adrenaline in actually discovering his biological roots. The excitement will drown out any underlying feelings about the adoption and ingrained issues that lie in the heart of the individual affected by it. This leads to the denial of all major issues, as the parties who have been reunited overlook questions such as why the child was given up, why previous contact had not been made, or why one did not search for the other first. The child or parent may not want to ruin the excitement of the moment and may therefore avoid addressing serious topics. This stage may feel like resolution, but it is actually several steps removed from it.

Anger and confusion, the second stage, may set in when the newness of the moment has worn off and the child has the ability to see that the parent she has found has flaws and imperfections like everyone else, or the parent who had been searching for a child once lost may realize that the fantasies he envisioned about the child are not valid and the child is a simple, basic human, with simple obligations, responsibilities, and goals. One sibling may feel anger that she, but not the others, was the last to be reunited or the only one to be given up for adoption. Eventually the thrill of the reunion will fade away, and the baggage that has been left sitting at the curb will have to be dealt with. Every individual will bring his own baggage and perceptions to the table, and each person will deal with the reunion in different stages, at varying times. What one person feels may be what another person has already felt, which complicates things even more.

One or the other parties may feel anger when the issues that have dwelled just below the surface come rising slowly to the top. More often than not the anger remains dormant, but sometimes it will escalate into a confrontation between the reunited. It is also possible that dredging up memories of the period when the adoption occurred means remembering a negative time in a birth parent's life—a time of youth, confusion, and recklessness when the world was spinning out of control. This is a common situation, and parents and children everywhere are trying to work through the entanglements of the past.

The third stage, sadness or distress, may not appear for a very long time, perhaps even years. The feelings of despair may be related to something that was learned during the search process or result from prolonged feelings of abandonment or loss of time, the years that were missed as a result of the adoption. There may be other family members, or siblings even, who have experienced events together, events that the searcher has missed. Sadness may come when the searcher realizes there is no way to recapture the time that has gone by.

The last stage toward the course of resolution is acceptance. Acceptance comes only when the one who has searched and found has come to terms with all of the issues involved in the adoption or search process. Acceptance means that, good or bad, the relevant parties will grow to accept that what has happened is a part of who they are, a thread in the fabric of their being. Acceptance will pave the path to greater understanding and will allow for a process of healing to begin and continue forever. The process of acceptance means that a child will learn to forgive the mother for the relinquishment, the mother will learn to accept the relationship the child has had with someone else, and both will strive to comprehend the questions and confusion the child has about her life, her past.

Reunion and Loss

The feelings enveloping a person who is reunited with a family member can be stronger than any other. An adult child will approach the reunion with a birth parent on two levels: the first as a child searching for love, acceptance, and answers; and the second as an adult in search of facts such as medical history, nationality, and family background.

When the reunion occurs, it is the culmination of all things. The searcher will sometimes feel as if the one he has found is a precious object that was once lost and must therefore be grasped tightly so that it is never lost again. Conversely, the searcher may be ambivalent about forging a connection with someone who was absent from his life for so many years, and he may harbor unconscious anger toward that person.

A parent searching for a child will feel hesitant to interrupt the child's life, guilt for giving the child up, and worries about whether the child will accept her. Even after the questions have been answered, a feeling of loss can develop. The reunion process is associated with loss when the reunion is unsuccessful or when the person the searcher was hoping to find has passed away. This is one possibility that many do not think about, especially if they have fantasized about what the person they hope to find will look like, act like, and be like. One birth mother who has shared her story on the Internet thought of her daughter every day of her life for thirteen years, unable to forget the infant she gave up in hopes of providing it a better life. The mother grieved on the child's birthday, feeling the loss and emptiness as strong as the day on which she let the little baby go. When she could stand it no more, she composed a letter to the adoption agency to forward to the child's adoptive parents and registered her name in the adoption search registry in hopes that her daughter would register, too. When she received a letter back from the agency, her spirits soared, but the message within it broke her heart, as she learned that her child had died in an accident many years before.

Searching for someone who has long since passed on is not as uncommon as it may seem. It's ironic, perhaps, that someone would feel a void for someone who is not even living, but the loss associated with searching for a biological family member may be more of a need for a connection than a need for that specific person. Though the search is for that one individual, if the searcher has found that the individual has died, often the searcher is able to learn much more along with the information of the death. Some who have searched have found entire families after learning that their mother, father, or siblings have passed away. The need for connection can sometimes be met through the re-creation of the past life that the one they have searched for has lived, giving the searchers insight into their own past.

Feeling a physical link to the past is just as important as finding an emotional one. Those who seek the past are comforted by physical reminders of it such as a watch from a father, a letter from a mother, or old photographs that tell stories about their lives. A seventy-year-old self-described orphan depicted an event she witnessed while working for a child welfare organization in the sixties. A brawny man in a flannel work shirt had come to the building looking for information on his birth mother. He was about fifty, and in his hand he held a stone, an ordinary-looking rock with ragged edges. He had found the stone in the yard of a rooming house where his mother once lived, and he held it tightly in his large hands, the only remembrance he had of his past.

Any evidence of the past is a priceless find and a conduit which further explains the mystery. Scientist and layman alike seek answers to the multitude of mysteries that surround us. The solar system, our existence after death, life on other planets, and even the differences between men and women are all cause for examination. No mystery, however, is as great as one that speaks to our hearts. The mystery of a family not found can be staggering and difficult to accept, for happiness, love, and family are all tied up in one emotional bundle. Like happiness and love, resolution is a mysterious entity and may come immediately or may never come at all. If it eludes us, we must strive to weave it into our lives somehow or endeavor to understand that sometimes in life, there are no answers. Those exact words were spoken at a funeral I attended for a sixteen-year-old child. The officiating pastor offered words of wisdom on resolution and how, sometimes, it never appears. "I find it hard to understand that this is the way God meant it to be," he said of the child's passing, "but sometimes, there are no answers and we must simply accept that there will be none in order to continue living."

The lack of resolution is a hard thing to accept. Wouldn't it be easier if there were answers for every question and the riddles in life were solved effortlessly? If we were provided with tangible survival tools to tackle the world, life would be a breeze. Tools like a map of our past or a crystal ball to predict our future would demystify the unknown and the unpredictable. We do not have such things, but each of us has a reservoir of untapped determination and a capacity to handle much more than we believe. These mental tools become evident during troubling times when, to endure, we need all the inner strength we can manage. They will also reveal themselves during the search, during the moments when you think there will be no answers. Reflect on your goals and aspirations, and look inside yourself for the truth. Don't be held back by fears, people, or inhibitions. All of those things are external elements that cannot affect your inner world if you do not allow them to. Devote your time instead to resolving the issues that are holding you back, for an exhilarating future awaits!

CHAPTER FIVE

Progress

I'm living breathing here and now, life has been good to me,
But still remains deep in my heart . . . something I can't see

IN APRIL OF 1996, the Reverend Thomas F. Brosnan addressed the National Maternity and Adoption Conference in San Antonio, Texas. An adoptee himself, the Reverend offered a moving speech about the effects of adoption in his own life and the need for access to open records for all adoptees. "The experience of loss and the need to belong are universal human experiences," remarked Reverend Brosnan. "When the truth is suppressed, forces are created that weaken and destabilize the family unit."

Truth and the development of relationships go hand in hand. You expect that your spouse or significant other will be truthful, and when you find that she hasn't been, your trust in her is damaged. The relationship suffers and must be repaired, or the injury it has sustained will threaten the life of the entire union. The family unit is very much the same, and adoptive families who are open and honest with their adoptive child need not fear the consequences of the truth, for it has already been addressed.

Reverend Brosnan is just one of many who have searched for a missing family member, who proposes fundamental changes in the laws that exist today prohibiting adoptees and others from obtaining the truth about their family history. Although it may seem obvious that as Americans all citizens should possess the right to know their heritage, it is not the case. Thousands of people across our great nation are engaged in some form of the search process at this very moment, yet thousands are being denied basic freedoms. Legislation such as the Freedom of Information Act, which provides access to public records, contains verbiage excluding adoptees from inclusion in these freedoms, eliminating the rights of one group of people.

Professional child advocacy organizations support the right to equal access of adoption information for adoptees across state lines, yet even with their backing, these records remain sealed in most states and access continues to be denied. Adoptees have limited rights when it comes to obtaining family history and genetic information that is basic and vital and a natural rite of passage for other adults.

The entire adoption experience has been embroiled in bitter controversy, with both sides of the dispute taking stringent, unflinching positions. There are several aspects to this debate, although privacy lies at the core of it, with the adoptee's right to know challenging the birth parent's right to privacy. Surprisingly, statistics support that most birth parents believe adoptees should have access to their adoption and birth records and contact should not be forbidden or prevented by law. Not so surprisingly, many birth parents support the sealed records laws being proposed in various states. The composition of the teams formed by both sides is heterogeneous and, at best, unpredictable. As with most causes, the individuals lobbying are passionate about their beliefs, which are founded on personal experiences, views, and agendas.

The one thing that can be said about existing adoption laws is that they vary greatly by state. The focus in recent years on the enactment of open records laws has been spearheaded by specific groups consisting of birth parents, adoptees, and even adoptive parents, backed by some organizations with a vested interest in adoption. This side of the fight advocates unsealing adoption and birth records for the adoptee, and some in this category also support allowing the adoptee or birth parent the option to search for a missing family member. Both propositions are vehemently opposed by those on the other side of the fence, the supporters of sealed records laws and detractors of the belief that it is the adoptee's right to know.

Some activists for open records allege that the deliberation has become a civil rights issue that will affect future adoptions. Sealed records, they say, will affect a birth parent who has relinquished a child and later desires to establish contact with that child and will also affect the adoptee who, at the age of maturity or beyond, desires to establish contact with a birth parent. The fact is that in most states today, even a hypothetical sixty-year-old who was adopted and raised in an abusive atmosphere would not be able to gain access to the records necessary to locate his birth parent. The elderly person would have no rights to his or her birthright, family history, or genetic background. If the sixty-year-old developed cancer and his only hope for survival was a bone marrow transplant by a living biological relative, he would have to endure additional trauma by instigating a court petition to unseal the adoption records that could provide him with identifying information about his biological family.

Although this example is not representative of the entire population of those who are searching for missing loved ones, it does represent the limitations and effects that the laws, or lack thereof, can have on an individual's life. Even more compelling is the argument that the adoptee suffers psychological and developmental oppression caused by the inability to explore his family history and genetic foundation.

The arguments for and against unsealed records laws are fueled by many diverse issues. Sharing of adoption or general missing persons information is not something that our country has resolved, and the complexities only augment the arguments being presented. Much like in the abortion or euthanasia debate, every conviction presented can be viewed as a log in the fire from which more sparks are created, multiplying and then soaring into the air. Before the argument is over, the air is filled with sparks, each one taking on a life of its own.

One religious leader affiliated with an organization backing the sealed records laws was quoted as saying that those who support the right to the truth, and the right to unsealed records laws, are the same people who believe in abortion. This is a sweeping generality and of course one that is untrue. The truth is continually distorted, while the laws of states and rights of individuals remain uncertain, and the debate involving public records continues. Adoption records are one small parcel of the entire open records package, for people across the nation are lobbying for access to records of every kind. Legal, medical, and government records are just a few that are continually being examined.

The National Institute for Missing and Exploited Children maintains a computer database on 367,000 missing children in the United States, but there is not yet a comprehensive vehicle for tracking missing adults. The general theory is that most adults who are missing prefer it that way and that any method to track them down would create a severe invasion of privacy. One database which does serve as a tracking mechanism for adults is off limits to the general public. The National Crime Information Center's (NCIC) computerized system for storing criminal activity is a powerhouse of information. This database will only store information on disabled adults, adults who are missing due to documented suspicious circumstances, or adults who have committed a criminal act. Maintained by the FBI, the NCIC database is linked to law enforcement agencies throughout the United States, with its primary goal being the apprehension of criminals.

If your husband or wife were to suddenly disappear, you would have to wait several days before the authorities would classify your spouse as a missing person, and even then the search would not be conducted with as much fervor as would a search for a missing child. Believe it or not, husbands and wives have disappeared, only to be found living on an island in the tropics with a new love.

Even in the adoption search, privacy is really what it's all about, and the argument centers very clearly on the right of the adoptee, or the child, versus the right of the adult who gave up the child. Currently the rights of the birth parent and adoptive parent prevail; however, residents of many states are seeking reform that could give equal rights to everyone in the process. Substantial arguments exist on both sides, and the debate is no closer to a clear-cut outcome than it was five years ago.

Proponents of sealed records generally argue on behalf of total confidentiality and the prevention of unsealing records to adoptees. Some of these advocates argue that the search or reunion process inhibits bonding between the adoptive parents and their adopted child. The National Council for Adoption (NCFA) is an organization that promotes adoption but opposes any attempts at reconciliation, search, or unsealing of records. The NCFA is one of the strongest supporters of sealed records laws and has led the fight for more stringent legislation in this area.

On the other side of the fight are organizations who have lobbied against sealed records laws and for bills to open such records in all states. Comprised of all branches of the adoption triad, these organizations propose consistent adoption laws from state to state, laws that would make it easier for an adoptee to obtain access to his birth and adoption records through the courts. One of the law's supporters, the American Adoption Congress, or AAC, is a carefully organized network of people who are proponents of open records laws and equal access for adoptees across state lines. This group comprises those who have lived through the adoption experience, and it supports the theory of truth in all facets of adoption. To that end, the AAC focuses on influencing legislation to make it easier for all members of the adoption triad to obtain basic information about their family member.

Although the AAC is continually fighting for the rights of children and adult adoptees, there are currently no set standards for establishing the rights of the adopted child beyond the adoption and care received by adoptive parents. This can be disconcerting to those who have acknowledged the truths behind their adoption and are ready to move forward and address the facts. A mature adult adoptee cannot gain access to birth records which could provide him with a perspective of his heredity. His adoptive mother may be able to talk about hers, his spouse or best friends about theirs, yet his own remains an uncertainty.

Progress with regard to the unsealing of records is noticeable in some states where legislation has been passed proposing increased access to records; however, even these previously enacted laws have continued to be the subject of legal controversy. Tennessee, for example, enacted a law permitting adoptees to view birth records if they were adopted before 1953. The law includes a contact veto which prohibits the adoptee from making personal contact with the birth parent if either birth parent elects to file this document. This law virtually guarantees privacy for both parties and ensures that the adoptee receives total access to her birth records; however, the implementation of it was immediately opposed by a small group of individuals and a religious organization that filed a complaint challenging Tennessee's open adoption records law as unconstitutional.

Several states are moving toward legislation of open records, and others are in the process of reviewing further restrictions on open records. Today, an adoptee's or searcher's success in finding the names of his family member will hinge largely on chance, depending on which state he was conceived in. In Virginia, for instance, an adoptee will have reasonable access to birth records with a little perseverance, while just across the border in Washington, D.C., he will have no access whatsoever. A brief geographic distance can make a world of difference in someone's life.

Some states have even migrated toward legislation of laws that protect and increase the rights of the birth father. This is a fairly recent issue, as birth fathers across the nation have started to assemble to air their views and lobby for their rights as parents. The birth father is often ignored and historically has been cut out of adoption transactions altogether. There are still birth fathers out there who choose to claim no responsibility for their offspring, but there are many more today who are interested in maintaining a connection with their children.

Other laws being considered for legislation involve employing affidavit systems, which would require dual consent. If an adoptee requests birth records, he or she would be required to wait until the birth parent gives written permission, via an affidavit, before access is granted. This affidavit would be kept in the adoptee's adoption file, and access would be granted if the birth parent had taken the appropriate action to provide written permission. Dual consent laws have become a popular mechanism to protect the rights of both parties involved.

Still other states offer what are referred to as passive registries, which allow access to information if the other individual has registered. More than fifteen states currently maintain passive registries, and more than twenty actually have search-and-consent procedures in place for those who are seeking contact with family members. By enacting legislation, these states have acknowledged the search process as a viable human issue, a victory for all in search.

A small handful of states allows total access to birth certificates for adult adoptees, with no permission necessary from the birth parent, adoptive parent, or courts. In this instance the birth certificate is released, but detailed information on the birth family remains completely confidential.

Various legislative options have been tossed about regarding the future of access to records. Some states have creatively addressed the issue by employing access to records with a security fence in the form of the contact veto. This type of veto acts as a legal firewall, preventing the adult child from contacting the parent if one or both parents submit a written veto to prevent it.

The adoption and search discussion is both legal and philosophical, for some argue that the unborn child is bonded with the mother while in the womb and that this bond is something no state can legally take away. Philosophically, this argument maintains that the right of the child to know his or her birth parent begins during the birth process, at the fetus stage, and continues on through the life of the person created. Psychologists and adoption professionals alike have taken this position. Medical professionals who have joined in the fight for open records have suggested that an infant who is going to be given up for adoption can feel the effects of this prior to entering the world. Furthermore, they maintain, the adopted child can suffer long-term psychological attachment disorders that stem from the early feelings of loss associated with adoption.

At the very least, the assertion is thought provoking. In Thomas Moore's spiritual book, *The Re-enchantment of Everyday Life,* the author stated, "I don't think for a moment that a child is a *tabula rasa,* an empty page, that life experiences and culture make into a person." If Moore's view is correct, it would suggest that a child is born with its own basic individuality, meaning the child has a life and personality of its own that it takes with it into adulthood. If indeed the child is born with its own aphoristic personality that cannot be molded completely by the parents who raise it, the genetic imprint, or biological plan, would appear to be omnipresent. Genetics and philosophy are intermingled in the adoption controversy despite the fact that genetics is based in science and philosophy, in theory and thought.

The argument against genetics as a primary factor would center around the belief that the child is a palette on which we can paint, create, and transfer our views and judgments about the world. An individual, yes, but an individual whose traits and characteristics have been shaped by environment more so than genetics. It is a fact that a large number of children who grow up in abusive households become abusers themselves, which would support this theory. However, it is also a fact that some who were raised in abusive homes become the best parents in the world, perhaps as a direct result of reacting against the environment they were raised in. Just as some children whose fathers are in the ministry grow up devoted to the church, there are just as many who reject a religious lifestyle. An argument can be molded to prove either point, and genetics versus environment is just one of the numerous components involved in the vast realm of adoption rights issues.

The question of whether a child is or is not molded by its upbringing and environment is not the singular issue. Ultimately the central argument is whether or not adoptees have the right, if they so desire, to pursue and discover the information that led to their genetic disposition. When these rights are denied and the questions pushed under the proverbial carpet, the adoptees feel misplaced in the world that belongs just as much to them as it does others.

This feeling of misplacement may not be tied to an individual's present state of mind but to the lack of familiar thoughts and surroundings, to the family that raised him. Brandon, age thirty-three, reports that he had always felt different, though he never really attempted to pinpoint the reason. He now attributes this feeling to his adoption, which he learned of when he was eighteen. It didn't change the love he felt for his parents, but Brandon finally felt as if he understood everything that had transpired through the years. The physical and mental differences, the differences in hobbies and interests, that he had encountered with the parents who raised him—all these things he found were distinct similarities with his birth parents, whom he located through a search firm.

I experienced something similar after locating the paternal side of my birth family. Everything about them was the same, and I instantly felt at home with their sarcastic humor, their beliefs, and interests that were uncannily parallel to my own. Even my love of flying seemed to be pre-destined. In looking through my father's belongings I discovered pho-tographs he had taken many years before his death—photographs of airplanes from the same airline that I worked for throughout my career in the airline industry. Coincidentally, my father had worked for the same company, and his love for flying was well known by his friends.

While it is arguable that children can ever discard their original genetic tendencies, it seems less arguable that children could ever be denied their God-given right to find the parts that make them whole. This basic information is available to every human being except the person who was conceived by parents who chose to place the child for adoption.

The laws that prevent access to open records have been the norm for many years and are therefore slow to change. Important to discern is the difference between the issue of open records for an adult and the issue of parental rights as it relates to the child. Some adoptive parents dread having the intrusion of the birth parent in their lives, fearing the consequences if the parent is allowed to reconnect with the child. Others have insecurities about the strength of the bond that develops between the adoptive parent and child, fearing it could be weakened by the birth parent who interrupts the child's life. Proposing that any union between the birth mother and child was extinguished the day the mother chose to give the child away, this side of the argument maintains that the adoptive parent should be pro-tected if the birth mother decides to reclaim her child. The importance of examining this issue lies in protecting the child and providing a consistent, healthy environment for that child.

The focus on sealed records is entirely removed from the maelstrom of diverse issues encompassing adoption. All of them are closely joined, yet those issues involving an adopted child must be looked at under a micro-scope separate from the one examining the rights of an adult, lest they con-taminate one another. Should a child under the age of eighteen have untamed legal access to birth records? Probably not. The adult adoptee, like other adults, has the capacity to make intelligent and mature decisions a child does not. Given this fact, it is difficult to comprehend why these adult adoptees are still treated like children in states where there are no concrete laws governing adoption and the adult adoptee's rights.

Some attorneys and backers of sealed records view all adoption issues as water in the same pool, proposing blanket legislation governing all facets of adoption. This is akin to viewing all Republicans as conservative types who drive Volvos, when the makeup of the Republican party is actually as diverse as the population of the United States itself. Each individual within it has his or her own ideals and lifestyle, just as adoption has several distinctly independent aspects to it.

The Uniform Adoption Act, or UAA as it is most often referred to, is a proposal to close adoption records for a term of ninety-nine years, thereby creating a thicker layer of privacy for the birth parents. The UAA also proposes utilizing false names in adoption proceedings and supports the continued practice of falsifying birth certificates of adoptees, a practice that started in the 1920s to conceal the identities of illegitimate children. The Uniform Adoption Act is being supported by the National Center for Adoption, an organization in favor of adoption but against open records. The NCFA also proposes making it a felony to search for a biological relative, meaning that someone who searches could be subject to a conviction, fine, and jail time, as well as a criminal record that would be communicated to potential employers who conduct background checks.

Approved by the National Conference of Commissioners on Uniform State Laws, an organization comprised of lawyers, the UAA seeks to enact uniform laws in every state. These lawyers are appointed by the governors of their respective states to oversee such legislation in hopes of simplifying our nation's complex legal system. No one can argue that this is not a goal worth chasing, but again, one concept erodes and contaminates others. By enacting laws that promote the sealing of adoption records in every state, we presume that every case of adoption is the same and that there will be no desire to search or need to unseal those records. The rights of adult adoptees are ignored, and the luxury of learning about their heritage taken away.

Specific verbiage within the UAA has been interpreted as detrimental to the rights of the adult adoptee, and for this reason the act is opposed by many, including the Child Welfare League of America, one of the oldest and most reputable children's advocate groups. Verbiage of particular concern to these groups and those on the adoption reform circuit is in the area of the birth father's parental rights. By allowing a birth mother the ability to relinquish a child without the father's consent, the act provides the father with virtually no say in the matter. The mother could maintain that she does not know who the birth father is or insist that he has left and his location is unknown.

In addition, the act makes it impossible for children who were adopted to be in contact with a birth parent who has previously raised them, even if the children are older. Any court orders that existed prior to an adoption would be deemed inactive, and any previous visitation or communication between the birth parent and child terminated. A child who was raised by its birth mother until the age of eight, then taken away and placed for adoption, would have no legal rights with regard to its desire to have visitation with the birth mother. In some cases this may be better for the child, and in some cases not good at all, but each case and relationship will vary and should be treated independently. We would never treat a migraine with vitamin C, as we would the flu. They are both illnesses, but very different ones requiring different care.

Adoption is a personal, individual experience, and every family relationship is unique. While specific laws must be enacted to govern the adoption process, certain human aspects cannot be mandated as off-the-shelf solutions. There cannot be one answer for every adoption, and each child should be given the right to a customized solution. Even suspected criminals have the right to a fair trial, with a neutral jury that analyzes the case to provide a recommendation leading to the outcome. In many states, the outcome is predetermined for the adult adoptee wishing to search.

Recognizing this, adoptees worldwide have united to create a force in numbers to prevent the enactment of the UAA. One group of vocal adoptees took their cause on-line, creating the Adoptees Internet Mailing List. The AIML web site offers adult adoptees the opportunity to subscribe to an e-mail list, whereby adoptees share various ideas and thoughts on the entire adoption process. Topics such as open records, reunions, and anxiety about searching are discussed. The AIML is focused first and foremost on search and support and second on preventing laws to close records, such as the UAA.

Adult adoptees view the UAA as a threat to their livelihood and an infringement of their rights. It has been introduced in several states already but has yet to be enacted as universal law. Some states have denied it, some will accept it, and other states, such as California, have modified their existing adoption laws to reflect more current times. California's public records bill was amended in April of 1995 to include a provision that allows adoptees access to general background information about their natural parents, provided that the information does not reveal their parents' actual identities.

The adult adoptee from California will have far more answers than adoptees from other states.

One notorious adoption case that was highly publicized was the case of Baby Jessica. This scenario involved a private adoption, sometimes referred to as an independent adoption. The child was then taken from the adoptive parents and given back to the birth parent by the court after a long and cumbersome legal battle. The case raised fear in adoptive parents across the nation as they watched a child who had been raised in the adoptive parents' home for many years get yanked away by authorities and placed back in the home of the birth mother. This case emphasizes the need for pre-adoptive counseling for the birth parents and strict enforcement of the legal agreements that provide the adoptive parent with legal custody of the child.

Though counseling will not always be possible, at its best, counseling for the birth parents should focus on the reasons for relinquishing the child. If the counseling explores the motives and actions of the parents at the deepest level, the birth mother and father will explore their own individual reasons for making the adoption decision, and the outcome will be beneficial to all parties involved. Post-adoption counseling is also available and something that many birth parents have relied on to help them long after the baby has been relinquished. Gina, a birth mother from Atlanta, recalls the effects of counseling in her life. "Before birth, I kept telling everyone that I was going to be fine, it would be no big deal," Gina recalls. "But after I had the baby, I realized I wouldn't be able to handle it on my own. I called the social worker right away, and she pointed me in the direction of a class for birth mothers, which I still go to twice a week."

The process of adoption is undoubtedly a lifelong journey. Though one side opposes searching and the other promotes it, both sides generally agree on one thing: a search due to a medical emergency. A life-or-death extreme medical emergency is usually considered a valid reason for conducting a search. However, the definition of *extreme* and definition of *medical emergency* have not been clearly defined, which causes some debate. If there is the possibility of death due to a lack of genetic information, most detractors of open records laws will submit to making them available. Not all, but most.

Adoptees facing life-threatening illnesses are also faced with limited options for receiving blood or organ donations. This creates a problem with much wider scope, as the adoptee is forced into a legal battle to obtain personal information that others already have. Medical and genetic history must be sought after, in order to preserve her life. A highly publicized case featured on various news programs involved a woman in her forties faced with cancer. The only hope for her survival would be a marrow donation by one of her biological parents, two people whom she knew nothing about. She had pursued many leads but couldn't find a match. The woman had been adopted and, in researching her adoption to locate critical medical information, found that the person who arranged it had been convicted of illegal baby brokering. The adoption records were falsified, along with hundreds of other adoption records, and nothing could be validated. Sadly, the woman may never know the identity of her true birth parents, even if they have been searching for her all along.

In most states, the power to unseal adoption records in the case of medical emergency lies with the courts. A sympathetic judge can hold the key to someone's medical future by allowing access to birth and adoption records that could lead the adoptee to his biological families. Though there have been many judges who have ruled favorably in such instances, others have refused such requests, denying information to adoptees in even the most heartbreaking of circumstances. This is an issue that has been brought to the forefront most recently in light of medical advances in the genetic field. Genetics can now determine an individual's predisposition to diseases such as Alzheimer's and breast cancer. An adult who knows that his mother or father was afflicted with a certain disease can take a test to determine if he shares the same gene. Being aware of the diseases that permeate a family lineage could help in prevention of the disease, a luxury that adoptees do not have. For some, having this basic information about themselves could be a matter of life or death.

"If a patient has some abnormality, it could be pinned down more quickly if there is a known family connection," offers Dr. Wayne Jenkins, Chief of Radiation Oncology at the M.D. Anderson Cancer Center in Orlando. Dr. Jenkins treats patients who have no family history of cancer and also those whose families have suffered from it for generations. Detecting a predisposition to cancer is more likely, though not guaranteed, if a history exists. If, for instance, a woman knows that her mother had breast cancer or some other affliction, this information, when provided to a medical professional, could lead to tests that would pinpoint the disease, leading to the early treatment of it.

Genetics pose many insights into our past and our futures. Survival, both emotional and physical, is incumbent upon genetics as we search not only for our histories but for understanding into the dynamics that shape our lives. A Harvard University genetic linkage study concluded that evidence exists to suggest that bipolar affective disorder, or manic-depressive illness, is a complex inherited trait among many in the Old Order Amish. This disorder is characterized best by episodes of mania interspersed with periods of depression. Manic-depressive illness afflicts approximately 1 percent of the nation's population and, if untreated, can lead to destruction. Bipolar disorder has been associated with a 20 percent risk of suicide in Americans. If an individual with this disease suffered frequent bouts of severe depression without understanding the reason, the depression could remain undiagnosed and untreated, drastically affecting the course of that person's life. Not knowing one's genetic makeup can lead to feelings of isolation, and the notion that one is the only person affected by this particular disorder may perhaps even contribute to the problem. To witness parents or other relatives experiencing the same diseases, thought processes, or symptoms provides greater understanding toward one's own self-improvement.

Our world has been on a self-improvement crusade for years. Spiritual and management gurus teach their own brands of self-improvement to the millions who invest in them each year. The goal, of course, is to learn more and improve ourselves so that we may become better, smarter, faster, and sexier. There are self-improvement manuals for lovers, self-improvement audiotapes that tell the secrets of highly successful people, books aimed at making CEOs better leaders, employees smarter workers, and men better husbands. You can now improve your memory, relationships, looks, and careers simply by going to the bookstore or following up on one of the multitude of advertisements in the papers. Everywhere you turn someone is telling you how you can improve yourself.

For the person without a foundation, improving means unearthing the past, genetic or otherwise, in order to improve internally. Understanding our intelligence, our characteristics, and the traits that make us who we are, are very basic elements to becoming whole. Each of us has cells and genes that form our individuality, but a person without medical information about her mother, father, or siblings has nothing beyond the fact that she is human and, of course, was incubated in a womb before being born.

The Human Genome Project is a task being undertaken by scientists throughout the world with the objective of understanding the hereditary instructions that make each of us complete. This project is really an investigation of ourselves, and by the year 2005 these scientists predict being able to read and comprehend the entire genetic script. This will open the door of molecular medicine, creating new developments in the area of gene therapy and the creation of precise guidelines for the prevention, diagnosis, and treatment of disease. Genes influence development and provide the recipe that determines our looks, our mannerisms, and the diseases we are afflicted by.

Even intelligence and IQ have been linked to genetics. For ages researchers sought to determine what, specifically, determines intelligence. Is intelligence actually inherited, or is it the result of an individual's environment? Much like the debate on homosexuality, some believe intelligence is ingrained genetically, while others believe it to be a direct result of one's surroundings. Future genetic findings could contribute greater insight into this phenomenon.

A researcher at the University of Minnesota has conducted extensive research on twins who were raised in separate households. Eighty-six pairs of adult twins were tested, with the results validating a correlation between IQ scores. These twins were raised in separate cities and states and, in some cases, separate countries, with some pairs not even aware that they were twins until they were united. Each twin was raised in a different environment, yet shared the same genetic material with the other twin, which led to the similarity in IQ scores.

Though the facts point to an everlasting biological imprint that remains with a child from cradle to grave, the validity of the role the birth family plays in the mind and the life of a child continues to be denied. The adoption reform movement is slowly attempting to change this. An organization called the Adoptees Civil Rights Association is in the process of exploring avenues to overturn the laws that prevent adoptees from obtaining the same information as the rest of the adult world. This organization believes that any genetically related information should be available to the adult adoptee and is currently exploring the viability of a class action lawsuit representing adult adoptees who have been denied identifying information.

The rights of the adoptee have been questioned for decades. The United Nations Commission on Human Rights held a convention in 1989 on the rights of the child, including the rights of the adopted child. This convention met with the goal of addressing issues that would positively contribute to the protection of children's rights. A document called the Convention on the Rights of the Child was drafted, establishing a framework for countries to live by, in dealing with their nation's children. This document mandates that the best interests of any child should be a primary consideration, thus protecting a child's rights. The document also maintains that a child shall have the right to a name and nationality and the right to know his or her parents and identity. Although these rights are outlined on paper, many adoptees argue that by being denied access to biological information, adoptees have not been afforded these basic rights. Article 7, item 1, delves deeper into the issue of the rights of the child and provides that, "The child shall be registered immediately after birth and shall have the right from birth to a name, the right to acquire a nationality and, as far as possible, the right to know and be cared for by his or her parents." In Article 8, the Convention goes on to declare that: "States parties undertake to respect the right of the child to preserve his or her identity, including nationality, name and family relations as recognized by law without unlawful interference."

Another document giving thought to the rights of the child is The Hague Convention on Intercountry Adoption. This draft outlines provisions for acceptable standards and guidelines for adoption transactions between countries. Seen as a positive step toward protecting children of adoption, the convention was endorsed by several major agencies, including the Joint Council on Children's Services, North American Council on Adoptable Children, and the U.S. Department of State. It addresses guidelines for adoptive parents, accreditation of agencies, and requirements, and it even includes provisions for displaced refugee children in foreign countries who may be candidates for adoption in a country other than their own.

Other noteworthy acts include the Adoption and Stability Act of 1996, which proposes that adoptive parents be eligible for a federal tax credit of up to five thousand dollars. This encourages adoption by offering a financial incentive to offset some of the costs associated with it. This act also seeks to remove ethnic barriers to adoption by mandating that interracial and ethnic adoptions can occur, whereby the parent and child are of different races, religions, or origins. The Indian Child Welfare Act is yet another bill which addresses the rights of the Native American child, providing for such aspects as mandatory visitation rights for the tribe or Indian family after the adoption, time limits for intervention by the tribe post-adoption, and specific requirements with regard to any adoption transaction.

Innumerable acts and proposed legislation exist to govern the rights of a child and other parties involved during the actual adoption transaction. Some of these laws were legislated many years ago and are in the process of being amended, and many are valid and in the child's best interest. These efforts, while certainly worthwhile, do not address the aspect of adoption involving the child as he or she reaches the age of adulthood, the issue of access to sealed records.

In a positive ruling on the rights of adoptees in the state of South Carolina, Judge Wade S. Weatherford, Jr., proclaimed that, *"For many, the future is blind without a sight of the past."* The window to the past can open the door to the future, enabling us to travel the same roads that were traveled by our ancestors, if we so choose, and to explore and better understand our innermost desires. The connection to family and heritage is just as important as the connection to spirituality and as integral to a prosperous and healthy development of self. All over the world, people enjoy the freedom to express their love for their individual religions, books, and activities. We enjoy these freedoms even more so in the United States, as our country is one in which Jews mix with Catholics and Buddhists, and atheists and Protestants alike work side by side. Everybody has the option to worship whichever religion they choose or to read whatever they want, but not everybody has the option to know the truth about their parents, the two people whose actions brought them into this world. This inalienable right is denied to the adult whose birth records are sealed.

Ultimately, the parents have the final word on what their child will be taught and what their child will be told. For an adoptive parent to hide the truth from the adopted child is currently acceptable by law. Some parents have elected to keep the secret until the child reaches the age of legal maturity, while others have kept it forever. "I don't think I ever want him to know," says one adoptive mother of her decision not to tell her son he is adopted. "Why rock the boat and ruin the relationship that we have built over the years? His mother didn't want him, so what if he finds her and she rejects him? It could end up to be devastating."

Most adoptees and illegitimate children will confirm that the truth is much easier to handle than living with questions and falsehoods. As the Reverend Brosnan, an adoptee, revealed in his speech at the adoption conference, he was actually told he was adopted at the age of twelve, though he can remember knowing it as early as five. I mentioned this once during a speaking engagement for an audience of prospective adoptive parents. Afterward, an adoptive father approached me at the front of the room to talk more about this one thing, which he couldn't believe was possible. "How could that be true?" he asked, perplexed by the idea. "If the parents did not tell him, how would he have known?" I don't know how Father Brosnan knew, but many adults can remember early feelings of loss and confusion associated with adoption. Some attribute these feelings to intuition, while others believe they absorbed shards of secret conversations that were held by the adults in their lives.

As adults we like to believe we have far more wisdom than the children who will walk in our footsteps, but in believing this we often underestimate the wisdom contained within a child. We cannot ignore the truth, because eventually children will come to discover it on their own. A child will metamorphose into an adult with his or her own beliefs and philosophies and will grow to view the world in his or her own way.

A parent cannot strive to shelter the child from the truths that inevitably surface. Try as we might to prevent it, our children will suffer as we did, with fear, rejection, adolescence, and all of the hardships that make each of us human. Rejection is always a possibility in the search process, but so are many other things that we must face in this world. Death is imminent for all of us, but do we cease to go on living because of it? Surely death is a negative, but not so much so that the thought of it prevents us from pursuing a fulfilling life. We cannot ignore the truth simply because of our fears or the fears of others. To live such a fearful, quiet existence would be far worse than encountering troubles along the road to a festive, passionate life. Controlling one's destiny by withholding the truth that can open doors, allowing an individual to bloom and prosper, is far worse.

Sherry Eldridge is an adoptee and the editor of *Jewel Among Jewels,* an adoption newsletter aimed at anyone touched by adoption. She was reunited with her biological mother after years of searching, yet was rejected by her mother and now has no contact with her. It continues to be a painful experience that touches every part of her being, yet she still feels freer than ever in knowing the truth: "The most important thing is that I know I would do it all over again, even though I was essentially rejected. I learned about my past, my nationality, and I learned critical medical information that will help me and my own daughter." Sherry recalled the time she attended a conference and met an elderly gentlemen who had experienced the same thing. As he recounted his story of being rejected by the mother he had found thirty years prior, he wept openly. "It was at that moment that my own healing process began," she said. "After thirty years his pain was still fresh, and I felt validated that someone else had been through the same thing. The man said just five words that brought forth a flood of tears, and I'll always remember them. He said, *'It really hurts, doesn't it?'*"

The search and its eventual outcome are the beginning of the healing process for those who have been living without answers. The conclusion cannot be predicted but most often results in a harmonious awareness of self and emotional advances in a life that had previously endured questions and chaos about the past. If you do not find what you're looking for during your search, perhaps you can discover something along the way that will lead to inner peace. At the very least, may your search open your eyes to new and exciting people and some image of the past. Keep your eye on the ball, and don't delay. You have everything you need to take that first step forward toward finding the family that is yours.

CHAPTER SIX

Search and Support Resources

DURING THE SEARCH process think of the resources at hand as a diverse portfolio of investments. The more you diversify, the greater your chances of success, as long as the best options are used most frequently and common sense prevails. You may elect to use good, old-fashioned techniques like the telephone, the library, or the yellow pages, yet also register with a nationwide computer search data bank. Or you may decide to hire a private investigator or attorney who specializes in finding missing persons. The more resources you use, the greater your chances for finding your family member.

This section contains a comprehensive listing of some of the resources available and organizations that are out there to assist you in your search. Although it is quite expansive, it's just the tip of the iceberg. Adoption- and search-related organizations are popping up every day. Your first inclination may be to contact an organization in your area, but don't limit yourself; request information from several sources and have them fax or mail it to you. Keep everything that comes in organized in your search file, and use it throughout the search process. Proceed at your own risk, and gather as much information as possible. Do your research or ask for references if you are planning on hiring any organization to conduct your search for you.

Internet Resources

Browsing the World Wide Web

The following are lists of Internet addresses and web sites with access to family search–related information. Keep in mind that web addresses can frequently change, but you can still search for information by entering a keyword. If you prefer to browse the Internet by using a keyword, an excellent starting point is to enter the word *reunion* to find all that is offered on family searches. Once you have gotten to the list of initial offerings, you can drill down through the various topics presented to find information on family searches, support, adoption, and reunions. Other relevant keywords to use are *adoption, genealogy, family,* and *birth.*

- Parent Finders, a search page for those looking for a biological parent
  http://www.idir.net/~pbrown/

- Sibling search site for those in search of a brother or sister
  http://www.tiac.net/users/rkytyk/KYT/A/siblings/siblings.html

- A web page in support of adoptees' rights, written by Anne Babb, activist and adoptive parent. This page provides links to various adoption- and search-related resources
  http://pages.prodigy.com/adoptreform/refwelci.htm

- Adult Adoptees Web Chat. This is a free on-line chat room where adult adoptees can speak on-line with other adoptees who are searching for parents
  http://wbs.net/webchat3.so?Room=Adult_Adoptees_Chat&last_read_para=193493&visit=1&fsection=input&join.x=1

- The Independent Adoption Center. This site provides state by state information on adoption
  http://www.webcom.com/nfediac

- The National Adoption Information Clearinghouse (NAIC) web site. This site provides excellent resources for adoptees, adoptive parents, and birth parents. The NAIC will send you a list of search and support organizations within your state and will also provide search assistance for a fee
  http://www.adoption...adopt/birthpar.html

- NAIC page on issues facing adoptees
  http://www.infi.net/adopt/adoptees.html

- Information for people who are searching for family members.
  This site is specifically aimed at adoptees
  hartung@crl.ucsd.edu *or*
  http://psy.ucsd.edu/~jhartung/down.txt

- Adoption Policy Resource Center
  http://www.fpsol.com/adoption/advocates.html

- American Law Sources On-Line
  http://www.lawsource.com

- Adoptees Internet Mailing List (AIML)
  http://www.webreflection.com/aiml/contribute.html

- Internet site for all members of the adoption triad. Information is
  available on a wide array of adoption subjects. Send a message to
  subscribe to their mailing list
  owner-adoption@listserv.law.cornell.edu

- Hillhouse Investigations paranormal detective agency
  http://ic.net/~dunstan/hh.htm

- Toll-free telephone number directory available on the Internet
  http://www.tollfree.att.net/dir800/

- Instant technologies missing persons page
  http://www.instantech.com:80/missing_person/

- Genealogist who specializes in people searches for a fee
  http://www.janyce.com/psearch/search.html

- Nationwide Investigations
  http://www.nwin.com

- Paragon Investigations people finder search
  http://www.usaor.com/affiliates/paragon.html

- People Finders database search firm
  http://www.xpressinfo.com/peoplefinder

- PVI Search Firm. Has successfully found over 500 people. Charges just $10 per search
  http://www.instantech.com/users/martin/adoptees.htm

- Tracer Net, specializes in locating people
  http://www.ipmg.com/tracernet/

- Adoption legislation information
  http://www.daily.iastate.edu/volumes/Fall95/Oct-17-95/
  laws-hollnd.html

- Web page that offers an adoptee's passionate and thought-provoking letter to Ann Landers
  http://www.ibar.com/ann.html

- Adoption information, laws and reform
  http://www.webcom.com/kmc

- Search agency specializing in family reunions
  http://www.digi-all.com/2315/Jerry-Walters-Drawstring-
  Incorporated/

- ReuNet reunion bulletin board
  http://www.reunion.com/

- Reunions, a free adoption registry
  http://www.absnw.com/reunions/ *or*
  http://www.execpc.com/~reunions

- Ancestry page which offers products and services for tracing your heritage, for a fee
  http://www.worldshop.com/cgi-bin/v551/itemlist.html

- Lady Teviot Census Searches. Offers search information and is based in the UK
  http://www.bwh.co.uk/familyhistory.htm

- Seekers of the Lost home page. Offers information to adoptees and anyone in search
  http://www.seeklost.com/seeklogo2.htm

- People Finder Free Search Database
  http://www.infospace.com/mage/people.html

Additional Web Site Listings by Name

- Adopting Resources and Online Support
  Pre- and post-adoption information including personal stories and
  magazine articles

- Adoption Advocate
  A web page for the organization Adoption Advocates. This site
  offers information to adoptive parents

- AdoptioNetwork
  A site providing information from all members of the adoption
  triad and from adoption professionals

- Adoption Interlink—UK
  Information on adoption and searching in the UK

- Adoption in the Computer Age
  A web page composed by an adoptee, covering several areas of
  interest

- Everton Genealogical Helper Online
  Genealogical magazine available on-line

- Family History Research Center
  Access to family history information, genealogy, census records,
  and Social Security Administration information

- Freedom of Information Act
  Information on this act, which provides access to public information

- GenServ: Genealogical GEDCOM Server System
  Web site offering access to over three million surnames. Allows a
  free trial search

- Military Information Enterprises
  Web site created by military personnel, offering information on
  discharge and nationwide military records

- National Reunion Registry
  Web site that lists dates and locations of reunions for retired military personnel serving in WWII, Vietnam, and the Korean War

- Parent Finders
  This web site is maintained by an adoptee who successfully searched for and found his birth parents. Paul Brown now provides his expertise to others on a per-fee basis. Searches exclusive to North America

- People Finder Free Search Database
  This web site is a free search database designed to trace people

- ReunionNet
  Web site for posting information on a family or organization's reunion

- Seekers of the Lost
  On-line search database service

- Tracing Friends and Relatives in Britain. A web page exclusively for searching in the UK

- The Veteran's Archive
  Listing of information for those who are searching for a veteran

- University Microfilms International, Inc.
  Go to this site to view a dissertation on adoption entitled *A Study of Ethics in Contemporary Adoption Practice in the United States*, dissertation number LD-03361

- Vietnam Veterans Home Page
  On-line forum for veterans to meet and discuss the war, exchange ideas, search for other veterans, and display poems, artwork, and other information

Adoption Laws by State

The following listings are adoption laws by state. Bear in mind that adoption laws get revised from time to time and that it is in your best interest to investigate the laws in your state before requesting information. Also be aware that if you are searching for your birth parent, he or she may not know that the following vehicles exist. Therefore, if you have registered your name with a registry in the state in which you were adopted and do not receive contact from your birth parent, do not assume that it is due to indifference. The rules are complicated and varied and far too cumbersome for everyone to sort through. Even the officials may not be aware of the precise current rulings, and may be unable to communicate them properly.

Nonidentifying information will vary by definition in each state but is generally limited to general family history; any medical history that was available leading up to the time the adoption took place; physical descriptions of the birth parent, child, or adoptive parent; and known interests. Identifying information is much more detailed and may even provide the requesting party with specific names, addresses, and access to vital statistics and court documentation.

A search-and-consent program means that an adoptee can register to have a third party search for the birth parent, who will or will not consent to having identifying information released to the adoptee. Some states require the permission of the adoptive parent before any information is released to the adoptee. All state laws will differ, and it is advisable to familiarize yourself with the law before trying to file a request for information.

Alabama

This state releases nonidentifying information to the adoptee, birth parent, and adoptive parent. Passive registry is available for the birth parent, and if the adoptee were to register by name with the state, a match would occur. Adoptees are also entitled to search and consent through the state, meaning that they can register their names to have a third party search for a birth parent, who will or will not consent to having identifying information released to an adoptee.

Alaska

Nonidentifying information is released to the adoptee and adoptive parent only. A passive registry is available for the birth parent who wishes to locate a child, and access is available to the birth records by the adoptee. Alaska is more liberal than a lot of states in providing vehicles for families who wish to be reunited.

Arizona

Nonidentifying information is released to all three members of the adoption triad: the adoptee, adoptive parent, and birth parent. Arizona also allows for search and consent for all parties wishing to obtain contact for identifying information.

Arkansas

All three members of the triad have access to nonidentifying information. A passive registry is available to the adoptee and birth parent.

California

All three members of the triad have access to nonidentifying information. A passive registry is available for all three members of the triad.

Colorado

The adoptee and adoptive parent have access to nonidentifying information; the birth parent does not. A search-and-consent program is available, as well as a registry for all three members of the adoption triad.

Connecticut

All three members of the triad have access to nonidentifying information. A search-and-consent program is available, as well as a registry for all three members of the adoption triad.

Delaware

All three members of the triad have access to nonidentifying information. A search-and-consent program is available for all three members of the triad. A state registry is not offered.

District of Columbia

The District of Columbia does not have adoption laws in place allowing access to any nonidentifying or identifying information for the adoptee, adoptive parent, or birth parent.

Florida

The adoptee and adoptive parent both have access to nonidentifying information; the birth parent does not. A passive registry exists for all three members of the adoption triad.

Georgia

The adoptee and adoptive parent both have access to nonidentifying information; the birth parent does not. A search-and-consent program is in place for the adoptee, and a passive registry exists for the birth parent who wishes to reestablish contact with the relinquished child.

Hawaii

All members of the adoption triad have access to nonidentifying information. This state offers a consent program whereby the other party is notified that someone is searching for him or her. This exists for adoptions that occurred prior to a certain year and also includes a contact veto whereby a birth parent, adoptee, or adoptive parent can establish the desire not to be contacted under any circumstances.

Idaho

The adoptee and adoptive parent have access to nonidentifying information by law. A passive registry is maintained for the adoptee and birth parent who wish to reconnect.

Illinois

The adoptee and adoptive parent have access to nonidentifying information. A passive registry exists for the adoptee and birth parent.

Indiana

The adoptee, birth parent, and adoptive parent all have access to nonidentifying information. The state offers a search-and-consent program as well as a registry, and both involve adoptions that took place prior to a specific year. Consult the state to determine the exact year. Indiana also recognizes the contact veto for those who wish to file it.

Iowa

The adoptee and adoptive parent have access to nonidentifying information. A passive registry exists for the adoptee and birth parent.

Kansas

The adoptee and adoptive parent have access to nonidentifying information. The adoptee has total access to identifying information in this very progressive state, and there is also a search-and-consent program for the adoptee and birth parent.

Kentucky

The adoptee and adoptive parent have access to nonidentifying information. A search-and-consent program exists for the adoptee as well as a passive registry for the birth parent who wishes to be listed in case the adopted child instigates a search to make contact.

Louisiana

The adoptee and adoptive parent have access to nonidentifying information for adoptions that took place prior to a certain year. After that year, a person adopted in Louisiana would have to petition to have this information released. A passive registry exists for the adoptee and birth parent.

Maine

The adoptee and adoptive parent have access to nonidentifying information. A passive registry exists for the adoptee and birth parent.

Maryland

The adoptee, adoptive parent, and birth parent all have access to nonidentifying information. A passive registry exists for the adoptee and birth parent.

Massachusetts

The adoptee, adoptive parent, and birth parent all have access to nonidentifying information. A passive registry exists for the adoptee and birth parent.

Michigan

All three members of the adoption triad have access to nonidentifying information. A contact veto was established for adoptions occurring after a specific year, for adoptees, and a search-and-consent program was established for all three members of the triad for adoptions that occurred prior to a certain year. A search registry also exists for birth parents wishing to list themselves, should their relinquished child decide to register as well.

Minnesota

The adoptee, adoptive parent, and birth parent all have access to nonidentifying information. A search-and-consent registry is available for the adoptee, and an affidavit program is available for the birth parent.

Missouri

The adoptee and adoptive parent have access to nonidentifying information about the birth parent. A search-and-consent program is available for the adoptee, and a registry exists for the adoptee as well as the birth parent.

Mississippi

The adoptee and adoptive parent have access to nonidentifying information about the birth parent. A search-and-consent program is available for the adoptee as well as a registry for adoptions that occurred between specific years.

Montana

The adoptee and adoptive parent have access to nonidentifying information about the birth parent. A search-and-consent program is available for the adoptee, adoptive parent, and birth parent.

Nebraska

The adoptee and adoptive parent have access to nonidentifying information about the birth parent. A search-and-consent program is available for the adoptee for adoptions that occurred prior to 1988. This state also offers a contact veto and a registry for adoptees, adoptive parents, and birth parents.

Nevada

The adoptee has access to nonidentifying information. There is also a passive registry available for the adoptee and birth parent.

New Hampshire

The adoptee and adoptive parent have access to nonidentifying information. A search-and-consent program is in place for the adoptee and birth parent.

New Jersey

The adoptee has access to nonidentifying information.

New Mexico

The adoptee, birth parent, and adoptive parent all have access to nonidentifying information. A passive registry is available for the adoptee and birth parent, and a search-and-consent program is available for the adoptee and birth parent.

New York

The adoptee and adoptive parent have access to nonidentifying information. A passive registry is also available for the adoptee and birth parent.

North Carolina

All three members of the adoption triad have access to nonidentifying information.

North Dakota

The adoptee and adoptive parent have access to nonidentifying information. A search-and-consent program is available for the adoptee and birth parent.

Ohio

Ohio permits access to nonidentifying information for adoptions that take place anytime after June of 1996. Prior to that date, the laws vary by year and county.

Oklahoma

The adoptee, adoptive parent, and birth parent all have access to nonidentifying information. A passive registry is available for the adoptee and birth parent.

Oregon

All three members of the adoption triad have access to nonidentifying information. A search-and-consent program is available for the adoptee, adoptive parent, and birth parent. A registry is also available for all members of the triad.

Pennsylvania

The adoptee and adoptive parent have access to nonidentifying information. A search-and-consent program is available for the adoptee, and a passive registry is available for the birth parent.

Rhode Island

The adoptee, adoptive parent, and birth parent all have access to nonidentifying information. A passive registry exists for the adoptee and birth parent.

South Carolina

The adoptee, adoptive parent, and birth parent have access to nonidentifying information. A passive registry exists for the adoptee and birth parent.

South Dakota

The adoptee and adoptive parent have access to nonidentifying information. A passive registry is available to the adoptee and birth parent.

Tennessee

The adoptee and adoptive parent have access to nonidentifying information. This state has a progressive open records law for adoptions that occurred in certain years; however, it is being challenged.

Texas

The adoptee and adoptive parent have access to nonidentifying information. A passive registry exists for the adoptee and birth parent.

Utah

All three members of the adoption triad have access to nonidentifying information. A passive registry is in place for the adoptee and birth parent.

Vermont

All three members of the adoption triad have access to nonidentifying information. This state allows total access to information, as well as a contact veto for the adoptee. A search-and-consent program is also available, as well as access for the adoptee to identifying information if the birth parent has offered prior consent.

Virginia

The adoptee and adoptive parent have access to nonidentifying information. Adoptees and birth parents can apply through the court for identifying information and for contact with the other party, if they can prove just cause.

Washington

The adoptee, adoptive parent, and birth parent have access to nonidentifying information. A search-and-consent program is in place, as well as a registry for the adoptee and birth parent. The program applies only to those adoptions that occurred after a specific date. There is also a contact veto available for parties who wish to veto communication.

West Virginia

The adoptee and adoptive parent have access to nonidentifying information. A passive registry is available for the adoptee and birth parent.

Wisconsin

The adoptee and adoptive parent have access to nonidentifying information. A search-and-consent program is available for the adoptee and birth parent.

Wyoming

The adoptee and adoptive parent have access to nonidentifying information. A search-and-consent program is available for the adoptee and birth parent.

Addresses of Search- and Adoption-Related Organizations

AAC (American Adoption Congress)
1000 Connecticut Avenue NW
Suite 9
Washington, D.C. 20036
202-483-3399
508-379-0727

Adopt a Special Kid/Aask America
2201 Broadway
Suite 702
Oakland, CA 94612
510-451-1748

Adoptee Awareness
P.O. Box 23019
Anchorage, KY 40223

Adoptees Identity Discovery
P.O. Box 2159
Sunnyvale, CA 94087

Adoptees in Search (AIS)
P.O. Box 41016
Bethesda, MA 20014
301-656-8555

Adoptees in Search of Knowledge (ASK)
4227 S. Belsay Road
Burton, MI 48519

Adoption Circle of Hawaii
P.O. Box 61723
Honolulu, HI 96839-1723

Adoption Exchange Association
820 S. Monaco Parkway, #263
Denver, CO 80224
303-322-9592

Adoption Information Exchange
P.O. Box 1917
Matthews, NC 28106

Adoption Reunion Search/Support
P.O. Box 239
Moore, SC 29369

Adoption Search National Hotline
P.O. Box 100—444
Palm Bay, FL 32910
407-768-2222

Adoption Triad
10 W. Hollow Lane
Webster, MA 01570
508-949-1919

Adoption with Truth
66-C Panoramic Way
Berkeley, CA 94704

Adoptive Families of America
(publishes an annual magazine and
    hosts conferences on adoption)
3333 Highway 100 North
Minneapolis, MN 55422
612-535-4829

Adoptive Parents for Open Records
P.O. Box 193
Long Valley, NJ 07853

Adoptsearch
1940 Los Angeles Street
Berkeley, CA 94707

ALMA (Adoptee's Liberation
    Movement Association)
P.O. Box 727
Radio City Station
New York, NY 10101-0727
212-581-1568

American Association of Open
    Adoption Agencies
1000 Hastings
Traverse City, MI 49686
616-947-8110

American Fathers Coalition
2000 Pennsylvania Avenue NW
Suite 148
Washington, D.C. 20006

American Journal of Adoption
    Reform
1139 Bal Harbor Blvd.
Suite 184
Punta Gorda, FL 33950
941-637-7477

American WWII Orphans Network
P.O. Box 4369
Bellingham, WA 98227
206-733-1678

Ancestry, Inc.
P.O. Box 476
Salt Lake City, UT 84110-0476

BirthParent Connection
P.O. Box 230643
Encinitas, CA 92023-0643
619-753-8288

Birthparents, Adoptees, Adopted
    Parents United in Support (BUS)
P.O. Box 299
Victor, NY 14425
716-924-0410

Bonding by Blood, Unlimited
4710 Cottrell Road
Rural Route #5
Vassar, MI 48768

Center for Reuniting Families
51 Burke Drive
Buffalo, NY 14215

Central Coast Adoption Search &
    Support Group (CCASG)
P.O. Box 8483
Goleta, CA 93118

CERA (Council for Equal Rights
   in Adoption)
356 E. 74th Street
Suite 2
New York, NY 10021-3925
212-988-0110

Children Awaiting Parents
700 Exchange Street
Rochester, NY 14608
716-232-5110

Child Welfare League of America
440 First Street NW
3rd Floor
Washington, D.C. 20001
202-638-2952

Christian Adoptees Support
   Exchange
2354 Willard Street
Ft. Myers, FL 33901

Circle of Hope
P.O. Box 127
Somersworth, NH 03878

Coalition for Preservation of
   Fatherhood
14 Beacon Street
Suite 421
Boston, MA 02108

Committee for Single Adoptive
   Parents
P.O. Box 15084
Chevy Chase, MD 20815

Common Bonds
1217 Indigo Drive
Oshkosh, WI 54901

Cooperative Adoption Consulting
54 Wellington Avenue
San Anselmo, CA 94960
415-453-0902

CUB (Concerned United Birthparents)
2000 Walker Street
Des Moines, IA 50317
800-822-2777

Database Inc.
3600 American River Drive
Suite 100
Sacramento, CA 95864
800-452-3282

Executive Search Corporation
29 W. Thomas Road
Phoenix, AZ 85013
800-528-6179

Families First
1105 W. Peachtree Street NE
P.O. Box 7948, Station C
Atlanta, GA 30357

Family Finders
122 Bass Drive
Mount Juliet, TN 37122

Family Ties
3185 Lincoln
Eugene, OR 97405

Finders Keepers
P.O. Box 748
Bear, DE 19701-0748

Friend Finders International
314 Lloyd Building
Seattle, WA 98101
1-800-FINDERS

Friends in Adoption
P.O. Box 1228
Middletown Springs, VT 05757

Generation Journey
Genealogy Service
8220 Ambassador Row
Dallas, TX 75247

Greene Genealogy-Family Research
  Genealogy Service
P.O. Box 62124
Boulder City, NV 89006-2124
702-293-3451

Healing Hearts, Inc.
P.O. Box 136
Stanford, IL 61774
309-379-5401

Hope Cottage Adoption Center
4209 McKinney Avenue
Suite 200
Dallas, TX 75205
214-526-8721

Independent Search Consultants
P.O. Box 10192
Costa Mesa, CA 92627

Institute for Black Parenting
992 La Cienaga Blvd.
Englewood, CA 90301
310-348-1400

The International Locator
2503 Del Prado Blvd.
Suite 435
Cape Coral, FL 33904
1-800-368-3463

International Soundex Reunion
  Registry (ISRR)
P.O. Box 2312
Carson City, NV 89702
702-882-7755

Kammandale Library
57 N. Dale Street
St. Paul, MN 55102
612-224-5160

L.A. County Adoption Search
  Association
P.O. Box 1461
Roseville, CA 95661

Lambs in Search
3578D Parkmoor Village Drive
Colorado Springs, CO 80907

Living in Search of Answers
P.O. Box 215
Gilsum, NH 03448-0215

Love, Roots and Wings
10432 Achilles
El Paso, TX 79924

Marywood Search Support Group
510 W. 26th Street
Austin, TX 78705
512-472-9251

Musser Foundation
1105 Cape Coral Parkway
Cape Coral, FL 33904
941-542-1342

National Adoption Center
1500 Walnut Street
Suite 701
Philadelphia, PA 19102
1-800-TOADOPT

National Adoption Information
  Clearinghouse (NAIC)
5640 Nicholson Lane
Unit 300
Rockville, MD 20852
703-246-9095

National Adoption Registry
6800 Elmwood Avenue
Kansas City, MO 64132-9963
800-875-4347

National Adoption
  Reunion Registry
P.O. Box 2494
Danbury, CT 06813

National Adoption Search
    Registry, Inc.
P.O. Box 2051
Great Neck, NY 11022

National Congress for Men
    & Children
P.O. Box 171675
Kansas City, KS 66117-1675
913-342-3860

National Data Research Center
(research of real estate records)
2398 NW 119th Street
Miami, FL 33167
1-800-327-1072

Nationwide Locating Service
2949 Brantley Drive
Antioch, TN 37013
615-367-0230

Native American Adoption Resource
    Exchange
200 Charles Street
Pittsburgh, PA 15238
412-782-4457

Native American Child & Family
    Resource Center
1315 E. Wells Avenue
Pierre, SD 57501
605-945-2836

National Organization for Birthfathers
    & Adoption Reform (NOBAR)
1139 Bal Harbor Blvd
Suite 184
P.O. Box 50
Punta Gorda, FL 33951
941-637-7477

National Personnel Records Center
(for military searches)
9700 Page Blvd.
St. Louis, MO 63132
314-538-4261 Army
314-538-4141 Navy/Marines/Coast Guard
314-538-4243 Air Force

National Resource Center for Special
    Needs Adoption
16250 Northland Drive
Suite 120
Southville, MI 48075

National Resource Oasis
P.O. Box 3031
Kokomo, IN 46901

Oregon Adoptive Rights Association
P.O. Box 882
Portland, OR 97207
503-235-3669

Organized Adoption Search
    Information Services, Inc. (OASIS)
P.O. Box 530761
Miami Shores, FL 33153
305-758-5196

Origins
P.O. Box 556
Whipanny, NJ 07981-0556

Orphan Train Heritage Society
    of America
614 E. Emma, #115
Springdale, AR 72764
501-756-2780

Past Present Future
7290 W. Shaw Butte Drive
Peoria, AZ 85345

Post Adoption Center for Education
    and Research
1634 Walnut
Berkeley, CA 94704

Professional Adoption Search Team
P.O. Box 24095
San Jose, CA 95154

PURE, Inc.
P.O. Box 638
Westminster, CA 92684
1-800-USEARCH

PVI Search Firm
Kate Helms-Martin
P.O. Box 174
Bellbrook, OH 45305

Reunions: The Next Step
305 E. 40th Street, #12V
New York, NY 10016

Re-Unite
P.O. Box 7945
Aspen, CO 81612

The Right to Know
P.O. Box 1409
Grand Prairie, TX 75050

Roots
7110 Westway Center
Knoxville, TN 37919

Roots and Reunions
210 Barbeau Street
Sault Saint Marie, MI 49783-2402

Salvation Army
Missing Persons Bureau
(This organization provides assistance
   to the needy. If you presume your
   person could be homeless or
   seeking assistance, contact it.)
120 West 14th Street
New York, NY 10011

Search Finders of California
P.O. Box 24595
San Jose, CA 95154-4595

Search for Tomorrow, Inc.
P.O. Box 441
New Haven, IN 46774

Searching
P.O. Box 7446
Harrisburg, PA 17113-0446
717-985-1561

Severed Strings
P.O. Box 2203
Fullerton, CA 92633

Shadow Trackers Investigative
   Services
(specializes in missing person searches)
P.O. Box 190666
Boise, ID 83719
208-362-6030
Fax: 208-362-5643

Social Security Administration
Location Services
6401 Security Blvd.
Baltimore, MD 21235

Stop the Act Coalition (STAC)
306 Lenapi Drive
Franklin Lakes, NJ 07417
201-891-4234

TexCare
P.O. Box 832161
Richardson, TX 75083
214-699-8386

Tracers Limited
P.O. Box 18511
Tucson, AZ 85732

Triadoption Library
Westminster Community Service
   Center
7571 Westminster Avenue
Westminster, CA 92683
714-892-4098

Tri-County Genealogical Society
21715 Brittany
Eastpointe, MI 48021-2503
810-774-7953

Truth Seekers in Adoption
P.O. Box 286
Roscoe, IL 61073
815-765-2730

United States Children's Bureau
(This organization is the United
    States' oldest child welfare and
    advocacy group.)
P.O. Box 1182
Washington, D.C. 20013
202-205-8671

WARM
5950 6th Avenue South
Suite 107
Seattle, WA 98108
206-767-9510

Washington Adoptees Rights
    Movement
P.O. Box 2667
Olympia, WA 99507

Wichita Adult Adoptees
4551 S. Osage
Wichita, KS 67217
316-522-8772

Women's Adoptee Support Group
197 Hammond Avenue
Santa Cruz, CA 95062

Yesterday's Children
77 Homer Street
Providence, RI 02804

International Search Resources

Adoptee's Foreign Searchers
P.O. Box 360074
Strongsville, OH 44136
216-238-1004

ALMA—England
P.O. Box 10
Rainham, Essex
UK RM13 8JZ
0708 55 6961

Geborener Deutscher
805 Alvarado NE
Albuquerque, NM 87108
505-268-1310

International Concerns Committee for
    Children
(publishes an annual report on
    foreign adoption)
911 Cypress Drive
Boulder, CO 80303
303-494-8333

Overseas Brats
P.O. Box 29805
San Antonio, TX 78229
210-349-1394

Newsletters, Magazines, and Other Resources

Adoptalk
970 Raymond Avenue
Suite 106
St. Paul, MN 55114-1149

Adoption Helpletter
P.O. Box 5929
Lake Worth, FL 33466-5929
407-738-0921

Adoptive Families
3333 Highway 100 North
Minneapolis, MN 55422
612-535-4829

Birthparents Today
3423 Blue Rock
Cincinnati, OH 45239
513-741-0929

Concerned United Birthparents
    Communicator
2000 Walker Street
Des Moines, IA 50317
800-822-2777

Confidential Information Services
Public and Private
Butterworth, Inc.
10 Tower Office Park
Woburn, MA 01801

The Decree
1000 Connecticut Avenue NW
Suite 9
Washington, D.C. 20036
202-483-3399

Directory of Independent Search
    Consultants
P.O. Box 10192
Costa Mesa, CA 92627

Directory of Professional
    Genealogists
421 M Street NW
Suite 236
Washington, D.C. 20007

Family Tree Maker
39500 Stevenson Place
Suite 204
Fremont, CA 94539
510-794-6850

The Information Book
Superintendent of Documents
U.S. Government Printing Office
Department 33
Washington, D.C. 20402
202-275-2481

Jewel Among Jewels
    Adoption News
P.O. Box 502065
Indianapolis, IN 46250
317-849-5651

Looking for Someone
Tower Press
Folly Mill Road
P.O. Box 438
Seabrook, NH 03874

Names and Numbers
John Wiley & Sons, Inc.
605 Third Avenue
New York, NY 10158

National Directory of Addresses and
    Telephone Numbers
850 Third Avenue
New York, NY 10022

On the Vine
Sweet Pea Press
P.O. Box 1852
Appleton, WI 54913-1852

Open Adoption Birthparent
721 Hawthorne Street
Royal Oak, MI 48067
810-543-0997

Pact Press
3315 Sacramento Street
Suite 239
San Francisco, CA 94118
415-221-6957

People Searching News
P.O. Box 100444
Palm Bay, FL 32910-0444
407-768-2222

Reunions Magazine
    (available in hard copy or on-line)
P.O. Box 11727
Milwaukee, WI 53211-0727
800-373-7933 for charge orders

Roots and Wings
c/o Cynthia Peck
30 Endicott Drive
Great Meadows, NJ 07838
908-637-8828

Search Aftermath
Box 10192
Costa Mesa, CA 92627

The Search and Support Directory
TRIADOPTION Publications
P.O. Box 638
Westminster, CA 92684

Search- and Support-Related Videos and Audiotapes

The following search- and support-related tools are available from an organization called Silver Roze Productions. To order a video or audiotape, contact the organization directly at 513 East First Street, 2nd Floor, Tustin, CA 92680, or by phone at 714-573-8865. This adoption organization's video and audio library includes the following titles:

Why Might Adoptees Be Angry at Their Adoptive Parents? American Adoption Congress 1991 conference audiotape

Seven Core Issues in Adoption. A two-hour videotape featuring a group of adoptees, birth parents, and adoptive parents who unite to speak out on and improve understanding of the issues affecting all members of the triad

Ungrieved Losses: Psychological Ties in the Adoption Triad. The American Adoption Congress 1990 conference audiotape

Loss and Grief in the Triad. Adoptive Families of America 1993 conference audiotape

Healing Loss in the Triad. North American Council on Adoptable Children 1994 conference audiotape

Rituals & Their Importance in Healing Adoption Loss. Adoptive Families of America 1993 conference audiotape

Putting Down the Myths about Adoption. Audiotape

Understanding Birth Parents. Adoptive Families of America 1992 conference audiotape

Extended Families. Audiotape

Adoption: Ages & Stages. Audiotape

Who Searches & Why? Audiotape

The Gilbert Adoption Video. Available from Home Sweet Home Educational Media Company, Box 544444, Dallas, TX 75254

Agencies for Pursuing Records Related to Adoption

Use discretion and thought during conversations seeking information from adoption, social service, or government agencies. Several states have passed more liberal information access laws that make it easier to find someone, but most are still resistant to requests for information and have laws that prohibit divulging it. Therefore, the way you present something may be directly related to the amount of information you gain. There are also laws that convict those who falsely represent themselves, so be careful not to be deceptive when requesting information.

Alabama
State Department of Human
  Resources
50 N. Ripley
Montgomery, AL 36130
205-242-9500

Alaska
Department of Health and Social
  Services
P.O. Box 110630
Juneau, AK 99811
907-465-3633

Arizona

Confidentiality Intermediary Program
Arizona Supreme Court
1501 W. Washington
Phoenix, AZ 85007
602-542-9580

Arkansas

Division of Children and Family
 Services
P.O. Box 1437
Mail Drop 808
Little Rock, AR 72203
501-682-8462

California

Department of Social Services
744 P Street M.S. 19-69
Sacramento, CA 95814
916-445-3146

Colorado

Colorado Voluntary Adoption Registry
Department of Health
4300 Cherry Creek Drive South
Denver, CO 80222-1530
303-692-2227

Connecticut

Connecticut Adoption Resource
 Exchange
B2 Whitehall, Undercliff Road
Meriden, CT 06451
203-238-6640

Delaware

Division of Child Protective Services
1825 Faulkland Road
Wilmington, DE 19805
302-633-2660

District of Columbia

Child and Family Services Division
Adoption and Placement Resources
 Branch
609 H Street NE
Room 313
Washington, D.C. 20002
202-724-4602

Veterans' Benefits Administration
Department of Veterans' Affairs
Administrative Support Staff 20A52
810 Vermont Avenue NW
Washington, D.C. 20420

Florida

Department of Health and Rehabilitative Services
1317 Winewood Blvd.
Building 8
Room 317
Tallahassee, FL 32301
904-448-7721

Georgia

Department of Human Resources
Division of Family and Children
 Services
878 Peachtree Street NE
Atlanta, GA 30309
404-657-3559

Hawaii

Court Management Service
P.O. Box 3498
Honolulu, HI 96811
808-548-4601

Idaho

Department of Health and Welfare
450 W. State Street
Boise, ID 83720
208-334-5702

Illinois

Department of Children and Family
    Services
406 E. Monroe
Springfield, IL 62701-1498
217-785-2509

Indiana

Registrar, Vital Records
Indiana State Board of Health
1330 W. Michigan
Room 121
Indianapolis, IN 46202
317-633-0276

Iowa

Department of Human Services
Hoover State Office Building
Des Moines, IA 50319
515-281-5358

Kansas

SRS Children and Family Service
West Hall
300 SW Oakley
Room 226
Topeka, KS 66606
913-296-8133

Kentucky

Department of Social Services
275 E. Main Street
6th Floor West
Frankfort, KY 40621
502-564-2136

Louisiana

Department of Health and Human
    Services
P.O. Box 3318
Baton Rouge, LA 70821
504-342-4086

Maine

Department of Human Services
State House
221 State Street
Augusta, ME 04333
207-287-5060

Maryland

Mutual Consent Voluntary Adoption
    Registry
311 W. Saratoga Street
Baltimore, MD 21201
301-333-0237

Massachusetts

Department of Social Services
24 Farnsworth Street
Boston, MA 02114
617-727-0900, x559

Michigan

Department of Social Services
P.O. Box 30037
235 S. Grand Avenue
Lansing, MI 48909
517-373-4021

Minnesota

Adoption and Guardianship Section
The Department of Human Services
444 Lafayette Road
St. Paul, MN 55155-3831
612-296-2795

Mississippi

Department of Human Services
P.O. Box 354
Jackson, MS 39205
601-354-6671

Missouri

Missouri Division of Family Services
P.O. Box 88
Jefferson City, MO 65103
314-751-2502

Montana
Department of Family Services
P.O. Box 8005
Helena, MT 59604
406-411-5900

Nebraska
Department of Social Services
P.O. Box 95026
Lincoln, NE 68509
402-471-9254

Nevada
Adoption Specialist, Division of Child
    and Family Services
6171 W. Charleston Blvd.
Building 15
Las Vegas, NV 89158
702-486-7650

New Hampshire
Division for Children, Youth and
    Families
361 Lincoln Street
Manchester, NH 03103
603-668-2330, x356

New Jersey
Division of Youth and Family Services
50 E. State Street, CN 717
Trenton, NJ 08625

New Mexico
Children Youth and Families
    Department
P.E.R.A. Building
Room 252
P.O. Drawer 5160
Santa Fe, NM 87502-05160
505-827-8422

New York
Department of Health
Corning Tower
Room 208
Albany, NY 12237
518-474-1746

North Carolina
Division of Social Services
325 N. Salisbury Street
Raleigh, NC 27603
919-733-3801

North Dakota
Children and Family Services
600 East Blvd.
Bismarck, ND 58505
701-224-4805

Ohio
Department of Human Services
30 E. State Street
5th Floor
Columbus, OH 43215
614-466-9274

Oklahoma
Department of Human Services
P.O. Box 25352
Oklahoma City, OK 73521
405-521-2475

Oregon
Children's Services Division
500 Summer Street NE
Salem, OR 97310
503-945-6616

Pennsylvania
Office of Children, Youth and Families
P.O. Box 2675, DPW Annex
Harrisburg, PA 17105-2675
717-787-4756

Puerto Rico
Department of Social Services
P.O. Box 11398
Santurce, PR 00910
809-721-0086

Rhode Island

Department of Children, Youth and
    Families
610 Mount Pleasant Avenue
Providence, RI 02908
401-457-4993

South Carolina

Department of Social Services
P.O. Box 1520
Columbia, SC 29202-1520
803-734-6095

South Dakota

Department of Social Services
Richard F. Knei Building
700 Governors Drive
Pierre, SD 57501-2291
605-773-3227

Tennessee

Department of Human Services
400 Deaderick Street
Nashville, TN 37248-9000
615-741-5935

Texas

Department of Protective and
    Regulatory Services
P.O. Box 149030, M.C. W-415
Austin, TX 78714-9030
512-450-3412

Utah

Department of Health
Vital Statistics
288 N. 1460
West Salt Lake City, UT 84145-0500
801-538-6105

Vermont

Department of Social and
    Rehabilitation Services
103 S. Main Street
Waterbury, VT 05671-2401
802-241-2131

Virginia

Department of Social Services
730 E. Broad Street
Richmond, VA 23219-1849
804-692-1290

Virgin Islands

Department of Human Services
Knud Hansen Complex
Building A
1303 Hospital Ground
St. Thomas, VI 00802
809-774-7865

Washington

Department of Social and Health
    Services
P.O. Box 45713
Olympia, WA 98504
360-586-6070

West Virginia

Health and Human Resources
State Capital Complex
Building 6
Room 850
Charleston, WV 25303
304-558-7980

Wisconsin

Bureau for Children, Youth and
    Families
P.O. Box 7851
Madison, WI 53707
608-266-7163

Wyoming

Department of Family Services
319 Hathaway Building
Cheyenne, WY 82002-0490
307-777-6890

Departments of Vital Statistics

To obtain your original birth certificate, contact the Department of Vital Statistics in the state in which you were born. Each department has different rules for requesting this information, but normally a written request must be made and some proof of identification given. Send a photocopy of your driver's license along with a personal or cashier's check in the amount of the fee that the agency charges for producing a copy of a birth record. In some cases you must provide your mother's maiden name before you can obtain your birth certificate. Some states, such as Mississippi, have very current procedures and allow you to request by fax and pay with a credit card, and they will even send your birth certificate to you overnight and bill it to your credit card. Death, marriage, and divorce records are also kept on file with the Vital Statistics offices.

Alabama

Center for Health Statistics
P.O. Box 5625
Montgomery, AL 36103
205-242-5033
*Charges a fee of $12.00 for birth
    and death certificates.*

Alaska

Bureau of Vital Statistics
P.O. Box H-02G
Juneau, AK 99811
907-465-3391
*Charges a fee of $7.00 for birth or
    death certificates.*

Arizona

Department of Health Services
P.O. Box 3887
Phoenix, AZ 85030
602-255-3260
*Charges a fee of $8.00 for birth and
    $5.00 for death certificates.*

Arkansas

Division of Vital Records
Department of Health
4815 W. Markham Street
Little Rock, AR 72201
501-661-2336
*Charges a fee of $5.00 for birth and
    $4.00 for death certificates.*

California

Vital Statistics Section
Department of Health Services
P.O. Box 730241
Sacramento, CA 94244
916-445-2684
*Charges a fee of $12.00 for
    birth and $8.00 for death
    certificates.*

Colorado

Office of Vital Records
605 Bannock Street
Denver, CO 80204
303-436-7350
*Charges a fee of $15.00 for birth
    and death certificates.*

Connecticut

Bureau of Vital Records
550 Main Street
Room 10
Hartford, CT 06103
860-543-8538
*Charges a fee of $5.00 for birth and
death certificates.*

Delaware

Office of Vital Statistics
P.O. Box 637
Dover, DE 19903
302-739-4721
*Charges a fee of $5.00 for birth and
death certificates.*

District of Columbia

Vital Records Branch
425 I Street NW
Room 3009
Washington, D.C. 20001
202-727-9281
*Charges a fee of $12.00 for birth
and death certificates.*

Florida

Department of Health and
Rehabilitative Services
P.O. Box 210
1217 Pearl Street
Jacksonville, FL 32231
904-359-6900
*Charges $9.00 for birth and $5.00
for death certificates.*

Georgia

Department of Human Resources
Room 217-H
47 Trinity Avenue SW
Atlanta, GA 30334
404-656-4900
*Charges a fee of $10.00 for birth
and death certificates.*

Hawaii

State Department of Health
P.O. Box 3378
Honolulu, HI 96801
808-586-4533
*Charges $2.00 for birth and death
certificates.*

Idaho

Idaho Department of Health and
Welfare
450 W. State Street
Boise, ID 83720-9990
208-334-5988
*Charges $8.00 for birth and death
certificates.*

Illinois

Department of Public Health
605 W. Jefferson Street
Springfield, IL 62702-5097
217-782-6553
*Charges $15.00 for birth and death
certificates.*

Indiana

State Department of Health
1330 W. Michigan Street
P.O. Box 1964
Indianapolis, IN 46206-1964
317-633-0274
*Charges $6.00 for birth and $4.00
for death certificates.*

Iowa

Department of Public Health
Vital Records Section
Lucas Office Building
321 E. 12th Street
Des Moines, IA 50319-0075
515-281-4944
*Charges $6.00 for birth and death
certificates.*

Kansas

State Department of Health and
    Environment
900 Jackson Street
Topeka, KS 66612-1290
913-296-1400
*Charges $10.00 for birth and $7.00
    for death certificates.*

Kentucky

Offices of Vital Statistics
275 E. Main Street
Frankfort, KY 40621
502-564-4212
*Charges a fee of $7.00 for
    birth and $6.00 for death
    certificates.*

Louisiana

Office of Public Health
325 Loyola Avenue
New Orleans, LA 70112
504-568-5150
*Charges $5.00 for birth and death
    certificates.*

Maine

Office of Vital Statistics
Department of Human Services
State House
Station 11
Augusta, ME 04333
207-289-3184
*Charges $10.00 for birth and death
    certificates.*

Maryland

Division of Vital Records
Department of Health and Mental
    Hygiene
Metro Executive Building
4201 Patterson Avenue
P.O. Box 68760
Baltimore, MD 21215-0020
301-974-3914
*Charges $4.00 for birth and death
    certificates.*

Massachusetts

Registry of Vital Records and Statistics
400 70 Atlantic Avenue
Boston, MA 02111
617-727-2816
*Charges $6.00 for birth and death
    certificates.*

Michigan

Office of the State Registrar and
    Center for Health Statistics
Michigan Department of Public
    Health
3423 N. Logan Street
Lansing, MI 48909
517-335-8655
*Charges $13.00 for birth and death
    certificates.*

Minnesota

Department of Health
Vital Statistics
717 Delaware Street SE
P.O. Box 9441
Minneapolis, MN 55440
612-623-5121
*Charges $11.00 for birth and $8.00
    for death certificates.*

Mississippi

Vital Records
State Department of Health
2433 N. State Street
Jackson, MS 39216
601-960-7450
Charges $12.00 for birth and
$10.00 for death certificates.

Missouri

Department of Health
Bureau of Vital Records
1730 E. Elm
P.O. Box 570
Jefferson City, MO 65102
314-751-6400
Charges $10.00 for birth and death
certificates.

Montana

Bureau of Records and Statistics
State Department of Health and
Environmental Sciences
Helena, MT 59620
406-444-2614
Charges $10.00 for birth and death
certificates.

Nebraska

State Department of Health
301 Centennial Mall South
P.O. Box 95007
Lincoln, NE 68509
402-471-2871
Charges $8.00 for birth and $7.00
for death certificates.

Nevada

Division of Health and Vital Statistics
Capitol Complex
505 E. King Street, #102
Carson City, NV 89710
702-687-4480
Charges $11.00 for birth and $8.00
for death certificates.

New Hampshire

Bureau of Vital Records
Health and Welfare Building
6 Haze Drive
Concord, NH 03301
603-271-4654
Charges $10.00 for birth and death
certificates.

New Jersey

Bureau of Vital Statistics
S. Warren and Market Streets, CN 370
Trenton, NJ 08625
609-292-4087
Charges $4.00 for birth and death
certificates.

New Mexico

New Mexico Health Services Division
Office of Vital Statistics
P.O. Box 26110
Santa Fe, NM 87502
505-827-2338
Charges $10.00 for birth and $5.00
for death certificates.

New York

Vital Records Section
State Department of Health
Empire State Plaza
Tower Building
Albany, NY 12237-0023
518-474-3075
Charges $15.00 for birth and death
certificates.

New York City

Division of Vital Records
New York City
Department of Health
P.O. Box 3776
New York, NY 10007
212-619-4530
Charges a fee of $15.00 for birth
and death certificates.

North Carolina

Department of Environment, Health
and Natural Resources
Division of Epidemiology, Vital
Records Section
225 N. McDowell Street
P.O. Box 29537
Raleigh, NC 27626-0537
919-733-3526
*Charges $10.00 for birth and death
certificates.*

North Dakota

Division of Vital Records
State Capitol
600 E. Boulevard Avenue
Bismarck, ND 58505
701-224-2360
*Charges $7.00 for birth and $5.00
for death certificates.*

Ohio

Bureau of Vital Statistics
Ohio Department of Health
P.O. Box 15098
Columbus, OH 43215-0098
614-466-2531
*Charges a fee of $7.00 for birth
and death certificates*

Oklahoma

Vital Records Section
State Department of Health
1000 NE 10th Street
P.O. Box 53551
Oklahoma City, OK 73152
405-271-4040
*Charges $5.00 for birth and death
certificates.*

Oregon

Oregon Health Division of Vital Statistics
P.O. Box 14050
Portland, OR 97214-0050
503-731-4095
*Charges $13.00 for birth and death
certificates.*

Pennsylvania

Division of Vital Records
State Department of Health
Central Building
101 S. Mercer Street
P.O. Box 1528
New Castle, PA 16103
412-656-3100
*Charges $4.00 for birth and $3.00
for death certificates.*

Rhode Island

Division of Vital Records
Rhode Island Department of Health
Room 101
Cannon Building
3 Capitol Hill
Providence, RI 02908-5097
401-277-2811
*Charges a fee of $10.00 for birth
and death certificates.*

South Carolina

Office of Vital Records and Public
Statistics
2600 Bull Street
Columbia, SC 29201
803-734-4830
*Charges a fee of $8.00 for birth
and death certificates.*

South Dakota

State Department of Health
Vital Records
523 E. Capitol
Pierre, SD 57501
605-773-3355
*Charges a fee of $5.00 for birth
    and death certificates.*

Tennessee

Tennessee Vital Records
Department of Health
Cordell Hull Building
Nashville, TN 37247-0350
615-741-1763
*Charges a fee of $10.00 for birth and
    $5.00 for death certificates.*

Texas

Bureau of Vital Statistics
Texas Department of Health
P.O. Box 12040
Austin, TX 78711-2040
512-458-7111
*Charges a fee of $11.00 for birth and
    $9.00 for death certificates.*

Utah

Bureau of Vital Records
Utah Department of Health
288 N. 1460 West
P.O. Box 16700
Salt Lake City, UT 84116-0700
801-538-6105
*Charges a fee of $12.00 for birth and
    $9.00 for death certificates.*

Vermont

Vermont Department of Health
Vital Records Section
Box 70
60 Main Street
Burlington, VT 05402
802-863-7275
*Charges a fee of $5.00 for birth
    and death certificates.*

Virginia

Division of Vital Records
State Health Department
P.O. Box 1000
Richmond, VA 23208-1000
804-786-6228
*Charges a fee of $5.00 for birth
    and death certificates.*

Washington

Department of Health
Center for Health Statistics
P.O. Box 9709
Olympia, WA 98508-9709
206-753-5936
*Charges $11.00 for birth and death
    certificates.*

West Virginia

Vital Registration Office
Division of Health
State Capitol
Complex Building 3
Charleston, WV 25305
304-558-2931
*Charges a fee of $5.00 for birth
    and death certificates.*

Wisconsin

Vital Records
1 W. Wilson Street
P.O. Box 309
Madison, WI 53701
608-266-1371
*Charges a fee of $10.00 for birth and
    $7.00 for death certificates.*

Wyoming

Vital Records Services
Hathaway Building
Cheyenne, WY 82002
307-777-7591
*Charges a fee of $8.00 for birth and
    $6.00 for death certificates.*

International Birth Records

To obtain international birth records, contact the Office of Overseas Citizens Services at the United States Department of State, Washington, D.C. 20520. This office can assist in helping you locate the birth certificate of a birth that occurred outside of the United States.

Military Searches

If the one you are searching for is currently in the armed forces, contact the appropriate organization below to conduct a database search.

Retired Military Personnel
The Office of Personnel Management
1900 E Street SW
Washington, D.C. 20415

United States Air Force
Air Force Military Personnel Center
Worldwide Locator
Randolph Air Force Base
San Antonio, TX 78150
512-652-5775

United States Army
Worldwide Locator Service
U.S. Army Personnel Service Support
    Center
Fort Benjamin
Harrison, IN 46249
317-542-4211

United States Coast Guard
Coast Guard Locator Service
Room 4502
2100 2nd Street SW
Washington, D.C. 20593
202-426-8898

United States Marine Corps
Marine Corps Headquarters
Locator Service
Washington, D.C. 20380
202-694-1624

United States Navy
Navy Locator Service
Navy Annex Building
Washington, D.C. 20370
202-694-3155

State Motor Vehicle Registration Offices

Some states are flexible in offering information from the Department of Motor Vehicles to requesting parties. Most, however, will expect a written or in-person request and will require a valid reason for divulging the information to you. If your request is granted, you will receive a printout of your person's driving record, possibly a photograph, and, if you're lucky, a current address. Only a couple of states will not actually provide access to driver's license records, and very few others require the driver's written permission.

An information broker, private investigator, or attorney skilled in this area may have more success in obtaining the records on your behalf. DMV records can provide you with someone's most up-to-date information, including address, date of birth, and Social Security number.

Alabama
Title Section
2721 Gunter Park Drive
P.O. Box 1331
Montgomery, AL 36102
205-271-3250

Alaska
Department of Public Safety
5700 E. Tudor Road
Anchorage, AK 99507
907-269-5559

Arizona
Motor Vehicle Division
1801 W. Jefferson Avenue
Phoenix, AZ 85007
602-255-7011

Arkansas
Office of Motor Vehicles
P.O. Box 1272
Little Rock, AR 72203
501-682-4630

California
Department of Motor Vehicles
P.O. Box 944247
Sacramento, CA 94244-2470
916-732-7243

Colorado
140 W. Sixth Avenue
Denver, CO 80204
303-620-4108

Connecticut
Division of Motor Vehicles
60 State Street
Wethersfield, CT 06109
203-566-4410

Delaware
Division of Motor Vehicles
P.O. Box 698
Dover, DE 19903
302-736-3147

District of Columbia
Bureau of Motor Vehicle Services
301 C Street NW
Washington, D.C. 20001
202-727-6680

Florida
Division of Motor Vehicles
Neil Kirkman Building
Tallahassee, FL 32301
904-488-4127

Georgia
Motor Vehicle Division
126 Trinity-Washington Building
Atlanta, GA 30334
404-656-4100

Hawaii
Division of Motor Vehicle Licensing
1455 S. Beretania Street
Honolulu, HI 96814
808-955-8221

Idaho
Transportation Department
P.O. Box 34
Boise, ID 83707
208-334-8663

Illinois
Vehicle Records Inquiry Section
4th Floor, Centennial Building
Springfield, IL 62756
217-782-6992

Indiana
Bureau of Motor Vehicles
401 State Office Building
100 N. Senate Avenue
Indianapolis, IN 46204
317-232-2798

Iowa
Department of Transportation
Lucas State Office Building
Des Moines, IA 50319
515-281-7710

Kansas
Department of Revenue
Division of Vehicles
State Office Building
Topeka, KS 66629
913-296-3621

Kentucky
Department of Motor Vehicle
    Regulation
New State Office Building
Frankfort, KY 40622
502-564-7570

Louisiana
Department of Public Safety
P.O. Box 64886
Baton Rouge, LA 70896
504-925-6146

Maine
Department of State
Motor Vehicle Division
State House Station #29
Augusta, ME 04333
207-287-3071

Maryland
Motor Vehicle Administration
6601 Ritchie Highway NE
Glen Burnie, MD 21062
410-768-7000

Massachusetts
Registrar of Motor Vehicles
100 Nashua Street
Boston, MA 02114
617-727-3700

Michigan
Department of State
Bureau of Driver and Vehicle Services
7064 Crowner Drive
Lansing, MI 48918
517-322-1166

Minnesota
Driver and Vehicle Services Division
Transportation Building
St. Paul, MN 55155
612-296-6911

Mississippi
Department of Motor Vehicles
Title Division
P.O. Box 1140
Jackson, MS 39205
601-359-1248

Missouri
Motor Vehicle Bureau
P.O. Box 100
Jefferson City, MO 65701
314-751-4509

Montana
Registrar's Bureau
925 Main Street
Deer Lodge, MT 58722
406-846-1423

Nebraska
Department of Motor Vehicles
P.O. Box 94789
Lincoln, NE 68509
402-471-2281

Nevada
Department of Motor Vehicles
Carson City, NV 89711
702-855-5370

New Hampshire
Department of Safety
J. H. Hayes Building
Concord, NH 03305
603-271-2251

New Jersey
Bureau of Office Services
Certified Information Unit
25 S. Montgomery Street
Trenton, NJ 08666
609-292-4102

New Mexico
Motor Vehicles Division
P.O. Box 1028
Santa Fe, NM 87504
505-827-2173

New York
Department of Motor Vehicles
Empire Plaza
Albany, NY 12228
518-474-2121

North Carolina
Division of Motor Vehicles
1100 New Bern Avenue
Raleigh, NC 27697
919-733-3025

North Dakota
Motor Vehicles Department
Capitol Grounds
Bismarck, ND 58505
701-224-2725

Ohio
Department of Highway Safety
P.O. Box 16520
Columbus, OH 43216
614-752-7500

Oklahoma
Motor Vehicle Division
2501 Lincoln Blvd.
Oklahoma City, OK 73194
405-521-3221

Oregon
Motor Vehicle Division
1905 Lana Avenue NE
Salem, OR 97314
503-371-2200

Pennsylvania
Bureau of Motor Vehicles
Harrisburg, PA 17122
717-787-3130

Puerto Rico
Department of Transportation
P.O. Box 41243
Minillar Station
Santurce, PR 00940
809-723-9607

Rhode Island
Registrar of Motor Vehicles
Providence, RI 02903
401-277-2970

South Carolina
Motor Vehicle Division
Columbia, SC 29216
803-737-1114

South Dakota
Department of Revenue
118 W. Capitol
Pierre, SD 57501
605-773-3541

Tennessee
Motor Vehicle Division
500 Deaderick Street
Nashville, TN 37242
615-741-3101

Texas

Motor Vehicle Division
40th and Jackson Avenue
Austin, TX 78779
512-465-7611

Utah

State Tax Commission
Motor Vehicle Division
State Fair Grounds
1095 Motor Avenue
Salt Lake City, UT 84116
801-538-8300

Vermont

Department of Motor Vehicles
120 State Street
Montpelier, VT 05603
802-828-2000

Virginia

Department of Motor Vehicles
P.O. Box 27412
Richmond, VA 23269
804-367-0523

Washington

Department of Licensing
P.O. Box 9909
Olympia, WA 98504
206-753-6946

West Virginia

Department of Motor Vehicles
State Capitol Complex
Building 3
Charleston, WV 25317
304-348-3900

Wisconsin

Department of Transportation
P.O. Box 7909
Madison, WI 53707
608-266-1466

Wyoming

Motor Vehicle Division
122 W. 25th Street
Cheyenne, WY 82002
302-777-6511

Genealogical Resources

Founded in 1884, the Church of Jesus Christ of Latter-Day Saints is one of the largest genealogical information warehouses in the world today. There are more than 2,800 branches of this organization throughout the United States and the world. These branches offer information on families through generations past and will even provide you with access to microfilm by placing an order with the main branch in Salt Lake City, Utah. Contact the branch nearest you for reference information on genealogy. This organization specializes in records on the deceased and may not be willing to assist if your request is solely for adoption-related or search purposes.

Many of the Family History Center locations will be closed on Mondays, as some choose to do their cataloguing on that day and others honor the traditional family day by not working in the church. Their services are complimentary, and the centers are run by volunteers who give their time to the church. Informational pamphlets are also available by calling the headquarters located in Salt Lake City, Utah. One entitled *Where Do I Start?* outlines the steps you need to take to research your family history using the Family History Center's services. Two primary resources, the Ancestral File and International Genealogical Index, offer hundreds of lineage-linked lists of families.

Some locations do not accept mail service; they allow only in-person visits or telephone calls.

Alabama
5520 Ziegler Boulevard
Mobile, AL 36608

Alaska
2501 Maplewood Street
Anchorage, AK 99508
907-277-8433

1500 Cowles Street
Fairbanks, AK 99701
907-456-1095

5100 Glacier Highway
Juneau, AK 99821
907-586-2525

LDS Meetinghouse
Ketchikan, AK 99950
907-225-3291

159 Marydale Drive
Soldotna, AK 99669
907-262-4253

Corner of Delwood and Bogard Road
Wasilia, AK 99687
907-376-9774

Arizona
127 10th Street
Cottonwood, AZ 86326
520-634-2349

625 E. Cherry
Flagstaff, AZ 86001
520-425-9570

Highway 60
Globe, AZ 85501
520-425-9570

1600 N. 2nd Avenue
Holbrook, AZ 86025
520-524-6341

3180 Rutherford Drive
Kingman, AZ 86401
520-524-6341

464 E. First Avenue
Mesa, AZ 85204
602-964-2051

313 Lake Powell Boulevard
Page, AZ 86040

12951 North 83rd Avenue
Peoria, AZ 85345

4601 W. Encanto Blvd.
Phoenix, AZ 85035

8710 N. 3rd Avenue
Phoenix, AZ 85021

3102 N. 18th Avenue
Phoenix, AZ
602-265-7762

1001 Ruth Street
Prescott, AZ 86303
520-778-2311

501 Catalina Drive
Stafford, AZ 85546
520-778-3194

Main Street
St. David, AZ 85630
520-586-4879

35 W. Cleveland Street
St. Johns, AZ 85963
520-337-2543

W. Highway 60
Show Low, AZ 85901
520-537-2331

225 W. Freeman Avenue
Snowflake, AZ 85937
520-536-7430

500 S. Langley
Tucson, AZ 85710
602-298-0905

4300 W. 16th Street
Yuma, AZ 85365
520-782-6364

Arkansas
13901 Quail Run Drive
Little Rock, AR
501-455-4998

California
4075 Riverside Avenue
Anderson, CA 96007

316 A Street
Bakersfield, CA 93004

7600 Crescent Avenue
Buena Park, CA 90620

1201 Paseo
Camarillo, CA 93010

19513 Drycliff
Canyon Country, CA 93010

1981 Chestnut Street
Carlsbad, CA 92008

2430 Mariposa Avenue
Chico, CA 95926

656 S. Grand Avenue
Covina, CA 91724
818-331-7117

1280 S. 8th Street
El Centro, CA 92244
619-353-6645

1917 E. Washington
Escondido, CA 92027

2734 Dolbeer
Eureka, CA 95501

2700 Camrose Drive
Fairfield, CA 94533
707-425-2027

6641 E. Butler
Fresno, CA 93725

1130 E. Wilson Avenue
Glendale, CA 91206
818-241-8763

478 Cambridge Drive
Goleta, CA 93117

348 Spruce Street
Gridley, CA 95948

16750 Colima Road
Hacienda Heights, CA 91745

425 N. Kirby Avenue
Hemet, CA 92343

7000 Central Avenue
Highland, CA 92343

4550 Raymond Avenue
La Crescenta, CA 91214
818-957-0925

3150 W. Avenue K
Lancaster, CA 93536

4142 Ceritos Avenue
Los Alamitos, CA 90721
714-821-6914

10741 Santa Monica Blvd.
Los Angeles, CA 90025
415-325-9711

23850 Los Alisos Blvd.
Mission Viejo, CA 92688
714-364-2742

731 El Vista Avenue
Modesto, CA 95354

2316 Hillview Avenue
Monterey Park, CA 91756

15311 S. Pioneer Blvd
Norwalk, CA 90650

4780 Lincoln Avenue
Oakland, CA 94602

674 Yorba Street
Orange, CA 92669
714-997-7710

2120 E. Avenue R
Palmdale, CA 93550
805-947-1694

72-960 Park View
Palm Desert, CA 92261
619-340-6094

770 N. Sierra Madre Villa
Pasadena, CA 91107
213-351-8517

5845 Cretridge
Rancho Palos Verdes, CA 90274

3410 Churncreek Road
Redding, CA 96002
916-222-4949

401 Norma Street
Ridgecrest, CA 93555

5900 Grand Avenue
Riverside, CA 92504

4375 Jackson Street
Riverside, CA 92503

2745 Eastern Avenue
Sacramento, CA 95821
916-487-2090

3705 10th Avenue
San Diego, 92103

2175 Santiago Street
San Jose, CA 95112

55 Casa Street
San Luis Obispo, CA 93404
805-543-6328

875 Quince Avenue
Santa Clara, CA 95051
408-241-1449

908 E. Sierra Madre Avenue
Santa Maria, CA 93454
805-928-4722

1725 Peterson Lane
Santa Rosa, CA 95403
707-829-5965

1024 Nocha Buena
Seaside, CA 93955
408-394-1124

3979 Township
Simi Valley, CA 93063
805-522-2181

820 W. Brookside Road
Stockton, CA 95207
209-951-7060

1337 S. Dora Street
Ukiah, CA 95482
707-468-5746

785 N. San Antonio
Upland, CA 91785

3501 Loma Vista Road
Ventura, CA 93003
805-643-5607

12100 Ridgecrest Road
Victorville, CA 92392
619-243-5632

825 W. Tulare Avenue
Visalia, CA 93277
209-732-3712

255 Holm
Watsonville, CA 95077
408-722-0208

10332 on Bolsa W. of Ward
Westminster, CA 92683
714-554-0592

7906 South Pickering
Whittier, CA 90602

1470 Butte House Road
Yuba City, CA 95992
916-673-0113

Colorado
7080 Independence
Arvada, CO 80004
303-421-0920

701 W. South Boulder Road
Boulder, CO 80303
303-665-4685

1054 E. Lasalle
Colorado Springs, CO 80907

1800 E. Empire Street
Cortez, CO 81321
970-565-4372

2710 S. Monaco Parkway
Denver, CO 80222

#2 Hill Top Circle
Durango, CO 81302
970-259-1061

600 E. Swallow Drive
Fort Collins, CO 80525
970-226-5999

647 Melody Lane
Grand Junction, CO 81506
970-243-2782

2207 23rd Avenue
Greeley, CO 80631

718 Broadway
La Jara, CO 81140

6705 S. Webster
Littleton, CO 80123
303-973-3737

1939 E. Easter Avenue
Littleton, CO 80122
303-798-6461

100 E. Malley Drive
Northglenn, CO 80233
303-451-7177

4720 Surfwood
Pueblo, CO 81005

Connecticut
1000 Mountain Road
Bloomfield, CT 06002

682 South Avenue
New Canaan, CT 06840

39 Bonnie View
Trumbull, CT 06611

Delaware
143 Dickinson Lane
Wilmington, DE 19711
302-654-1911

Florida
1530 W. Camino Real
Boca Raton, FL 33486

3105 Broadway
Fort Myers, FL 33901

29600 SW 167th Avenue
Homestead, FL 33030

4087 Hendricks Avenue
Jacksonville, FL 32207
904-398-3487

1802 College Street
Marianna, FL 32446
904-482-8159

461 Blanding Boulevard
Orange Park, FL 32073
904-272-1150

45 E. Par Avenue
Orlando, FL 32804

3140 State Avenue
Panama City, FL 32405

5773 N. 9th Avenue
Pensacola, FL 32504

1801 Fisk Boulevard
Rockledge, FL 32955

570 62nd Avenue North
St. Petersburg, FL 33702

312 Stadium Drive
Tallahassee, FL 32304
904-224-6431

4106 Fletcher Avenue
Tampa, FL 33637

1958 9th Street SE
Winter Haven, FL 33880

Georgia
1155 Mount Vernon Highway
Dunwoody, GA 30338

1624 Williamson Road
Macon, GA 31206

613 Montgomery Cross Road
Savannah, GA 31406

1307 W. Alden Avenue
Valdosta, GA 31602
912-242-2300

Hawaii
13733 Kilauea Avenue
Hilo, HI 96721
808-935-0711

1560 S. Beretania Street
Honolulu, HI 96826
808-955-8910

1733 Beckley Street
Honolulu, HI 96819
808-841-4118

46-117 Halaulani Street
Kaneohe, HI 96744
808-247-3134

55-600 Naniloa Loop
Laie, HI 96762
808-293-2133

Idaho
101 N. 900 West
Blackfoot, ID 83221

325 W. State Street
Boise, ID 83702

12040 W. Amity Road
Boise, ID 83709
208-362-5847

224 E. 14th Street
Burley, ID 83318
208-678-7286

3015 S. Kimball
Caldwell, ID 83605
208-459-2531

2801 N. 4th
Coeur D'Alene, ID 83814
208-765-0150

221 N. 1st East
Driggs, ID 83422
208-354-2253

980 W. Central Road
Emmett, ID 83617

1155 1st Street
Idaho Falls, ID 83401
208-524-5291

3000 Central Avenue
Idaho Falls, ID 83406
208-529-4087

138 N. 6th Street
Montpelier, ID 83254
208-847-0340

143 Central Canyon
Nampa, ID 83686
208-467-5827

156 1/2 S. 6th Center
Pocatello, ID 83201
208-232-9262

325 E. Locust
Shelly, ID 83274
208-357-7831

281 E. Hooper Avenue
Soda Springs, ID 83276
208-547-2237

401 Maurice Street North
Twin Falls, ID 83303
208-733-8073

306 E. Main Street
Weiser, ID 83672
208-549-1575

Illinois
604 W. Windsor Road
Champaign, IL 61820
217-352-8063

402 Longwood Drive
Chicago Heights, IL 60620

25 W. 341 Ridgeland Road
Naperville, IL 60540

3700 W. Reservoir Boulevard
Peoria, IL 61615
309-682-4073

620 N. Alpine Road
Rockford, IL 61107
815-399-5448

1320 W. Schaumburg Road
Schaumburg, IL 60194

2801 Lake Avenue
Wilmette, IL 60091

Indiana
2411 E. 2nd Street
Bloomington, IN 47402
812-332-9786

519 E. Almstead
Evansville, IN 47708

5401 St. Joe Road
Ft. Wayne, IN 46835
219-485-9581

900 E. Stop 11 Road
Indianapolis, IN 46227
317-888-6002

777 Sanblest Boulevard
Noblesville, IN 46060

3050 Edison Road
South Bend, IN 46619
219-233-6501

1845 N. Center
Terra Haute, IN 47804
812-234-0269

Iowa

4300 Trailridge Road SE
Cedar Rapids, IA 52403
319-386-7547

4929 Wisconsin Avenue
Davenport, IA 52806
319-386-7547

1201 W. Clifton
Sioux City, IA 51101
712-255-9686

3301 Ashworth Road
West Des Moines, IA 50265
515-225-0416

Kansas

2506 6th Avenue
Dodge City, KS 67801
316-225-6540

15916 W. 143rd Street
Olathe, KS 66062
913-829-1775

3611 SW Jewell
Topeka, KS 66611
913-266-7503

7011 E. 13th Street
Wichita, KS 67206
316-683-2951

Kentucky

1789 Tates Creek Park
Lexington, KY 40502
606-269-2722

1000 Hurstborne Lane
Louisville, KY 40222
502-426-5317

320 Birch Street
Paducah, KY 42001
502-442-5317

Louisiana

611 Versailles Street
Alexandria, LA 71303
318-448-1842

5686 Winbourne Avenue
Baton Rouge, LA 70805
504-357-8385

909 N. 33rd Street
Monroe, LA 71201
318-387-3793

5025 Cleveland Place
Metairie, LA 70112
504-885-3936

200 Carroll Street
Shreveport, LA 71105
318-868-5169

Maine

639 Grandview Avenue
Bangor, ME 04401
207-942-7677

29 Ocean House Road
Cape Elizabeth, ME 04104
207-799-7018

Maryland

4100 St. Johns Lane
Ellicott City, MD 21043
301-465-1642

10000 Stoneybrook Drive
Kensington, MD 20895
301-587-0144

1400 Dulaney Valley Road
Lutherville, MD 21093
301-256-5890

Massachusetts
150 Brown Street
Weston, MA 02138
617-235-9892

Michigan
914 Hill Street
Ann Arbor, MI 48104
313-995-0211

425 N. Woodward Avenue
Bloomfield Hills, MI 48302
313-647-5671

431 E. Saginaw Street
East Lansing, MI 48906
527-332-2932

4285 McCandlish Road
Grand Blanc, MI 48439
616-949-0070

3181 Bradford NE
Grand Rapids, MI 49506
616-949-0070

1112 N. Drake Road
Kalamazoo, MI 49007
616-342-1906

1700 W. Sugnet Road
Midland, MI 48640
517-631-1120

7575 N. Hix Road
Westland, MI 48185
313-459-4570

Minnesota
521 Upham Road
Duluth, MN 55811
218-722-9508

2801 N. Douglas Drive
Minneapolis, MN 55422
612-544-2479

1002 SE 16th Street
Rochester, MN 55904
507-282-2382

1420 29th Avenue North
St. Cloud, MN 56302
612-252-4355

2200 N. Haley
St. Paul, MN 55119
612-770-3213

Mississippi
1301 Pinchaven Road
Clinton, MS 39202
601-924-2537

U.S. 11 South
Hattiesburg, MS 39401
601-544-9238

Missouri
904 Old Highway 36 South
Columbia, MO 65202
314-443-1024

10445 Clayton Road
Frontenac, MO 63141
314-993-2328

705 W. Walnut
Independence, MO 64050
816-461-0245

1120 Clayview Drive
Liberty, MO 64068
816-781-8295

3325 E. Bennett
Springfield, MO 65804
417-887-8229

Montana
1711 Sixth Street West
Billings, MT 59102
406-245-8112

1000 Wicks Lane
Billings, MT 59105
406-259-3348

2195 Coulter Drive
Bozeman, MT 58715
406-586-3880

3400 E. 4 Mile Road
Butte, MT 59701
406-494-9909

1401 9th Street NW
Great Falls, MT 59404
406-453-4280

1610 E. 6th Avenue
Helena, MT 59601
406-442-1558

3201 Bancroft Drive
Missoula, MT 59801
406-543-6148

Nebraska
212 W. 22nd Street
Grand Island, NE 68801
308-382-9418

3100 Old Cheney Road
Lincoln, NE 68516
402-423-4561

11027 Martha Street
Omaha, NE 68144
402-393-7641

Nevada
1651 College Parkway
Elko, NV 89801
702-738-4565

900 Avenue East
Ely, NV 89301
702-289-3575

750 W. Richards Street
Fallon, NV 89406
702-423-2094

509 S. Ninth Street
Las Vegas, NV 89104
702-382-9695

301 S. Center
Reno, NV 89501
702-785-4530

2955 N. Rock Boulevard
Sparks, NV 89431
702-359-5834

111 W. MacArthur Avenue
Winnemucca, NV 89445
702-623-4413

New Hampshire
90 Clinton Street
Concord, NH 03301
603-224-3061

303 Dunham's Corner Road
East Brunswick, NH 08816

283 James Street
Morristown, NH 07960
201-539-5362

110 Concord Street
Nashua, NH 03060
603-880-7371

New Jersey
W. Windsor Mtg. House
Alexander Road
Windsor, NJ
609-452-0802

New Mexico
1100 Montano Road NW
Albuquerque, NM 87107

5709 Haines Avenue NE
Albuquerque, NM 87110

1200 W. Church Street
Carlsbad, NM 88221

400 W. Apache
Farmington, NM 87499
505-325-5813

1010 Bondad
Grants, NM 87020
505-287-2548

1015 Telsher Boulevard
Las Cruces, NM 88001
505-522-2300

New York
851 Forest Avenue
Jamestown, NY 14702

411 Loudon Road
Loudonville, NY 12211

Two Lincoln Square
New York City, NY 10023

460 Kreag Road
Pittsford, NY 14534

160 Washington Avenue
Plainview, NY 11803

801 E. Colvin Street
Syracuse, NY 13214
315-478-8484

305 Murray Hill Road
Vestal, NY 13850

1424 Maple Road
Williamsville, NY 14204
716-688-9759

North Carolina
3020 Hilliard Drive
Charlotte, NC 28205
704-535-0238

3200 Scotty Hill Road
Fayetteville, NC 28303

3719 Pinetop Road
Greensboro, NC 27410

Highway 127 North
Hickory, NC 28601

3006 Carey Road
Kinston, NC 28501

5100 Six Forks Road
Raleigh, NC 27609

514 S. College Road
Wilmington, NC 27604

4760 Westchester Drive
Winston-Salem, NC 27103

North Dakota
1500 Country West Road
Bismarck, ND 58501

2502 17th Avenue South
Fargo, ND 58103

2025 9th Street NW
Minot, ND 58701

Ohio
735 N. Revere Road
Akron, OH 44313
330-864-0203

5505 Bosworth Place
Cincinnati, OH 45212
513-531-5624

3648 Leib Street
Columbus, OH 43209
614-451-0483

1500 Shiloh Springs Road
Dayton, OH 45426
513-854-4566

3080 Bell Drive
Fairborn, OH 45324
513-878-9551

8876 Chillicothe Road
Kirkland, OH 44094
216-256-8808

2135 Baldwin Road
Reynoldsburg, OH 43068
614-866-7686

1545 East Gate
Toledo, OH 43619
419-382-0262

25000 Westwood Road
Westlake, OH 44145
216-777-1518

Oklahoma
923 Hilltop Drive
Lawton, OK 73507
405-355-9946

3008 E. Hancock Road
Muskogee, OK 74403

5020 NW 63rd
Oklahoma City, OK 73132
405-721-8455

1720 E. Virginia
Stillwater, OK 74075
405-372-8569

12110 E. 7th Street
Tulsa, OK 74128

Oregon
4195 SW 99th
Beaverton, OR 97007
503-644-7782

1260 Thompson Drive
Bend, OR 97701
503-389-3559

3950 Sherman Avenue
Coos Bay, OR 97402
503-269-9037

4141 NW Harrison
Corvallis, OR 97330
503-752-2256

3550 W. 18th Street
Eugene, OR 97412
503-343-3741

1969 Williams Highway
Grants Pass, OR 97527
503-479-7644

3500 SE 182nd Street
Gresham, OR 97030
503-665-1524

850 SW 11th
Hermiston, OR 97838
503-567-3445

2200 NE Jackson School Road
Hillsboro, OR 97124
503-640-4658

2504 N. Fir
La Grande, OR 97850

1271 Overlook Drive
Lake Oswego, OR 97034

2900 Juanipero Way
Medford, OR 97504
541-773-3363

W. Alberta Avenue
Nyssa, OR 97913
503-773-3363

14340 S. Donovan Road
Oregon City, OR 97045
503-657-9584

2931 SE Harrison
Portland, OR 97214
503-235-9090

2215 NE 106th Street
Portland, OR 97220

1864 NW Calkins Road
Roseburg, OR 97470
541-672-4108

862 45th NE
Salem, OR 97301
503-371-0453

4550 Lone Oak SE
Salem, OR 97302
503-363-0374

1395 Lockhaven Drive NE
Salem, OR 97303
503-390-2095

15th and Oregon
The Dalles, OR 97058
541-296-4301

Pennsylvania
721 Paxon Hollow Road
Broomall, PA 19008

1101 S. Hill Road
Erie, PA 16505
814-866-3611

46 School Street
Pittsburgh, PA 15220
412-921-2115

3344 Reading Crest Avenue
Reading, PA 19606

842 Whitehall Road
State College, PA 16802
814-238-4560

2100 Hollywood Drive
York, PA 17315
717-854-9331

Rhode Island
1000 Narragansatt Parkway
Warwick, RI
401-463-8150

South Carolina
1310 Sam Rittenburg
Charleston, SC 29407
803-766-6017

4440 Fort Jackson Boulevard
Columbia, SC 29209
803-782-7141

1620 Maldin Drive
Florence, SC 29502
803-662-9482

South Dakota
2822 Canyon Lake Drive
Rapid City, SD 57702
605-341-8572

3900 S. Fairhall Avenue
Sioux Falls, SD 57106
605-361-1070

Tennessee
1019 N. Moore Road
Chattanooga, TN 37411
423-892-7632

100 Cannongate Road
Kingsport, TN 37660
423-245-2321

400 Kendall Road
Knoxville, TN 37919

107 Twin Hills Drive
Madison, TN 37115
615-859-6926

8150 Walnut Grove Road
Memphis, TN 38119
901-754-2545

Texas
3325 N. 12th Street
Abilene, TX 79603

5401 Bell Street
Amarillo, TX 79109

1000 E. Rutherford
Austin, TX 78753
512-837-3626

1200 Barak Lane
Bryan, TX 77802

6750 Woodridge Road
Corpus Christi, TX 78414

1801 Malone
Denton, TX 76201

1019 Big Stone Gap
Duncanville, TX 75137

3651 Douglas Avenue
El Paso, TX 79903
915-565-9711

5001 Altamesa Boulevard
Fort Worth, TX 76134
817-292-8393

505 Deseret
Friendswood, TX 77546
713-996-9346

10555 Mills Road
Houston, TX 77070
713-890-7434

3000 Broadway
Houston, TX 77017
713-893-5381

16331 Hafer Road
Houston, TX 77090
713-893-5381

1410 S. 2nd Street
Killeen, TX 77449
817-526-2918

4021 Deerbrook
Kingwood, TX 77339
713-360-1363

1700 Blueridge Parkway
Longview, TX 75605
214-759-7911

3211 58th Street
Lubbock, TX 79413
806-792-5040

2011 N. Washington
Odessa, TX 79761

2700 Roundrock
Plano, TX 75075

3939 Turtle Creek Drive
Port Arthur, TX 77642

2103 St. Cloud
San Antonio, TX 78228

Utah
The Family History Library
    Headquarters
35 NW Temple Street
Salt Lake City, UT 84150
1-800-346-6044

210 N. Main
Beaver, UT 84713
801-438-5262

225 E. 2nd North
Blanding, UT 84511
801-678-2024

50 N. Main Street
Logan, UT 84321
801-752-0546

300 N. Center Street
Moroni, UT 84646
801-436-8497

539 24th Street
Ogden, UT 84401

Brigham Young University
Provo, UT 84602
801-378-6200

447 E. Lagoon Street
Roosevelt, UT 84060
801-722-3794

269 B Street
Wendover, UT 84083
801-665-2220

Vermont
Rural Route #1
Box 2560
Montpelier, VT 05602

Virginia
3900 Howard Street
Annandale, VA 22003
703-256-5518

3000 Dale Boulevard
Dale City, VA 22193
703-670-5977

901 Denbigh Boulevard
Newport News, VA 23602
804-874-2335

2719 Hunter Mill Road
Oakton, VA 22124
703-281-1836

5600 Monument Avenue
Richmond, VA 23226
804-288-8134

6311 Watburn Drive
Salem, VA 24153

4760 Princess Anne Road
Virginia Beach, VA 23462
804-467-3302

Washington
10675 NE 20th Street
Bellevue, WA 98004

2225 Perry Avenue
Bremerton, WA 98315

2801 Mt. Vista Road
Centralia, WA 98531
206-736-5476

7309 228th Street SW
Edmonds, WA 98020

702 E. Main
Elma, WA 98541

9505 19th Avenue SE
Everett, WA 98201
206-337-0457

34815 3rd Avenue South
Federal Way, WA 98003

5800 Northwest Avenue
Ferndale, WA 98248

131 101st Avenue SE
Lake Stevens, WA 98258

1721 30th Avenue
Longview, WA 98632

1515 Division
Moses Lake, WA 98837
509-765-8711

1314 Goethals
Richland, WA 99352
509-946-6637

512 Valley Avenue
Sumner, WA 98390

10509 SE 5th Street
Vancouver, WA 98684
206-256-7235

667 10th Street NE
Wenatchee, WA 98801
509-884-3285

West Virginia
Route 73 South
Fairmont, WV 26555
304-363-0116

5640 Shawnee Drive
Huntington, WV 25705

Wisconsin
9600 W. Grange Avenue
Hales Corner, WI 53130
414-425-4182

1711 University Avenue
Madison, WI 53705
608-238-1071

910 E. Zingler
Shawano, WI 54166
713-526-2946

Wyoming
347 Jefferson
Afton, WY 83110
307-886-3526

Wyoming County Library
2800 Central Avenue
Cheyenne, WY 82001
307-634-3561

1407 Heart Mountain
Cody, WY 82001
307-634-3561

1500 O'Hara Street
Gillette, WY 82716

120 Shoshone Avenue
Green River, WY 82935
307-875-3972

520 E. Broadway
Jackson, WY 83001
307-733-6337

50 W. Main
Lovell, WY 82431
307-548-2963

923 Garfield
Riverton, WY 82501

2055 Edgar Street
Rock Springs, WY 82901
307-362-8062

2051 Colonial Drive
Sheridan, WY 82801

International Locations
910 70 Avenue SW
Calgary, Canada
403-244-5910

701 Mann Avenue
Victoria, Canada
604-479-3631

6666 Terre Bonne Street
Montreal, Canada
514-489-9138

670 Cherry Hinton Road
Cambridge, Cambridgeshire, England
0223-247-010

401 Holywood Road
Belfast, County Antrim, Ireland
0232-768250

35 Julian Avenue
Glasgow, Scotland
041-357-1024

Boecklinser 55
Vienna, Austria
0222-735-649

Nokelantie 38
Oulu, Finland
981-335714

5 Avenue Therese
Nice, France
9381-0669

Klingelhoefer Strasse 24
Berlin, Germany
030-262-1089

Eckenheimer Landstrasse 264
Frankfurt, Germany
069-546005

Rueckerstrasse 2
Munich, Germany
089-535176

Skolavordustig 46
Reykjavik, Iceland
91-28730

Casa Riunione
Milan, Italy
02-28-22-58

Herbstweg 120
Zurich, Switzerland
0041-1413598

101-105 Wattle Street
O'Connor
Canberra, Australia

308 Preston Point Road
Perth, Australia
09-330-3750

Avenue du Commandant Chesse
Papeete, Tahiti
42-55-94

H. Irigoyen 1230
Vicente Lopez, Bs. As.
Buenos Aires, Argentina
701-4881

Av. Prof. Francisco Morato 2430
Sao Paulo, Brazil
011-814-3492

Pedro de Valdivia #1423
Santiago, Chile
40083-741218

Carrera 38A, #57B-26
Bogota, Columbia

Barrio la Tropicana
Alajuela, Costa Rica
41-29-47

3A Av. 14-16 Zona 1
Ciudad de Guatemala
51-10-58

Carbonel #1301
Chihuahua, Mexico
14-13-11-92

2DA Avenida de Campo Alegra, #14
Urbanizacion Campo Alegre Chacao
Apartado 62569
Caracas, Venezuela

1 Hunter Street
Highlands
Johannesburg, South Africa
011-618-1890

5-10-30 Minami-azabu
Minato-ku
Tokyo, Japan
03-440-3244

#5 Lane 183, Chin Hua Street
Taipei, Taiwan
02-3210690

25 Greer Technical Street
University Hills
Caloocan City, Phillipines
362-28-85

Listing of Public Records by Department

Public records are those that can be researched and viewed by the public after submitting a written, verbal, or in-person request to the appropriate agency or government office. Below is a list of frequently sought records and the public agency where they are most likely to be found.

Chamber of Commerce

Corporation addresses and listings
Corporate listings by industry
Market share data by industry
Employee figures by corporation
Employment and growth statistics
Philanthropic organization information
Sports and entertainment information
Tourism

City Hall

Budget records
Building permits
Planning permits
Sales tax licenses
Zoning records

County Assessors

Plat maps and property numbers
Property ownership and assessed valuations

County Clerks

Amusement, liquor, and vending records
Board meeting minutes
Council and board member voting records
County enactments and resolutions
Municipal election records

County Medical Examiner

Autopsy reports

County Recorders

Foreclosure records
General partnership filings
Liens
Real estate deeds
Real estate conveyances
Union Commercial Code filings
Voter registration records

County Superior Courts

Civil judgments
Criminal conviction records
Divorce decrees
Marriage licenses
Probate records

County Treasurers

Property tax records

Fire Departments

Fire statistics
Fire and arson listings

Municipal and Justice Courts

Civil citations
Court orders of protection
Disorderly conduct citations
Drunken driving violations
Traffic convictions

Police Departments

Arrest records
Crime statistics
Investigative reports
Traffic accident reports

Secretary of State

Financial disclosure statements of elected officials
Limited partnership filings
State election records
Trade name registry
Uniform commercial code filings

State Banking Department

Banking industry regulations
Consumer complaints
Documentation on interest rates

State Building and Fire Safety Department

Building inspection records
City building codes and requirements
Fire safety violations and complaints
Manufactured housing regulatory records

State Corporation Commission

Annual corporate reports
Nonprofit corporation information
Utility regulations

Safety records of various industries and organizations
Securities information

State Department of Administration

Accounting records
Payroll records
Procurement documentation
State agency contracting records
Tax records

State Department of Education

Attendance figures
Curriculum documentation
Employee complaint records
Safety requirements
School district complaints
School district zoning records
School system graduation statistics by county
Standardized test scores
State board of education meeting minutes
State education spending and budgeting records

State Department of Environmental Quality

Air quality permits
Development and clean up projects
Emissions permits
Hazardous waste records
Landfill permits and requests
Minutes of environmental meetings and enactments
Water permits

State Department of Health

Day care licenses
Hospital rates
Medical facility complaints
Nursing home licenses
Nursing home complaints

State Department of Insurance

Consumer complaints against insurance companies
Legal actions filed against insurers
Insurance company rates
Insurance licenses

State Department of Real Estate

Investigative records
Licenses for cemeteries
Cemetery records and complaints
Real estate licenses

State Department of Transportation

Driver's license information
Highway development plans
Vehicle registration records

State Department of Vital Statistics

Birth certificates
Death certificates (not always available to the public)

State Industrial Commission

Administrative law records
Occupational safety records
Workers compensation records

State Land Department

Grazing permits
Land development records
Lease records
State land sales and transactions

State Legislature

Legislative voting records
Proposed laws and pending legislation

State Liquor Department

Investigative reports and complaints
Liquor board records and meeting minutes
Liquor license applications

State Professional Licensure Boards

Accountancy
Appraisal
Barber shops
Behavior health professionals
Chiropractic examiners
Cosmetology industry
Dental professionals
Embalmers
Funeral directors
Homeopathic medical examiners
Law
Medical examiners
Nursing
Occupational therapy professionals
Opticians
Osteopathic
Pest control
Pharmaceutical industry professionals
Physical therapy workers
Podiatry
Private postsecondary education professionals
Psychologists
Respiratory care examiners
Veterinary medicine

State Registrar of Contractors

Consumer complaints
Contracting license permits

Weights and Measures Department

Inspection reports for gasoline pump inspections
Inspection reports for meat scale requirements
Inspection reports for general industry requirements

Psychologists and Search Support

If you would like to contact a psychologist who specializes in issues related to the search, the following organizations can provide you with a referral to a specialist. Psychologists are available in all states who deal specifically with issues of family separation, adoption, and post-adoption support, including the treatment of relational disorders. A psychologist can assist before, during, or after the search.

The American Psychological Association (APA)
1200 17th Street NW
Washington, D.C. 20036
202-336-5500

The American Psychiatric Association
1400 K Street NW
Washington, D.C. 20005

The American Association of Marriage and Family Therapists
1100 17th Street NW
10th Floor
Washington, D.C. 20036
202-452-0109

The National Association of Social Workers
750 First Street NE
Suite 700
Washington, DC 20002
202-408-8600

Sample Letters for Use During the Search Process

Baron Lytton, an English writer, once wrote that the pen is mightier than the sword, and he may have been correct. The following tools are samples of letters and documents to aid you in your search. Modify them to suit your specific needs, and use them as a guide, adding your own personal touches. Written correspondence has been around since the beginning of time, and people are generally responsive to a nicely composed, professional letter. If you're not sure how to express your feelings in person, putting them on paper is the best alternative. If you write to an agency requesting information and don't receive a favorable response, try the same letter on a different person within the organization.

Sample Letter to Request Information from Your Adoption Agency

Dear [name of agency or contact at agency],

My name is Dana Lynn Dean, and your agency handled my adoption in 1955. I was born on December 3, 1953, and placed with [adoptive parents' full names] when I was three years old.

I'm writing to request any nonidentifying information that may exist from my adoption file. Any information you could provide regarding medical conditions, medical history, or family heritage would be greatly appreciated. I am also asking for any information you can provide on the date that I was discharged from the hospital, and if I was in one or multiple homes prior to placement.

Please forward to me any information that you can on my birth mother, birth father, and their extended relatives such as their parents or siblings. If possible please include their ages, physical descriptions, religions, medical history, nationality, education, and any other information on their life histories.

I would specifically be interested in knowing:
- When did my birth mother contact your agency?
- What were the circumstances that led her to choose adoption?
- Were there any special requests given to the family that adopted me?

- Did she have contact or visit me after I was born?
- Did my birth father have knowledge of my birth or the adoption?
- Do I have siblings?
- Has your agency had contact with any of my birth relatives after my placement?
- Do you have any records, letters, or pictures that you can forward to me?

If you have a registry to match adoptees with their birth parents, I would be extremely interested in enrolling as soon as possible. Thank you very much for taking the time to respond to my request for information, as this knowledge is very important to me at this time in my life.

Best Regards,
Dana L. Dean
Phone: _____
Fax: _____
Address: _____

Sample Letter to a Birth Parent

If you are at a point where you are certain of the identity of one or both of your birth parents but have not yet contacted them, a personal letter may be the best place to start. It's less threatening than a phone call, gives the recipient time to think about things and reread it, and will allow you to put your thoughts down on paper. If you don't receive a response to the letter you send, it is advisable to make that phone call, because otherwise you'll never really know if your letter got there and reached the hands of the person it was addressed to.

Mr. James Johnson
125 Saranac Way
Lake Saranac, NY 12435

Dear Mr. Johnson,

My name is Michael Davidson, and I was raised by a single mother in Chicago, Illinois. Neither my mother nor anyone else in my family would tell me who my biological father was, though I asked many times. It always bothered me, and I continued to wonder who my father was, what he was like, and where he was living.

After my mother passed away last year, I found several papers in her personal belongings with your name on them. These papers were dated back to the year that I was born, and there were also old photographs that lead me to believe that you are the one I have been searching for all of my life, my birth father.

I realize that you must have your own life now and possibly even children whom you have raised. I've considered this and many other possibilities and want you to know that my intentions are nothing more than to know where I came from, know who my biological father is, and have peace in my life at last. I will understand if you tell me you do not want or cannot have a relationship with me, and I will understand if this is a part of your life that you have long since put behind you.

I have searched for the answers to my beginnings ever since childhood and have lived with the secret behind my birth for thirty-five years now. It's very difficult not knowing the basics and not knowing my medical history. In hoping that you will contact me, I'd like to share with you a few things about myself.

I'm thirty-five years old and have a solid career in the investment banking industry. I paid my way through Cornell University and majored in business. I have had a very good life and enjoyed several activities throughout high school and college. I played baseball in college and continue to play in a men's league one night a week after work. I wonder if you, too, have the same love for all sports that I do. I love watching college and pro football and am a big Bears fan. I grew up in Chicago and moved to New York to live and work after college.

I can be reached at 212-222-2222 if you would like to give me a call (even collect is fine), or you can write me at 121 53rd Place, New York, NY 10012.

I'm looking forward to hearing from you.

Sincerely,
Michael Davidson

Sample Letter to a Sibling

Dear Morgan,

My name is Kim Howard, and I was raised with one brother in Lexington, Kentucky. When I was thirteen, an older cousin told me that he thought I had a younger sister, but he didn't know anything more. Since that time, I have heard the same thing from a few other relatives in my family.

I am now forty-three and have sat down with an older aunt who has given me a lot more information than I ever had. She gave me your name and some photographs of you when you were an infant. We have the same mother, but different fathers, and I was told that you were taken by your biological father after he and our mother split up. I am anxious to know more about you and to hear if you know about me.

I have two small children, a three-year-old named Jessica and a five-year-old named James. They are both precocious little toddlers and would love to have an aunt in their lives! Please contact me at the phone number enclosed, or feel free to write if that's better for you. I look forward to making your acquaintance.

Sincerely,
Kimberly Howard

Sample Letter to Friends and Family

If your search results in a reunion, the aftermath could last for a lifetime. If things go really well, you may have an entirely new family and circle of friends. Your Christmas shopping list will increase and you'll have less income than you previously had now that there are additional birthdays and anniversaries to recognize. Don't laugh—it happened to me!

Everyone is different in terms of how they will react once the search is over. More than likely your closest friends and family members will know from you that you have found your family or will hear of it through the grapevine. Others may find out months or even years later, or perhaps never. If you are a very private person, you may wish to keep it all inside. If you feel comfortable communicating in writing and think a letter is appropriate, the following is a sample letter for disseminating the good news.

Dear Aunt Jane,

I know it's been years since I've seen you, and I hope you are well. I received your Easter card last week and thought I'd drop you a note to tell you how I'm doing.

A lot has happened in my life the last few years. I learned I was adopted at a very young age, as you probably know (the entire family did, it seems!), and I was always very curious about my biological parents. I decided to search for them after college and went through a series of steps until I finally found them. They are married now (they weren't when they gave me up for adoption) and have two other children, whom they raised. They were teenagers when my birth mother became pregnant, and they didn't feel they could raise me properly at that time.

Everything has gone fine since we met, and they have even met Mom and Dad. We all had dinner last Sunday, and everyone gets along great! You should see my new sisters—they look exactly like me! I can't tell you how peaceful I feel now and how much of an adventure it has been for me.

My new job in Nashville has been keeping me busy as of late. I'm working on a special task force to find ways to clean up the environment for the Environmental Protection Agency.

Please keep in touch. I'd love to hear from you.

Lynn

Sample Letter to Your Child

Dear Ron,

I hope you accept this letter for what it is, an attempt to reach you and explain the reasons behind why I placed you for adoption. When I was seventeen and a senior in high school, I became pregnant with you by my high school boyfriend, your father. I was far too young to handle being a mother and too immature to even handle the things that were going on in my own life.

I'm not trying to make excuses, because the fact is, I simply could not care for a baby at that point in my life. My parents, your grandparents, arranged for the adoption, and it all took place very quickly, as soon as you were born. The moment I held you in my arms I knew that I would think of you every day for the rest of my life. I was depressed for many months afterwards. Through the years I thought of you and wondered if your family was taking care of you the way I had hoped for. I never tried to contact you, I have to admit, because I thought that I would in some way ruin your life by entering it again.

I came to the conclusion that I had to find you last year when I contacted the adoption agency and they said that you had contacted them looking for me as well! I can't tell you how excited I was to learn that. I always wanted you to know how much I love you and have thought of you through the years. I never wanted you to feel abandoned by me, because I do not see it that way. I hope that I gave you a better life, a life with two loving parents who could give you everything you needed. I am placing this letter with them in hopes that you will respond to me. I look forward to telling you everything about my life and to hearing everything about yours!

Please contact me at 501-888-9900.

Sincerely,
Sharon James
Your Birth Mother

Classified Advertisements

A classified ad can be placed in the newspaper or on the Internet with the intention of reaching the person you are looking for or someone who knows them. Regardless of where you place the ad, keep it concise, to the point, and somewhat general. Leave any detailed personal information such as your home address out of it to avoid unwanted visits from strangers. Remember that a lot of people, not just your target market, will view the message.

Searching for:

*Mr. Brandon Michael Brown
from Austin, Texas
I am his son, born
11/2/61 in Plano, Texas.
Anyone with information please
call 972-333-3544, direct or collect.*

The goal of a personal ad is to reach your target while giving him or her an easy method of responding to you. If you make the response process too cumbersome, you're giving the individual you are searching for a roadblock. If the ad is placed on the Internet, leave an e-mail address where a message can be electronically sent for an immediate reply. You may also elect to leave a fax number or alternate telephone number. The following message was an actual posting on the Internet by a birth mother searching for the child she had given up for adoption many years before.

Hi:

   I am trying to find my daughter that was adopted in August 1960. I was 16 years old at the time, and I was born and raised in England. She was born in Cambridge, England. My parents would not allow me at the time to raise a baby in their home. I had no choice. I have been wondering about her for the past 30 years. I never knew at that time there would be such a thing as computers. Does anyone have any ideas how I may find her? Thanks.

There are others like this mother, reaching out for help in hopes of finding their children. There are just as many children searching for birth parents, siblings looking for each other, and friends in search of those they lost touch with long ago. If you have access to the Internet, begin by searching the numerous ads placed on search bulletin boards. Remember that the chances of actually seeing an ad that was posted by someone related to you is rare, and achieving an immediate response probably won't be that simple. Although some families have been reunited through the Internet, the world is a large place and is growing rapidly every second. The United States Census Bureau predicts that by the year 2000 the world will have grown to six billion people. Finding one person amongst everyone else will probably take more than just searching for a classified posting in the paper or on the Internet.

Adoption Attorney Referrals

The American Bar Association offers a list of attorney referral services as a guide for finding competent legal assistance. Although it does not endorse any particular attorney that is referred, this service is a step in the right direction toward locating an adoption or open records specialist. Contact the American Bar Association for the location nearest you to obtain the name of an attorney who specializes in assisting with the legal aspects of records and family searches.

American Bar Association
750 N. Lake Shore Drive
Chicago, IL 60611
312-988-5000

International Adoption Agencies Based in the United States

If you were born in another country or are searching for someone who was, the following list of adoption agencies with experience in international adoptions may be of assistance. There are agencies that specialize in certain countries and have employees based in those countries with the goal of providing their children with homes in the United States. The International Concerns for Children publishes an annual report on international adoption that is an excellent resource as well. *The Report on Intercountry Adoption* can be obtained through ICC by writing to them at 911 Cypress Drive, Boulder, CO 80303.

ABC Adoption Agency Inc.
417 San Pedro Avenue
San Antonio, TX 78212-5592
512-227-7820

Accept
339 S. San Antonio Road, #1a
Los Altos, CA 94022
415-917-8090

Adopt-A-Child
Maxon Towers
Suite L-111
6315 Forbes Avenue
Pittsburgh, PA 15217
412-421-1911

Adopt International
121 Springdale Way
Redwood City, CA 94062-3909
415-369-7300

Adoption Advisory Council
2448 Stuart Street
Brooklyn, NY 11229-5816

Adoption Advocates Inc.
2601 Crossroads Drive
Madison, WI 53701
608-246-2844
Fax: 608-246-2875

Adoption Advocates International
401 E. Front Street
Port Angeles, WA 98362-3113
360-452-4777

Adoption—A Gift of Love
35 Rolling Hills
Denton, TX 76205

Adoption Alliance
P.O. Box 581
Sellersville, PA 18960-0581

Adoption Alliance
17 Main Street
Sayville, NY 11782
516-567-7789

Adoption Alliance
3090 S. Jamaica Court
Suite 106
Aurora, CO 80014
303-337-1731

Adoption Associates
1901 Sylvan SE
Grand Rapids, MI 49506
616-957-0581

Adoption Associates
100 N. Euclid Avenue
Suite 306
Saint Louis, MO 63108-1543

Adoption by Choice
4102 W. Linebaugh Avenue
Suite 200
Tampa, FL 33624
813-960-2229

Adoption Center of WA
1816 Jefferson Place NW
Washington, D.C. 20036
202-452-8278
202-452-8280

Adoption Center of Washington
1990 M Street NW
Suite 380
Washington, D.C. 20036
202-452-8278
Fax: 202-452-8280

Adoption Centre, Inc.
110 N. Orlando Avenue
Suite 5
Maitland, FL 32751
407-740-0044

Adoption Connection
11223 Cornell Park Drive
Cincinnati, OH 45242
513-489-1616

Adoption Counselors Inc.
130 Temple Street
West Newton, MA 02165

Adoption Horizons
899 Petersburg Road
Carlisle, PA 17013-9218

Adoption Horizons
302 4th Street
2nd Floor
Eureka, CA 95501-1147
707-444-9909
Fax: 707-443-9580

Adoption Links Worldwide
3528 Dodge
Omaha, NE 68131-3202

Adoption Option Inc.
2600 S. Parker Road
Suite 2-320
Aurora, CO 80014-1613
303-695-1601

Adoption Option, Inc.
1804 Chapman Drive
Waukesha, WI 53186-7219
414-544-4278

Adoption Resource Center at Brightside
2112 Riverdale Street
West Springfield, MA 01089-1063
413-788-7366
Fax: 413-747-0182

Adoption Service Info Agency
7720 Alaska Avenue NW
Washington, D.C. 20012-1461
202-726-7193

Adoption Services
28 Central Blvd.
Camp Hill, PA 17011-4209

Adoption Services Association
8703 Wurzbach Road
San Antonio, TX 78240-1160
210-699-6094

Adoption Services Inc.
3500 Overton Park West
Fort Worth, TX 76109-2505
817-921-0718
Fax: 817-924-0066

Adoption Services International
2021 Sperry Avenue
Suite 41
Ventura, CA 93003-7446
805-644-3067

Adoption Services of Green Bay
529 S. Jefferson Street
Suite 105
Green Bay, WI 54301-4125

Adoption Unlimited
2770 Weston Road
Lancaster, PA 17603
717-872-1340

Adoptions from the Heart
1525 Oregon Park
Suite 501
Lancaster, PA 17601
717-691-9686

Adoptions from the Heart
18 A Trolley Square
Wilmington, DE 19806
302-658-8883

Adoptions from the Heart
76 Rittenhouse Place
Ardmore, PA 19003
610-642-7200

Adoptions from the Heart
451 Woodland Avenue
Cherry Hill, NJ 08002
609-795-5400

Adoptions Together
6 Sudbrook Lane
Baltimore, MD 21208
410-653-3446

Advocates for Children and Families
16831 NE 6th Avenue
Miami, FL 33142
305-653-2474

Agape Social Services
8500 N. Stemmons, #2080
Dallas, TX 75247
214-631-6784

Alaska International Adoption Agency
3605 Arctic Blvd., #1177
Anchorage, AK 99503
907-264-6678

All God's Children International
4114 NE Freemont Street
Suite 1
Portland, OR 97212
503-282-7652

Alliance for Children
40 William Street
Suite G80
Wellesley, MA 02181-3902
617-431-7148

Alternative Adoption Advisors
P.O. Box 353
Augusta, MI 49012-0353

American Adoption Agency
1228 M Street NW
2nd Floor
Washington, D.C. 20005-5197
202-638-1543

Americans for African Adoption Inc.
8910 Timberwood Drive
Indianapolis, IN 46234-1952
317-271-4567

Americans for International Aid
P.O. Box 6051
Spokane, WA 99207-0901

Americans for International Aid and
    Adoption
P.O. Box 290
Plainville, NY 13137
315-638-9449
315-635-7270

Americans for International Aid and
    Adoption
887 S. Adams Road
Birmingham, MI 48009-7025
810-645-2211

Americans for International Aid and
    Adoption
42 Mitchell Blvd.
San Rafael, CA 94903

Americans for International Aid and
    Adoption
3080 Shields Drive, #101
Eagan, MN 55121
612-687-0259

Americans International Family Service
3724 Boca Chica Blvd., #C194
Brownsville, TX 78521-4022

Amor Adoptions Inc.
4208 Rancho Centro NW
Albuquerque, NM 87120
1-800-596-2273

Associated Catholic Charities of East
    Tennessee
119 Dameron Avenue
Knoxville, TN 37917
423-524-9896

Bal Jagat—Children's World Inc.
Farralone Avenue
Chatsworth, CA 91311-4703
818-709-4737

Barker Foundation
1200 18th Street NW
Suite 312
Washington, D.C. 20036
202-363-7751

Barker Foundation
1495 Chain Bridge Road
Suite 201
McLean, VA 22101
703-536-1827

Bay Area Adoption Services
465 Fairchild Drive
Suite 215
Mountain View, CA 94043
415-964-3800

Beacon Adoption Center, Inc.
66 Lake Buel Road
Great Barrington, MA 01230-1450
413-528-2749

Beech Brook/Spaulding Adopt Project
3737 Lander Road
Cleveland, OH 44124-5712
216-464-4445

Bensenville Home Society
331 S. York Road
Bensenville, IL 60106-2600
708-766-5800

Bensenville Home Society
318 N. Church Street
Rockford, IL 61101-1006

Bensenville Home Society
6100 Center Grove Road, #9
Edwardsville, IL 62025-3308

Bensenville Home Society
905 S. Russell Street
Champaign, IL 61821-4419

Berkshire Center—Families & Children
480 West Street
Pittsfield, MA 01201-5730
413-448-8281

Bethany Christian Services
P.O. Box 15569
Asheville, NC 28813-0569
704-274-7146

Bethany Christian Services
8786 Goodwood Blvd.
Suite 103
Baton Rouge, LA 70806
504-927-3235

Bethany Christian Services
901 Eastern Avenue NE
Grand Rapids, MI 49503
616-459-6273

Black Adoption Placement/Research
1801 Harrison Street, #200
Oakland, CA 94612-3403
510-839-3678

Boston Children's Services
867 Boylston Street
Boston, MA 02116-2666
617-267-3700

Burlington United Methodist Home
P.O. Box 370
Scott Depot, WV 25560-0370
304-757-9127

Cambridge Adoption & Counseling
    Associates, Inc.
P.O. Box 190
Cambridge, MA 02142-0002
617-923-0370

Care Connection, Inc.
400 Harvey Street
San Marcos, TX 78666-5504
512-396-8111

Caring Alternatives/Volunteers of
    America
3900 N. Causeway Blvd.
Suite 700
Metairie, LA 70002-1746
504-836-5225

Catholic Charities
2045 Lawton Street
San Francisco, CA 94122-3243

Catholic Charities
P.O. Box 296
Ogdensburg, NY 13669-0296
315-393-2255

Catholic Charities
15 Ripley Street
Worcester, MA 01610-2598
508-798-0191

Catholic Charities
1276 University Avenue
Saint Paul, MN 55104
612-641-1180

Catholic Charities Adoption Agency
349 Cedar Street
San Diego, CA 92101-3112
619-231-2828

Catholic Charities Inc
P.O. Box 610
Crookston, MN 56716-0610
218-281-4224

Catholic Charities Inc.
P.O. Box 2248
Jackson, MS 39225-2248
601-355-8634
Fax: 601-960-8493

Catholic Charities of Chicago
126 N. DesPlaines Street
Chicago, IL 60661
312-655-7076

Catholic Charities of DC
1438 Rhode Island Avenue NE
Washington, D.C. 20018-3709
202-526-4100

Catholic Charities of Indiana
425 N. Michigan
Suite 222
South Bend, IN 46601-1236
219-234-3111

Catholic Charities of Richmond
1512 Willow Lawn Drive
Richmond, VA 23230-0565
804-285-5900
Fax: 804-285-9130

Catholic Charities of TN Inc.
30 White Bridge Road
Nashville, TN 37205-1401
615-352-3087

Catholic Social Service
2546 20th Street
Great Bend, KS 67530-2412
316-792-1393

Catholic Social Service
603 N. Center Street
Bloomington, IL 61701-2981

Catholic Social Service
617 S. Belt West
Belleville, IL 62220-2482
618-277-9200

Catholic Social Service Bureau
3629 Church Street
Covington, KY 41015-1430
606-581-8974

Catholic Social Services
P.O. Box M
Fall River, MA 02724-0388
508-674-4681

Catholic Social Services
P.O. Box 1457
Biloxi, MS 39533-1457
601-864-7917

Catholic Social Services
347 Rock Street
Marquette, MI 49855-4783
906-228-8630

Catholic Social Services
225 Cordova Street
Building B
Anchorage, AK 99501-2409
907-277-2554

Catholic Social Services
100 E. 8th Street
Cincinnati, OH 45202
513-241-7745
Fax: 513-241-4333

Catholic Social Services
4925 Packard
Ann Arbor, MI 48108
313-971-9781

Catholic Social Services
433 Elmwood Avenue
Providence, RI 02907-1793
401-467-7200

Catholic Social Services
1065 Fairington Drive
Sidney, OH 45365-8130

Catholic Social Services for Montana
P.O. Box 907
Helena, MT 59601-5732
406-442-4130
Fax: 406-442-4192

Catholic Social Services Inc.
680 W. Peachtree Street NW
Atlanta, GA 30308-1931
404-881-6571

Catholic Social Services Inc.
1771 N. Semoran Blvd.
Orlando, FL 32807-3544
407-658-1818

Catholic Social Services of Wyoming
P.O. Box 1026
Cheyenne, WY 82003
307-638-1530
Fax: 307-637-7936

Catholic Social Services/St. Vincent
    Home
2800 W. Willow Street
Lansing, MI 48917-1833
517-323-4734

Child Placement Center
2212 Sunny Lane
Killeen, TX 76541-8273
817-690-5959
Fax: 817-690-4314

Children of Light
102 E Blithedale Avenue
Mill Valley, CA 94941-2024

Children of the World
685 Bloomfield Avenue, #201
Verona, NJ 07044-1602

Children's Adoption Network
245 Bradley Court
Holland, PA 18966
215-860-3353
Fax: 215-860-3522

Children's Aid and Adoption
575 Main Street
Hackensack, NJ 07601
201-487-2022

Children's Aid and Adoption
196 Speedwell Avenue
Morristown, NJ 07960-2934

Children's Aid Home Society
P.O. Box 1195
Somerset, PA 15501-0320

Children's Aid Society of Utah
652 26th Street
Ogden, UT 84401-2546
801-393-8671

Children's Bureau of Los Angeles
3030 Tyler Avenue
El Monte, CA 91731-3352
818-575-5897

Children's Choice
International Plaza Two
Suite 325
Philadelphia, PA 19113
610-521-6270
Fax: 610-521-6266

Children's Home of North Kentucky
200 Home Road
Covington, KY 41011-1942

Children's Home of Pittsburgh
5618 Kentucky Avenue
Pittsburgh, PA 15232-2606
412-441-4884

Children's Home Society
3200 Telegraph Avenue
Oakland, CA 94609-3077
510-655-7406

Children's Home Society
7695 Cardinal Court
San Diego, CA 92123-3399
619-278-7800

Children's Home Society
15535 San Fernando Mission Blvd.
Mission Hills, CA 91345
818-837-8100

Children's Home Society
300 S. Sycamore Street
Santa Ana, CA 92701-5730
714-542-1147

Children's Home Society of Florida
P.O. Box 10097
Jacksonville, FL 32247-0097
904-396-4084

Children's Home Society of MN
2230 Como Avenue
Saint Paul, MN 55109
612-646-6393
Fax: 612-646-0436

Children's Home Society of NC
P.O. Box 14608
Greensboro, NC 27415-4608

Children's Home Society of WA
201 S. 34th Street
Tacoma, WA 98408-7895
206-472-3355

Children's Home Society of WV
P.O. Box 2942
Charleston, WV 25330-2942

Children's Hope Adoption Services
7823 S. Whiteville Road
Shepherd, MI 48883-9566
517-828-5842

Children's Hope Int'l—China's
   Children
9229 Lackland
Saint Louis, MO 63114
314-427-0790

Children's House International
P.O. Box 2321
Salt Lake City, UT 84110-2321

Children's Services Center
648 Pine Avenue
Pacific Grove, CA 93950-3347
408-649-3033

Children's Service Society
124 S. Fourth East
Salt Lake City, UT 84111
801-355-7444

Children's Service Society of WI
1212 S. 70th Street
West Allis, WI 53214-3105
414-453-1400

China Adoption Services
P.O. Box 19764
Portland, OR 97280
503-245-0976

China's Children
2343 E. 71st Street, #586
Tulsa, OK 74136-5407

China's Children
8776 E. Shea Blvd., #3A-216
Scottsdale, AZ 85260
602-816-0725

Chinese Children Adoption
    International
805 W. Peakview Circle
Littleton, CO 80120-3323
303-347-2224

Christian Adoption Services
624 Matthews Mint Hill Road, #134
Matthews, NC 28105-2797
704-847-0038

Christian Child Help Foundation
710 N. Post Oak Road
Suite 500
Houston, TX 77024-3840
713-850-9703

Christian Child Placement Service
HC 69, Box 48
Portales, NM 88130-9805
505-356-4232

Christian Counseling Services
P.O. Box 60383
Nashville, TN 37206
615-254-8341

Christian Family Life Services
1201 12th Avenue North
Fargo, ND 58102-3530
701-237-9464

Christian World Adoption, Inc.
270 W. Coleman Blvd. #100
Mount Pleasant, SC 29464-3489
803-856-0305
Fax: 803-856-0350

Chrysalis House
2134 W. Alluvial Avenue
Fresno, CA 93711-0441
209-432-7170

Coleman Adoption Services
615 N. Alabama Street
Suite 419
Indianapolis, IN 46204-1434
317-638-0965

Colorado Adoption Center
1136 E. Stuart Street
Suite 4206
Fort Collins, CO 80525-1193

Colorado Adoption Center
4175 Harlan Street
Suite 101
Wheat Ridge, CO 80033-5150

Commonwealth Adoptions
    International
201 N. Jessica Avenue
Tucson, AZ 85710-2100
602-886-1396
Fax: 602-885-6396

Community Adoption Center
R1619 Wolf River Avenue
Shawano, WI 54166
715-524-4222

Community Adoption Center
101 E. Milwaukee Street
Suite 424
Janesville, WI 53545-3005

Community Adoption Center
3701 Kadow Street
Manitowoc, WI 54220-5449

Community Adoption Center
215 Allen Avenue
Green Bay, WI 54302
414-465-0818

Community Counseling & Adoption
    Services
323 Allumbaugh Street
Boise, ID 83704-9208
208-322-1262

Community Maternity Services
27 N. Main Avenue
Albany, NY 12203
518-482-8836

Comprehensive Studies
111 Patterson Street
Charleston, WV 25302-3124

Concern for Children
746 Grove Avenue
Kent, OH 44240-3408

Concern Professional Services
1 E. Main Street
Fleetwood, PA 19522-1411
215-944-0445

Concerned Persons for Adoption
P.O. Box 179
Whippany, NJ 07891

Concord Family Service
111 Ornac
Concord, MA 01742
508-369-4909
Fax: 508-371-1463

Covenant International, Inc.
2055 Angelo Drive, #104
Colorado Springs, CO 80918
719-531-5100
Fax: 719-531-6931

Cradle of Hope Adoption Center
1815 H Street NW
Suite 1050
Washington, D.C. 20006
202-296-4700

Cradle Society
2049 Ridge Avenue
Evanston, IL 60201-2794
708-475-5800

Creative Adoptions
10750 Hickory Ridge Road
Suite 109
Columbia, MD 20782
301-596-1521
Fax: 301-596-0346

Creative Adoptions
3331 Toledo Terrace, #D-108
Hyattsville, MD 20782
301-559-6296

Creative Adoptions, Inc.
10711 SW 104th Street
Miami, FL 33176-8162
305-596-2211

Crittenton Services Center
1229 Sunbury Road
Columbus, OH 43219-2047

Crossroads, Inc.
4640 W. 77th Street
Suite 179
Minneapolis, MN 55435-4914
612-831-5707

Crown Child Placement
    International, Inc.
82–851 Kamakiani Street
Captain Cook, HI 96704
808-323-2625
Fax: 808-323-2286

D. A. Blodgett Service for Child
    & Family
805 Leonard Street NE
Grand Rapids, MI 49503-1198
616-451-2021

Datz Foundation
875 Walnut Street
Suite 275
Cary, NC 27511-4215
919-319-6635

Datz Foundation
16220 S. Frederick Avenue
Suite 404
Gaithersburg, MD 20877-4021
301-258-0629

Deaconess Home
5401 N. Portland Avenue
Oklahoma City, OK 73112-2061
405-942-5001

Dillon International Inc.
7615 E. 63rd Place
Suite 100
Tulsa, OK 74133-1248
918-250-1561
Fax: 918-250-2030

Dillon Southwest
P.O. Box 3535
Scottsdale, AZ 85271-3535
602-945-2221

Dove Adoptions International, Inc.
3735 SE Martins
Portland, OR 97202
503-774-7210
Fax: 503-771-7893

East–West Concepts, Inc.
414 Plainsboro Road
Plainsboro, NJ 08536
609-275-7211
Fax: 609-799-8654

Ecumenical Refugee Services
190 E. 9th Avenue
Suite 420
Denver, CO 80203-2738

Evangelical Child & Family Agency
2401 N. Mayfair Road
Suite 302
Milwaukee, WI 53226-1408
414-476-9550

Fairbanks Adoption and Counseling
P.O. Box 71544
Fairbanks, AK 99707-1544

Fairbanks Counseling & Adoption
753 Gaffney Road
Fairbanks, AK 99701-4609
907-456-4729

Families Are Special
Box 5789, 2200 Main
N. Little Rock, AR 72119
501-758-9184

Families for Children
55 5th Street E.
Suite 1400
Saint Paul, MN 55101-1715
612-545-1750

Family Adoption Center
8536 Crow Drive
Suite 218
Macedonia, OH 44056-1900
216-468-0673
Fax: 216-468-0678

Family Adoption Consultants
310 W. University Drive
Rochester, MI 48307-1937
313-652-2842
Fax: 313-652-6241

Family Adoption Consultants
P.O. Box 489
Kalamazoo, MI 49005
616-343-3316
Fax: 616-343-3359

Family and Children's Counseling
P.O. Box 314
Elizabeth, NJ 07207-0314

Family and Children's Exchange
6630 Baltimore Nat'l Pike, #100-B
Baltimore, MD 21228
410-744-6393

Family & Children's Service
210 23rd Avenue North
Nashville, TN 37203-1502
615-320-0591

Family & Children's Services
204 W. Lanvale Street
Baltimore, MD 21217-4121
301-669-9000

Family Connections
4609 E. Illinois Avenue
Fresno, CA 93702-2532

Family Connections
P.O. Box 576035
Modesto, CA 95357-6035
209-524-8844
Fax: 209-524-2139

Family Connections
1010 Hurley Way, #300
Sacramento, CA 95825
916-568-5966

Family Extension, Inc.
P.O. Box 1458
Longmont, CO 80502

Family Focus Adoption Services
5440 Little Neck Parkway
Little Neck, NY 11362-2205

Family Life Services
1000 Villa Road
Lynchburg, VA 24503-2624
804-384-3043

Family Network
9378 Olive St. Road
Room 320
Saint Louis, MO 63132
314-567-0707
Fax: 314-567-7064

Family Network
333 Monticello Drive
Greenwood, IN 46142
317-887-3288

Family Network, Inc.
282 Sirena Del Mar Road
Marina, CA 93933-4306

Family Service & Children's Aid
716 E. 2nd Street
Oil City, PA 16301-2330
814-677-4005

Family Service Agency
915 Vermont Street
Quincy, IL 62301-3049
217-222-8254

Family Service of Decatur
247 W. Prairie Avenue
Decatur, IL 62523-1220

Family Service of Westchester
1 Summit Avenue
White Plains, NY 10606-3011

Family Services, Inc.
610 Coliseum Drive
Winston-Salem, NC 27106-5393
919-722-8173

Family Services of Tidewater, Inc.
3720 Virginia Beach Blvd., #200
Virginia Beach, VA 23452-3414

Family Tree
1743 Route 9
Clifton Park, NY 12065
518-371-1336
Fax: 518-371-3097

Florence Crittenton League
119 Hall Street
Lowell, MA 01854-3634

Florida Adoption & Children's Center
11410 N. Kendall Drive
Miami, FL 33176-1031

Forever Families International
2004 Highway 37
Eveleth, MN 55734-9664

Friends of Children Various Nations
1756 High Street
Denver, CO 80218-1306

Future Families, Inc.
1671 The Alameda
San Jose, CA 95126-2222
408-559-0203

Future Families, Inc.
3233 Valencia Avenue
Suite A6
Aptos, CA 95003-4127
408-662-0202

Gentle Shepherd
6310 Lamar Avenue, #140
Overland Park, KS 66202-4247
913-432-7353

Gentle Shepherd
P.O. Box 30341
Kansas City, MO 64112

Gift of Love
P.O. Box 447
Johnston, IA 50131
515-276-9277
Fax: 515-265-0834

Gladney Center
2300 Hemphill Street
Fort Worth, TX 76110-2651
817-922-6000
Fax: 817-926-8505

Global Adoption Service Inc.
204 S. Custer
Sheridan, WY 82801
307-672-7605
Fax: 307-672-7605

Globe International Adoption
6334 W. Villa Theresa Drive
Glendale, AZ 85308-1022

Golden Cradle International
1660 Cliffs Landing, #3
Ypsilanti, MI 48103
800-566-5368
Fax: 313-663-0784

Good Samaritan Agency
450 Essex Street
Bangor, ME 04401-3937
207-942-7211

Graham-Windham Services
33 Irving Place
New York, NY 10003-2332
212-529-6445

Growing Families Inc.
1 Tall Timber Drive
Morristown, NJ 07960-2614
201-984-7875

Growing Families, Inc.
8 Hopi Drive
Middletown, NJ 07748-3750

Growing Thru Adoption
306 Congress Street
Portland, ME 04101-3645

Hall Neighborhood House Inc.
52 Green Street
Bridgeport, CT 06608-2490
203-334-3900
Fax: 719-632-8428

Hand in Hand
3102 N. Country Club
Tucson, AZ 85716
602-327-5550
Fax: 602-327-1430

Hand in Hand
1617 W. Colorado Avenue
Colorado Springs, CO 80904
719-473-8844

Hawaii Int'l Child Placement
P.O. Box 240486
Honolulu, HI 96824-0486
808-377-0881
Fax: 808-373-5095

Heart International Adoption
    Services, Inc.
2951 Marina Drive, #130
League City, TX 77573
713-326-3063
Fax: 713-532-1987

Heart International Adoption
    Services, Inc.
5335 Merle Hay Road
Johnston, IA 50131
515-278-4053
Fax: 515-278-2618

Heaven Sent Children
P.O. Box 2514
Murfreesboro, TN 37133
615-898-0803
Fax: 615-898-0803

Help the Children
41 W. Yokuts Avenue, #107
Stockton, CA 95207
209-478-5585
Fax: 209-478-5586

Heritage Adoption Services
516 SE Morrison
Suite 714
Portland, OR 97214
503-233-1099
Fax: 503-233-0587

Heritage Adoption Services
P.O. Box 188408
Sacramento, CA 95818-8408

Hold International Children's
    Services—New Jersey
340 Scotch Road
Trenton, NJ 08628
609-882-4972

Holston United Methodist Homes
    for Children
1165 S. Church
Cleveland, TN 37311
615-476-8238
Fax: 615-624-1228

Holt International Children's Services
P.O. Box 2880
Eugene, OR 97402-0375
503-687-2202
Fax: 503-683-6175

Holt International Children's Services
3807 Pasadena Avenue
Suite 170
Sacramento, CA 95821
916-487-4658

Holt International Children's Services
2200 Abbott Drive
Carter Lake, IA 51510-1551
712-347-5911

Holy Cross Child Placement
    Agency, Inc.
929 Olive Street
Shreveport, LA 71104
318-222-7892
Fax: 318-222-7647

Holy Families Services
1403 S. Main Street
Santa Ana, CA 92707-1790
714-835-5551

Holy Family Services
155 N. Occidental Blvd.
Los Angeles, CA 90026-4641
213-387-1600

Holy Family Services
6851 Lennox Avenue
Van Nuys, CA 91405-4043
818-908-5069

Homes for Children
1447 Peachtree Street NE
Suite 511
Atlanta, GA 30309-3031
404-897-1766

Homestudies, Inc.
1182 Teaneck Road #101
Teaneck, NJ 07666-4825

Hope Adoption & Family Services
    International, Inc.
421 S. Main Street
Stillwater, MN 55082-5172
612-439-2446

Hope for Children, Inc.
1511 Johnson Ferry Road
Suite 100
Marietta, GA 30062
404-977-0813
Fax: 404-973-6033

Hope's Promise
309 Jerry Street, #202
Castle Rock, CO 80104-2442
303-660-0277

House of Samuel
2430 N. Sycamore Blvd.
Tucson, AZ 85712-2517

Idaho Youth Ranch Adoption Service
P.O. Box 8538
Boise, ID 83707-2538
208-342-6805

Infant of Prague
149 N. Fulton Street
Fresno, CA 93701-1607
209-237-3700

Innovative Adoptions, Inc
1850 Race Street
Denver, CO 80206-1116
303-355-2107

Institute for Black Parenting
3233 Arlington Avenue
Riverside, CA 92506-3246
714-782-2800

International Adoption Services
4940 Viking Drive
Suite 388
Minneapolis, MN 55435
612-893-1343
Fax: 612-893-9193

International Adoption Services
  Centre
P.O. Box 55
Alna, ME 04578
207-586-5058
Fax: 207-586-5057

International Alliance for Children
23 S. Main Street
New Milford, CT 06776-3507

International Assistance Group
21 Brilliant Avenue
Suite 201
Pittsburgh, PA 15215
412-781-6470

International Children's Services
2130 E. 4850 South
Salt Lake City, UT 84117-5252
801-272-0707

International Christian Adoptions
41745 Rider Way, #2
Temecula, CA 92590-4826
909-695-3336
Fax: 909-308-1753

International Concerns Committee
  for Children
911 Cypress Drive
Boulder, CO 80303
303-494-8333

International Families, Inc.
5 Thomas Circle NW
Washington, D.C. 20005-4153

International Family Services
700 S. Friendswood Drive
Suite B
Friendswood, TX 77546
713-992-4677
Fax: 713-992-3179

International Mission of Hope
3080 Shields Drive, #101
Eagan, MN 55121
612-687-0259
Fax: 612-688-6639

International Mission of Hope
8060 Emerson
Thornton, CO 80229
303-657-1875
Fax: 303-287-3325

International Social Services
390 Park Avenue South
New York, NY 10016
212-532-6350
Fax: 212-532-8558

Jewish Child Care Association
575 Lexington Avenue
New York, NY 10022
212-303-4722
Fax: 212-371-1275

Jewish Family and Children Services
1600 Scott Street
San Francisco, CA 94115-3014
415-567-8860

Jewish Family and Children's Service
10125 Verree Road
Suite 200
Philadelphia, PA 19116-3611

Jewish Family and Community
  Service
3601 Cardinal Point Drive
Jacksonville, FL 32257-5582

Jewish Family Services
1605 W. Peachtree Street NE
Atlanta, GA 30309-2641
404-487-2277

Jewish Family Services of Greater
  Springfield
5 Lenox Street
Springfield, MA 01108-2606
413-737-2601

Jewish Family Services of New Haven
1440 Whalley Avenue
New Haven, CT 06515-1144
203-777-6641

Journeys of the Heart Adoption
  Services
905 E. Main Street
Hillsboro, OR 97123
503-681-3075

Lake/Geauga Adoption Services
8 N. State Street, #445
Painesville, OH 44077-3904
216-946-7264

LDS
4320 Stevens Creek Blvd.
Suite 129
San Jose, CA 95129-1266
408-243-1688

LDS Social Services
5624 Executive Center Drive
Suite 109
Charlotte, NC 28212-8832
704-535-2436

Leap of Faith
22601 SE 322nd Street
Kent, WA 98042-7147
206-886-2103

Lee & Beulah Moor Children's Home
1100 E. Cliff Drive
El Paso, TX 79902-4625
915-544-8777

Life Adoption Services, Inc.
440 W. Main Street
Tustin, CA 92680-4324
714-838-5433
714-838-1160

Life Anew, Inca
2635 NE Loop 286
Paris, TX 75460-3444
903-785-7701

Lilliput Children's Services
1540 River Park Drive
Suite 107
Sacramento, CA 95815-4608
916-923-5444

Lilliput Children's Services
130 E. Magnolia Street
Stockton, CA 95202-1412
209-943-0530

Limiar
2373 Brunswick Lane
Hudson, OH 44236-1402
216-653-8129

Los Ninos International
1600 Lake Front Circle
Suite 130
The Woodlands, TX 77380-3600
713-363-2892
Fax: 713-363-2896

Love Basket
4472 Goldman Road
Hillsboro, MO 63050
314-789-4100
Fax: 314-789-4978

Love the Children
221 W. Broad Street
Quakertown, PA 18951-1267
215-536-4180

Love the Children
2 Perry Drive
Duxbury, MA 02332-3726

Lund Family Center
P.O. Box 4009
Burlington, VT 05406-4009
802-864-7467

Lutheran Child & Family Services
333 W. Lake
Addison, IL 60101
708-628-6118

Lutheran Children and Family
    Services
2278 Mt. Carmel Avenue
Glenside, PA 19038
215-881-6816
Fax: 215-884-3110

Lutheran Community Services
27 Park Place
New York, NY 10007-2589

Lutheran Counseling & Family Service
3800 N. Mayfair Road
Milwaukee, WI 53222-2213
414-536-8333

Lutheran Family & Children's Service
4625 Lindell Blvd.
Suite 501
Saint Louis, MO 63108-3796
314-361-2121

Lutheran Family Services in the
    Carolinas
P.O. Box 12287
Raleigh, NC 27605
919-832-2620
Fax: 919-832-0591

Lutheran Family Services of VA
Rt. 1, Box 417
McGaheysville, VA 22840
703-289-6141
Fax: 703-289-6141

Lutheran Family Services in the
    Carolinas
P.O. Box 21728
Columbia, SC 29210
803-750-0034
Fax: 803-731-1263

Lutheran Home
1 S. Home Avenue
Topton, PA 19562-1399
215-682-1504

Lutheran Ministries of Georgia Inc.
756 W. Peachtree Street NW
Atlanta, GA 30308-1138
404-607-7126

Lutheran Service Society
1011 Old Salem Road #107
Greensburg, PA 15601-1034
412-837-9385

Lutheran Social Ministries of NJ
120 Route 156
Yardville, NJ 08620-2202
609-585-0303

Lutheran Social Service
1855 N. Hillside Street
Wichita, KS 67214-2399
316-686-6645

Lutheran Social Service of Iowa
3116 University Avenue
Des Moines, IA 50311-3818
515-277-4476

Lutheran Social Services
57 E. Main Street
Columbus, OH 43215-5115

Lutheran Social Services
2414 Park Avenue
Minneapolis, MN 55404-2599
612-871-0221

Lutheran Social Services of the
    South, Inc.
314 Highland Mall Blvd., #200
Austin, TX 78752
512-454-4611

Lutheran Society Services of Illinois
6525 North Avenue, #212
Oak Park, IL 60302-1019
708-445-8341
Fax: 708-445-8351

Maine Adoption Placement Service
Market Square
Houlton, ME 04730-0772
207-532-9538
Fax: 207-532-4122

Maine Adoption Placement Service
1 Forest Avenue
Portland, ME 04101-3315
207-775-4101
Fax: 207-775-1019

Maine Adoption Placement Services
P.O. Box 2249
Bangor, ME 04402-2249
207-941-9500

Methodist Home of KY/Mary
    Kendall Home
193 Phillips Court
Owensboro, KY 42303
502-683-3723
Fax: 502-926-0817

Methodist's Children's Home Society
26645 W. 6 Mile Road
Detroit, MI 48240-2319
313-531-4060

Metrocenter for Family Ministries
P.O. Box 34
Edmond, OK 73083-0034
405-359-1400

Mid-South Christian Services
3100 Walnut Grove Road
Suite 104
Memphis, TN 38111-3530
901-454-1401

Morning Star Adoption Resource
    Services
2300 N. Woodward Avenue
Suite 9
Royal Oak, MI 48073-3752
810-399-2740

National Adoption Center
1500 Walnut Street
Suite 701
Philadelphia, PA 19102-3507

Nebraska Children's Home Society
3549 Fontenelle Blvd.
Omaha, NE 68104-3698
402-451-0787
Fax: 402-451-0360

New Beginnings Family & Children
141 Willis Avenue
Mineola, NY 11501-2655
516-747-2204

New England Home
161 S. Huntington Avenue
Boston, MA 02130
617-232-8610
Fax: 617-232-7925

New Families
15959 SW 172nd Avenue
Miami, FL 33187-1302

New Family Foundation
3408 Wisconsin Avenue NW
Suite 217
Washington, D.C. 20016
202-244-1400
Fax: 202-244-4029

New Hope Child and Family Agency
2611 NE 125th Street
Suite 146
Seattle, WA 98125-4357
206-363-1800
Fax: 206-363-0318

New Hope Family Services
3519 James Street
Syracuse, NY 13206-2350
315-437-8300

New Horizons Adoption Agency
P.O. Box 623
Frost, MN 56033
507-878-3200
Fax: 507-878-3132

New Horizons Foreign Adoption
	Service
2823 Woodland Drive
Bismarck, ND 58504-8925
701-258-8650

New Partners Inc.
8905 Bradley Blvd.
Potomac, MD 20854-4602
301-469-0476
Fax: 301-469-0361

New York Home Study Service
515 Oxford Street
Westbury, NY 11590-2428

North Bay Adoptions
9068 Brooks Road South
Windsor, CA 95492-7811
707-837-0277
Fax: 707-837-0280

Nurturing Family Growth
2960 N. Main Street
Danville, VA 24540
804-836-5433

Nurturing Family Growth
P.O. Box 4645
Lynchburg, VA 24502-0654
804-237-4195

Oliver/Sorano Group, Inc.
3343 Peachtree Road NE, #200
Atlanta, GA 30326-1022
803-370-2523

One Child at a Time
4040 Crabapple Lake Court
Roswell, GA 30076

Open Arms
6816 135th Court NE
Redmond, WA 98052-1829

Open Door Adoption Agency, Inc.
P.O. Box 4
Thomasville, GA 31799-0004
912-228-6339
Fax: 912-228-4726

Option of Adoption
504 E. Haines Street
Philadelphia, PA 19144-1215

Parent and Child Development
	Service
21 E. Broad Street
Savannah, GA 31401
912-238-2777
Fax: 912-238-2777

Parents and Adoptive Children
	Together (PAACT)
703 N. Market
Liverpool, PA 17045
717-444-3629
Fax: 717-697-1830

Parsons Child & Family Center
60 Academy Road
Albany, NY 12208-3103

Partners for Adoption
P.O. Box 2791
Santa Rosa, CA 95405-0791

Partners in Adoption
1050 Little River Lane
Alpharetta, GA 30201
404-740-1371

Pauquette Children's Services
P.O. Box 162
Portage, WI 53901-0162

Plan International Adoption Services
P.O. Box 667
McMinnville, OR 97128-0667
503-472-8452

Project Adopt
2915 N. Classen Blvd.
Suite 215
Oklahoma City, OK 73106-5471

Project S.T.A.R.
6301 Northumberland Street
Pittsburgh, PA 15217-1360
412-521-9000

Protestant Social Service Bureau
776 Hancock Street
Wollaston, MA 02170-2724
617-773-6203

Quality of Life, Inc.
10242 Crestover Drive
Dallas, TX 75229-6114
214-350-1637

Rainbow House International
19676 N. Highway 85
Belen, NM 87002-6381
505-865-5550

Rootwings Adoption Exchange
P.O. Box 96
Barre, VT 05641
802-223-0605

Sharing in Adoption
2 Springbrook Lane
Gorham, ME 04038
207-839-2934

Sierra Adoption Services
8912 Volunteer Lane
Suite 130
Sacramento, CA 95826-3224

Sierra Adoption Services
P.O. Box 361
Nevada City, CA 95959-0361

Small Miracles International
7430 SE 15th
Suite 204
Midwest City, OK 73110
405-732-7295
Fax: 405-732-7297

Small Miracles International, Inc.
550 S. Oliver Street
Wichita, KS 67218-2351

Small World Ministries
401 Bonnaspring Drive
Hermitage, TN 37076
615-883-4372
Fax: 615-885-7582

Small World Ministries
5213 Montrose Road
P.O. Box 5550
Knoxville, TN 37918
615-281-9499

Small World Ministries
130 E. Main Street
Maple Shade, NJ 08052
609-779-2776

Southeastern Adoption Services
P.O. Box 356
Marion, MA 02738-0356

Special Children, Inc.
910 N. Elm Grove Road
Suite 2
Elm Grove, WI 53122-2531

Spence-Chapin
6 E. 94th Street
New York, NY 10128-0612
212-369-0300

St. Andre Home
283 Elm Street
Biddeford, ME 04005
207-282-3351

St. Elizabeth's
2500 Churchman Avenue
Indianapolis, IN 46203-4613
317-787-3412

St. Mary's Services
717 W. Kirchhoff Road
Arlington Heights, IL 60005-2358
708-870-8181

Suncoast International Adoptions
P.O. Box 332
Indian Rocks Beach, FL 34635-0332
813-596-3135
Fax: 813-593-0106

Suncoast International Adoptions, Inc.
14277 Walsingham Road
Largo, FL 34644
813-596-3135

Sunny Ridge Family Center
3215 E. State Street
Rockford, IL 61108-1803

Sunny Ridge Family Center
9105a Indianapolis Blvd., #301
Highland, IN 46322-2504
219-838-6611

Sunny Ridge Family Center
2 S. 426 Orchard Drive
Wheaton, IL 60187

Tabor Children's Services
601 New Britain Road
Doylestown, PA 18901-2707

Tara Berkland
1003 Burleigh Street
Yankton, SD 57078
605-665-2036
Fax: 605-665-2036

Tennessee Baptist Children's Home
P.O. Box 728
Brentwood, TN 37024-0728
615-371-2000

Tessler Lutheran Services
836 S. George Street
York, PA 17403-3124
717-845-9113
Fax: 717-852-8439

Thursday's Child
227 Tunxis Avenue
Bloomfield, CT 06002
203-242-5941

Today's Adoption Agency
P.O. Box G
Hawley, PA 18428-0178
717-226-0808
Fax: 717-226-3760

Travelers Aid Adoption Services
909 4th Avenue
Room 630
Seattle, WA 98104-1194
206-461-3888

Triad Adoption, Inc.
100 N. 6th Street
Suite 402
Waco, TX 76701-2032
817-690-5959

Triad Adoption Services
2811 Indian School Road NE
Albuquerque, NM 87106-1825
505-266-0456

Trinity Adoption Services
    International
7610 Clublake Drive
Houston, TX 77095
713-855-0042

Unified Pan American
772 Congress Street SE
Washington, D.C. 20032-4105

United Methodist Counseling
    Services
1933 NW 23rd Street
Oklahoma City, OK 73106-1201

United Methodist Family Services
3900 W. Broad Street
Richmond, VA 23230-3958
804-353-4461

Universal Adoption Services
124 E. High Street
Jefferson City, MO 65101-2965

Universal Aid for Children
P.O. Box 610246
North Miami, FL 33261-0246
305-754-4886
Fax: 305-754-4725

Universal Family Services
P.O. Box 2505
Mill Valley, CA 94942
415-388-3561
Fax: 415-388-5923

Vermont Catholic Charities
351 North Avenue
Burlington, VT 05401-2921
802-658-6110

Vermont Children's Aid Society
32 Pleasant Street
Woodstock, VT 05091
802-457-3084

Vermont Children's Aid Society
P.O. Box 127
Winooski, VT 05404-0127
802-655-0006

Vermont International Adoption
    Agency
12 Pearl Street
Essex Junction, VT 05452
802-872-8434
Fax: 802-872-8233

Villa Hope
4 Office Park Circle
Suite 303
Birmingham, AL 35223-2539
205-870-7359
Fax: 205-871-6629

Vista Del Mar Child and Family
    Services
3200 Motor Avenue
Los Angeles, CA 90034-3710
213-836-1223

Voice of International and
    Domestic Adoption
354 Allen Street
Hudson, NY 12534
518-828-4527
Fax: 518-828-0688

Volunteers of America
    Maternity/Adoption Program
3900 N. Causeway, #700
Metairie, LA 70002
504-836-5225
Fax: 504-836-5233

Welcome House Adoption Services
P.O. Box 181, Green Hills Farm
Perkasie, PA 18944-0181

Wellspring Adoption Agency
1219 University Avenue SE
Minneapolis, MN 55414-2038
612-333-0489

Wide Horizons for Children
99 W. Main Street
New Britain, CT 06051-4222

Wide Horizons for Children Inc.
282 Moody Street
Waltham, MA 02154-5219

Williams-Illien Adoptions
3439 Venson Drive
Memphis, TN 38135
901-373-6003
Fax: 901-373-0130

WI Lutheran Child & Family Service
P.O. Box 23980
Milwaukee, WI 53223-0980
414-353-5000

Work Family Directions
930 Commonwealth Avenue
Boston, MA 02215-1274

World Association for Children
& Parents
315 S. 2nd
Renton, WA 98055

World Association for Children
& Parents
P.O. Box 88948
Seattle, WA 98138-2948
206-575-4550

World Child
13525 Point Pleasant Drive
Chantilly, VA 22021
202-829-5244
Fax: 202-291-4516

World Child
4300 16th Street NW
Washington, D.C. 20011-4228
202-829-5244

World Child
1400 Spring Street
Suite 410
Silver Spring, MD 20910
301-589-3271
Fax: 301-608-2425

World Wide Adoptions
P.O. Box 1073
14 Cleveland Avenue
Lily Dale, NY 14752
716-595-2060

Thomas Brosnan's Public Address

The following is the speech delivered by the Reverend Thomas F. Brosnan to the 1996 National Maternity and Adoption Conference. It is printed in its entirety and is a must-read for adoptees and anyone searching for a family member. Reverend Brosnan found his birth mother and father and continues to help others in their spiritual and emotional journeys for family by devoting his time to the quest for open records laws.

❖

This presentation is entitled Strengthening Families. *Through references to history, literature, film, and personal experience I will attempt to offer some suggestions on how adoptive families might fight the subtle and not-so-subtle forces which seek to weaken and destabilize the family unit. I will suggest that strength is born of the acknowledgment of truth, specifically an acknowledgment of truth about the experience of loss and the nature of belonging.*

By way of introduction, my name is Tom Brosnan. I am a Roman Catholic priest of the Diocese of Brooklyn, New York, where I presently live and work with Korean Catholics. I am no psychologist, pastoral counselor, or social worker; in other words, I'm no expert. My remarks come from my experience concerning my own adoption and that of other adopted persons, birth parents, and adoptive parents with whom I have worked over the past fifteen years. This presentation is, I suppose, a "confession" of sorts regarding my journey of discovering who I am—a process which, I would suggest, is the vocation of every human being, adopted or not.

Permit me to begin with a little background. In 1952 a young woman of twenty-five was living in a boardinghouse connected with the Peabody Conservatory of Music in Baltimore, Maryland. She was not a music student like her roommate or the rest of the inhabitants of the house, but was invited to stay there because there were few female boarders. She met a music student from Toronto, and they fell in love. She realized she was pregnant after her boyfriend had returned to Toronto at semester's end. She visited, she pleaded, but he said he could not, he would not marry her. Meanwhile another student from Peabody, a gallant young man from Virginia, who knew she was pregnant, offered to marry her. The other students, not knowing she was pregnant, had a bridal shower for her in their boardinghouse. Within a few weeks, however, she informed her friends that they decided not to marry. Becoming desperate, the young woman told her older brother she was pregnant with no hope of marrying. The brother, a Jesuit priest, arranged for her to go to New York to deliver and relinquish the baby for adoption. The priest, the boyfriend, the gallant Southerner, and her loyal roommate, Sophia, were the only ones who knew of her pregnancy. She delivered her child on January 10th, 1953, at Misericordia Hospital, then located in Manhattan, and immediately relinquished the boy to adoption. He waited in a foster home for six months and was eventually adopted by a couple from Brooklyn where he lived with them and his adoptive mother's parents in a small row house in Flatbush.

My parents told me I was adopted when I was twelve, though I can remember knowing since I was five. We never talked about adoption, yet it seems to me these many years later that adoption, with all its cumbersome baggage, was the air we breathed. We never acknowledged to each other the truth about the loss each of us suffered. We were, I believe, victims of the closed adoption system which exerts an extraordinarily powerful hold on all members of the triad. It is a cruel taskmaster and demands untold sacrifices. It is merciless in its destructive power. Like the razed Berlin Wall that divided a city for a generation, like the dismantled statues of Lenin across the Russias, I pray for the demise of the closed adoption system. And I offer these words in the hope to effect that outcome by alerting you who are adoptive parents, adoption specialists, social workers, and clergy to the dangers that secrecy and lies can wield on the family.

I love the movies. It's one of the few places I lose my self-control and permit myself to feel those difficult emotions which the experiences of loss and belonging evoke. One of my favorite films of all time is Cinema Paradiso, *an Italian film of a few years ago about a fatherless young boy from a small Sicilian town who befriends the movie-house projectionist. The boy learns to love movies while learning to love the older man who teaches him so much. When he is eighteen, he joins the army, and we see him standing with his mother and sister at the train station waiting for the good-byes to end. The old man is there, too. He whispers in the boy's ear: "Go, and never, never come back." The boy obeys. He goes to Rome and becomes a famous film director. He calls his mother now and then but keeps his promise never to return to his hometown. Then the old man dies, and the mother leaves a message on the son's answering machine telling him the day and time of the funeral. "You know he'll never come back," the skeptical sister tells the mother. But he does.*

On the day of his return the camera is focused on the mother as she sits in a rocker, nervously knitting. Slowly the camera closes in on the knitting needles, deftly moving back and forth, twining yarn and space. The camera focuses on her wrinkled hands and the long needles when in the background we hear a car pull up on the gravel path. Suddenly the hands stop, the woman quickly stands, unconsciously catching a piece of the yarn on her dress. The camera stays focused on the yarn as it unwinds with every step the mother takes toward the door. Then we hear the car door slam and the yarn ceases to unravel. We know without a word being spoken, or any visual image given besides the unraveling yarn, that mother and son have embraced after many lost years.

With this simple yet beautiful image I wish to remind you of something you already know: that the experience of loss and the need to belong are universal human experiences. But none of us likes to face the pain of loss, and we don't like to be reminded of it in others. When we are reminded, our immediate reaction is to make it go away, to lessen its obvious import to the person, to hopelessly put a mere bandage on what is doubtless a gushing wound.

The Catholic Bishops of the United States have done just that in their recently published Book of Blessings. *Among the many rituals is one entitled "Blessing for Parents and an Adopted Child." The prayer begins: "It has pleased God our heavenly Father to answer the earnest prayers of [this couple] for the gift of a child . . ." Despite the feeling of joy the words are meant to instill, there remains the unasked question, have the events which preceded this adoption ritual, namely the relinquishment of the child by his mother, has that also pleased God? What is missing is any reference to what has had to have taken place in order for this joyful blessing to occur. There is no mention, no acknowledgment of loss, of the relinquishment that had to have occurred in order for the adoption to have taken place.*

Although difficult, it is essential to acknowledge this fundamental truth about the experience of loss in adoption. It is not easy, however, and it is not a one-shot deal. It will have to be acknowledged at different times during the adoptee's maturing process, but I believe it to be essential in the building of strong, healthy families. Acknowledging truth about loss means first of all to give up the lies about what actually happened. It means giving up myths like the chosen baby story so many adoptees were told. It means to accept the events as are known, not fabricating explanations which we think might lessen the blow. You know what I mean: like the "your parents were killed in a car crash" story, intended to save the adoptee from the truth which we presume to be far worse: a truth like "your parents weren't married; or, your mother was raped; or even, you're the product of incest." If the adoptive parents truly have the best interest of their child at heart, I would suggest that the truth is the only choice they really have in attempting to do what's best for their son or daughter.

"There is no truth existing which I fear," Thomas Jefferson once wrote, "or [that I] wish unknown to the whole world." Another Thomas, many centuries prior to Jefferson, placed truth at the heart of what it means to be a human being. "For [Thomas] Aquinas, the most decisive human trait is that human beings are truth-seeking animals, moved by love for the truth [come what may]. . . . So inherent is this drive for the truth in human nature that it is an imperative . . . to address a human being in any lesser mode is to do his nature violence."

As H. David Kirk explained in his groundbreaking book on adoption, Shared Fate, *published nearly thirty years ago, there is at least one condition that each member of the adoption triad shares, and that is the experience of loss. Acknowledging the truth about loss is the beginning of mutual respect and love.*

There's a beautiful scene at the end of James Joyce's short story, The Dead. *Gabriel and his wife Gretta, married a number of years, have attended a dinner party. It's time to leave and Gabriel is about to call his wife, whom he sees at the top of the stairs. Her expression seems melancholy as she listens to the music coming from the next room. Gabriel knows that something profoundly important is taking place within Gretta at that moment. Observing her from the shadows kindles a renewed passion in Gabriel, for he assumes that he is the cause of her wistful look and tearful eye. Later in their hotel room Gabriel is keen on renewing that passion. He confidently asks Gretta what she was thinking about when he saw her as she listened to the old Irish ballad. It is then that Gretta breaks down and begins to sob uncontrollably. She tells her bewildered husband how long before she met him she was courted by a young man named Michael Fury who sang that same ballad to her beneath her window in the drenching rain the night before she was to leave for a convent school. Young Michael Fury caught his death that night, and she knew he died for love of her. This poignantly sad yet beautiful memory was Gretta's, but it was not Gabriel's. The cold reality that Gretta had a history before him is like a slap in the face to the middle-aged Gabriel. It was the tune of the ancient ballad that triggered the memory, and Gabriel realized he had no right to transgress such a sacred place.*

Not all, but many adoptive parents come to the adoption process through the loss we call infertility. Whether couples decide to adopt when they are first diagnosed or whether they come to that decision only after they have endured the horrors and humiliations of the fertility clinics, once they decide to adopt they have acknowledged the terrible reality that they will never have their own children. The decision to adopt marks the moment they give up their dream of seeing "flesh of their flesh and bone of their bone." What the infertile couple needs to do is acknowledge that the choice to adopt is their second choice. To admit to themselves that if they had their way adoption would most likely not be a part of their lives. They choose to adopt because there is no other way to become parents.

Acknowledging the truth of loss is also a part of the birth parents' lives, especially the mother. I believe there is no closer relationship than a mother and her unborn child. Perhaps you saw the movie Losing Isaiah. *Whether or not you liked the scenario, perhaps you would agree with me that even a crack-addicted woman feels that powerful bond with her child. The act of relinquishment is so wrenching an event that young women have told me that they chose to abort their babies rather than relinquish them to adoption. Some of us may judge this to be the height of selfishness, but I wonder if there is not some instinctual response involved in making that drastic decision. No matter what the reasons for relinquishment might be, the emotional response to the act of relinquishment is analogous to abortion, an unbloody abortion if you will, but as one prominent psychiatrist has written, "a psychological abortion" nonetheless.*

Maybe you remember the scandal that broke a few years back about the Irish bishop, Eamon Casey, who fathered a child some twenty years previous with a young American woman named Annie Murphy. Annie's family had sent her to the bishop to straighten out her life, but she ended up having an affair with the bishop and getting pregnant. The bishop arranged for her to go to a home for unwed mothers. When the time for delivery came they had a heated argument. Annie told the bishop she wanted to keep their child. The bishop was furious and said she must give the baby up for adoption. "The child was a mistake," Annie remembered the bishop saying. "He made it clear," she said, "that through the [relinquishment] of the child [she] would be cleansed." Thus the bishop believed, as do many religiously inclined people, that relinquishment is tantamount to the purifying fires of purgatory—a notion I would suggest not far removed from the response of those young women who chose abortion over adoption. There is, of course, another possible reason for the bishop's insistence on relinquishment. Once placed in the closed adoption system, his son would not be able to identify the bishop as his father.

In my biased opinion the greatest loss is suffered by the adopted person. I want to make it very clear, however, that adoption may indeed be in many, many cases a wonderful blessing for all involved. It may indeed be the only merciful solution to a seemingly impossible situation. Adoption can be one of the noblest of human achievements, but for the adopted person it is always, always the result of a tragic loss. I am not suggesting that problems within the adoptive family are the result of any lack of love on the part of parents, but simply saying that we must acknowledge the truth and not believe the false premise, the myth, which suggests that love conquers all. Because love does not conquer all, love cannot, love should not. "Love can neither eradicate biology," as one writer-adoptee has put it, "nor can love alter events which have already occurred." Let's not pretend that love can or should.

Adoption is a lifelong process, and it is at times hard work. The adoptive parents must acknowledge the truth of their infertility not only when first adopting, but years later when their child enters puberty and they begin to witness his or her sexual awakening with all its potential fecundity. They must face it each time their adoptive children have children. Adoption can make an infertile couple into the greatest of parents, but it can never make them fertile.

Adoption as relinquishment is a lifelong process for the birth mother. I've met a number of birth mothers who have never had any more children and others, like my mother, who had one child every year, year after year. Some birth mothers feel so guilty, it has been observed, they punish themselves by suppressing their fertility, while others seek to replace what was lost.

For the adoptee, life is adoption. I think this is true whether an adopted person admits it or not. There is always either an active curiosity about where you came from or a strong denial of any desire to know. If anyone asked me while I was in my teens or twenties if I wanted to know who my birth mother was, I would have vehemently said, "no, of course not." It took me over thirty years to realize what I needed to do. It is the adoptee's dilemma of belonging and not belonging, struggling between the need to know and misguided feelings of loyalty and gratitude.

I can never forget the experience I had when I began my search for my mother over ten years ago. Before I found her I discovered that her brother was a Jesuit priest who had died rather young at Georgetown University. One day I got in the car and drove down to Georgetown. I visited my uncle's grave and decided to ring the bell of the Jesuit residence. The priest who answered turned out to be not only my uncle's classmate but his best friend, having grown up with him in Philadelphia. Father Dineen was a very kind man, and I spent the entire day with him, listening to the many stories he longed to tell of my uncle and their friendship. After dinner he invited me to his room, "to see some old photos," he said. As we were about to open the album, it suddenly dawned on me that this would be the first time in my thirty-three years of life that I was to see someone related to me.

Just last week I had a similar experience when I met with my mother's room-mate, Sophia, the roommate she was living with when carrying me. This was our third meeting since my mother's death, and Sophia said she had brought me a present. She took out a photograph she said she found accidentally. It was a picture of both my mother and father, cheek to cheek, posing in one of those quick-picture booths. I secretly wondered as I studied their faces whether I was there, too, still unseen, but forever a part of their lives. The losses suffered in adoption are also always there, whether we acknowledge them or not.

Those of you not adopted no doubt take for granted the importance of growing up with people related to you, who look and act like you. Adoptees miss that very primal experience. I would suggest it is at the heart of the dilemma of the adopted person who feels on some level that he does not belong in his adoptive family. This does not necessarily have anything to do with either the abundance of love within the adoptive family or lack of it. It exists quite apart from the material well-being provided by the adoptive family. In adoption groups you often hear adoptees clas-sify themselves as "good adoptees" or "bad adoptees." The good ones never searched while their parents were alive; the bad ones were always running away. But when the adopted person does decide to search, he is looking to belong. The adoptee feels himself to be a literal misfit, not quite fitting in, misplaced somehow; in another manner of speaking, he feels himself to be an exile. Belonging and identity are synonymous for the adoptee, but he must initiate his search or at least acknowl-edge the desire to search for his identity, in order for the healing to begin.

A priest friend of mine once told me of his jarring experience when visiting a home for emotionally disturbed adolescents in Brooklyn. The priest walked into the home as a young man was singing the Irish ballad "Danny Boy." The young man had his back to the priest. When he finished, the priest went over and tapped the young man on the shoulder, thanking him for such a beautiful rendition of the sad song. The young man quickly turned, revealing an Asian face. The priest instinctively laughed: "I'm sorry," he said. "I thought you were Irish." The boy's eyes filled with tears and he angrily shouted back: "I am Irish. My name's Michael O'Brien."

The American Jesuit, John Courtney Murray, considered by many the greatest Catholic theologian America has yet produced, wrote this about identity: "Self-understanding is the necessary condition of a sense of self-identity and self-confidence . . . the peril is great. The complete loss of one's identity is, with all propriety of theological defin-ition, hell. In diminished forms it is insanity." Let me repeat that important insight: "The complete loss of one's identity is, with all propriety of theological definition, hell. In diminished forms it is insanity."

I suspect that everyone in this room today knows of Erik Erikson and his impor-
tant contribution to the knowledge of human development by his investigation
of developmental crises surrounding identity. Indeed, it was Erikson who
invented the term identity-crisis. *But I wonder how many know of his own*
experience of not belonging.

"Erikson's mother, a Danish Jew, never told Erik the true story of his origins,
wanting him to believe that her husband, the pediatrician Theodor Homberger,
was his father. As a boy growing up 'blond, blue-eyed, and flagrantly tall' in
Germany, Erik thought it strange that his father was short and dark. He was
acutely aware that he was referred to as a goy in his father's temple, while to
his schoolmates he was a Jew. He thought of himself as a 'foundling.' " Erikson
related this experience to Betty Jean Lifton, which she recounts in her recent
book Journey of the Adopted Self.

"Erik was in the Black Forest watching an old peasant woman milking a cow,
when she looked up and said, 'Do you know who your father is?' He was taken
by surprise. It was the first time anyone had said such a thing to him. He knew
she must have noticed how different he looked from his father. Like Oedipus, he
rushed to his mother to ask for the truth, [but] was given a half-truth. She
admitted he had been adopted by Homberger, whom she married on the day
Erik turned three. She spoke vaguely about having been abandoned by her for-
mer Danish-Jewish husband in Copenhagen while she was pregnant, and going
to Germany to give birth. Sensing her discomfort, and responding to his own
anxiety, Erikson submerged his need to know more about his father at that time.
In his adolescence he would hear rumors that his father was not his mother's for-
mer husband, but rather a Danish aristocrat whose name her brothers had sworn
never to reveal. When Erik journeyed to America he renamed himself on his
application for citizenship, calling himself Erik Erik-son. He had settled to cre-
ate himself." The search for identity and belonging can indeed be a very cre-
ative and fruitful process.

Names are an important aspect of the search to belong. Names are powerful and
mysterious entities. My mother told me she named me Thomas for her brother,
the priest. The story of that most famous of adoptees, Moses, is given in the Book
of Exodus. In Hebrew, however, the book is not called Exodus but rather the
Book of Names. In it the divine name is revealed, the revelation of who God
is. But it is also the story of who Moses is, a Hebrew raised Egyptian, and how
his search to belong was pivotal to the history of salvation. "My name is Michael
O'Brien," the young Asian man defiantly asserted. "The complete loss of one's

identity is, with all propriety of theological definition, hell. In diminished forms it is insanity."

In the acknowledgment of the truth about loss and the need to belong a word must be said about anger. The anger of the infertile couple at the loss of their dream: their intended children. The anger of the birth mother at the loss of her child: the relinquishment. In recent years we have seen, thank God, the anger of birth fathers whose rights are so often violated in the adoption process. And most significantly perhaps, the anger of the adopted person, who feels the extra-ordinary loss of parents, heritage, and genetic connection.

For some adoptees, anger remains suppressed; for others, it becomes destructive and even violent. I can never forget the day I went to the Catholic Home Bureau in Manhattan to see if I could get any information regarding my adoption. The nun sat calmly behind the desk, reading from the papers in front of her. She read me an account of my adoption and gave me the nonidentifying informa-tion I had requested. I knew she was not supposed to tell me my mother's name but I asked just the same. She said, of course, she could not give me the name but then asked in a tone of voice that triggered in me a cascade of rage: "Why would you want to know? Didn't you have a good adoption?" I realized that at that moment if I had had a gun I would have killed her. I am not exaggerat-ing here. I know for certain I would have killed. Perhaps that's what happened to Moses the day he saw the Egyptian beating the Hebrew, an event which trig-gered in him a cascade of rage, an anger that had been welling up all his life, intimately connected with his struggle over identity and belonging, and absolutely pivotal in the history of salvation.

Anger is a natural reaction to being hurt. Since adoption always involves loss for each member of the triad, and loss is a deep hurt, is it any wonder that there is a lot of anger permeating adoption? But anger can be a catalyst for positive change. In that great classic of western literature, The Odyssey, Homer gives us Odysseus, a man who is struggling to return to the place he belongs. Indeed, the theme of The Odyssey *could be summed up in one word: nostalgia, literally meaning the pain for home. The etymology of words here is interesting. The root of* nostal-gia *is* nostos, *meaning* home. It is also the root of noos, which may be rendered consciousness. At the end of the saga Odysseus confronts his enemy, Antinous, who was conspiring to rob Odysseus of wife, home, and property while Odysseus was on his journey. The bloody scene in which Homer describes how Odysseus kills Antinous is quite powerful. And what does the name Antinous mean? It means anti-noos, against consciousness; Antinous stands for oblivion. It is

Odysseus' anger, his brutal rage, that enables him to slay Antinous. In this Odysseus rejects oblivion, that state of unawareness, and comes to consciousness— he regains home and family. Anger can be the catalyst which brings to consciousness the acknowledgment of the deep loss the adopted person has experienced, and so lets him begin the healing process, his odyssey towards home.

A word of anger must be raised against what might be called the mark of illegitimacy. Society labels those born illegitimate bastards. *You may think it strange that I, as an illegitimately born individual, am ambiguous about this designation. On the one hand, I disdain the state and the church for creating such a designation because of its repercussions. In order for me to be ordained a priest I had to request special dispensation because bastards could not receive Holy Orders. That has recently changed, but the psychological effects of such a designation always remain. On the other hand, it is argued that the closed adoption system was created to protect the child from the mark of illegitimacy. If that is true (though I am not convinced it is the real reason for sealed records), then I would prefer to be labeled a bastard and be able to see my birth certificate than continue to be denied that fundamental right. In any event, my parents were not married, and so I am born in different status. But I am in good company and feel a certain kindred spirit with other bastards of history. And there are many: Erasmus, Leonardo da Vinci, Pope Clement VII, to name a few.*

"I'll tell you something," a famous American once wrote a friend in strictest confidence. "I'll tell you something, but keep it a secret while I live. My mother was a bastard, was the daughter of a nobleman so-called of Virginia. My mother's mother was poor and credulous, and she was shamefully taken advantage of by the man. My mother inherited his qualities and I hers. All that I am or hope ever to be I got from my mother, God bless her. Did you never notice that bastards are generally smarter, shrewder, and more intellectual than others? Is it because it is stolen?"

So wrote Abraham Lincoln of his mother, Nancy Hanks. But there's still more to the story. Lincoln always feared that his mother never properly married Thomas Lincoln. President Lincoln died before the marriage certificate he had requested years before had been found. It was discovered some years later, but some now think that document a forgery. And still a further twist to Lincoln's story. Many people and, according to his closest friend, even Lincoln himself believed not only that Nancy Hanks never really married Thomas Lincoln, but that Thomas Lincoln was not his actual father. A few years back I was touring the South with a friend who was visiting from England. As we were visiting the home of Jefferson Davis, the President of the Confederacy, I remarked to my friend that I couldn't believe they had the gall to hang a picture of Abraham Lincoln in the hallway. The guide overheard me and said, "Oh, so many people say the same thing, but that's not Lincoln, it's Jefferson Davis." The resemblance was uncanny, and indeed some believe that it was Samuel Davis who fathered both Jefferson Davis and Abraham Lincoln. How does the radio commentator put it: "Now you know the rest of the story."

I can't fail to mention Jesus himself in this regard, because I believe Jesus knew the mark of illegitimacy. I think there is ample proof in the gospel texts to suggest that many believed Jesus to be a bastard, as is asserted in later Jewish apologetic works written to refute Christianity. For those of you who are Christian and have a hard time accepting the Virginal Conception, that is, the belief that Jesus' father was God Himself, and so settle for accepting Joseph as Jesus' real father, I would submit you are on shaky ground, because the gospels suggest, for some unmentioned reason, that it was obvious Joseph could not have been Jesus' father. This poses a dilemma for the struggling believer: either Jesus was Son of God or he was the bastard son of a Roman soldier, as the later Jewish texts assert. In any event, Jesus would have known what it felt like to bear the mark of illegitimacy.

A word of anger must also be raised against the closed adoption system and sealed records. Closed records, while purporting to insure confidentiality for the birth mother, mean that I as an adopted person have no right to my own name. Sealed records rob me of my name, my heritage, my medical history, and any connection to those related to me by blood. My question is this: Is the practice of closed adoption, which separates child from mother without the child's consent, which suppresses knowledge of family heritage and genetic connection, which refuses to reveal the child's name even to the child himself, are these any different from the methods employed by the institution of slavery? Who can honestly deny that it constitutes, at the very least, a psychological slavery or, as Dr. Leston Havens of Harvard put it, "a psychological possession of the human being"?

And a word of anger must be raised against the myth of confidentiality. Lawyers, social workers, and church officials assert that confidentiality was promised to the birth mother, and a promise given cannot be breached. But then, I ask, why was my name, that is, the name given to me at birth by my birth mother, that is, my mother's surname—why was that name printed on the very adoption papers given to my adoptive parents if indeed the state wished to assure my birth mother of confidentiality? Why? Because confidentiality for the birth mother was not really ever intended. It is a myth.

When I testified some months ago before the New Jersey Legislature in favor of a bill to open records, the most vocal and powerful opponent was the New Jersey Catholic Conference, representing the Catholic Bishops of New Jersey. A word of anger must be raised against the hypocrisy of the Catholic Bishops of New Jersey who testified that the "dark secret"—these are their words, not mine—the "dark secret" of the relinquished child's birth must remain so because of the supposed confidentiality promised to the birth mother. Thus the bishops argue that a woman does indeed have a right to privacy from her own child. I wonder if Planned Parenthood and the abortion rights movement realize they have such powerful allies in the Catholic Bishops of New Jersey?

Further, maintaining that "dark secret" permits church officials to release false baptismal certificates, misleading the adopted person either into believing he was baptized twice or leading him to believe that the name he now uses is indeed his baptismal name, while in many cases it is not. How do church officials, particularly the Catholic Bishops of New Jersey, justify such hypocrisy and outright lies? All because a mother has a right to privacy from her own child, the bishops argue.

If the National Council for Adoption lobby gets its way and the proposed Uniformed Adoptions Acts are legislated across this country, virtually anyone will be permitted to contract adoption with little or no supervision. Vacant wombs will be rented out, babies will continue to be contracted for, children bought and sold: all protected under the guise of confidentiality. The scenario of a Lisa Steinberg may not be the exception, but the rule.

The adoption reform movement has attempted over the years to correct what seems to many members of the triad a terrible injustice. I would suggest that the injustice of closed adoption is based on a philosophy of life we call dualism. Dualism sees everything in black and white; everything is reduced to an either/or dichotomy. This virus of dualism invaded the psychology of adoption early on and remains active yet: "Psychology emphasized environment rather than heredity as a more important factor in child development," Linda Burgess reminds us in her book The Art of Adoption. *"Parents saw the chance to erase in their adopted children the hereditary components which, it was assumed, were of dubious quality . . . the personality and character of the child could be molded and their adopted children would become as if born to them."*

Today, as near-daily discoveries are made in genetic research, we are coming to appreciate the great impact of heredity in human development, not only in its obvious physical results but in the psychological and even emotional temperament of the individual. And it becomes increasingly obvious that the human person is not the isolated product of either genetics or heredity, but rather the continuing result of a very complex interplay of inherited traits and environmental conditioning.

Dualist thinking invades our religious life and beliefs about human life. It undermines the proper relationship between body and soul, spirit and flesh. It distorts our vision and teaches us to disdain the body. It abhors the flesh; it loathes things sexual. And if adoption is about anything, it is about sex, about the uncontrollable urges of first love or even the violent urges of adolescence. Dualist thinking teaches us to regard everything in the adoptees' history prior to the adoption as dark and dirty, to be forgotten and purged. Dualism is the preeminent denier of truth. True religion, on the other hand, seeks to embrace the tension between body and soul, spirit and flesh. Religion, according to the great Catholic theologian von Balthasar, is "the renewed bonding of previously separated parts." St. Teresa of Avila, the great Spanish mystic, put it this way: "For never, however exalted the soul may be, is anything else more fitting than self-knowledge. . . ." The adopted person's search for his origins is then a religious experience. It is a spiritual journey, a pilgrimage of self-knowledge, a holy endeavor.

The search is undergone in order to gain the experience of integrity, of wholeness, of health. The Latin root of the word salvation *is* salus, *meaning* health. *And the English words* wholeness *and* holiness *are more closely related than simply their shared sound. In the adopted person's search for origins, in his drive for the truth, and through his desire to belong, he becomes the paradigm, the sacrament if you will, of Everyman. "You have made us for Thyself, O Lord," St. Augustine wrote some fifteen hundred years ago, "and our hearts are restless until they rest in Thee."*

Malcolm Muggeridge, the British journalist turned Christian, wrote in his memoirs: "the first thing I concluded about the world—and I pray it may be the last—is that I was a stranger in it. . . . For me," Muggeridge said, "there has always been—and I count it the greatest of blessings—a window that never finally blacked out, a light never finally extinguished. Days or weeks or months might pass. Would it never return—the lostness? I strain my ears to hear it, like distant music; my eyes to see it, a very bright light far away. Has it gone forever? And then—ah! the relief. Like slipping away from a sleeping embrace, silently shutting the door behind one, tiptoeing off in the gray light of dawn— a stranger again. The only ultimate disaster that can befall us, I have come to realize, is to feel ourselves at home here on earth. . . ."

Walker Percy, another Catholic writer, touches on this parallel feeling of belonging and not belonging in his novel The Moviegoer. *It is a story about a man who is searching for meaning in life. It takes place in 1960 or so in New Orleans over the course of the week which ends on Ash Wednesday. Near the end of the novel the main character is sitting with a friend in his car in front of a church. He notices a car driven by a black man pull up behind them.*

> *A florid new Mercury pulls up behind us and a Negro gets out and goes into the church. He is more respectable than respectable; he is more middle-class than one could believe: his Archie Moore mustache, the way he turns and, seeing us see him, casts a weather eye at the sky; the way he plucks a handkerchief out of his rear pocket with a flurry of his coattail and blows his nose in a magic placative gesture (as if to say "you see, I've been here before, it's a routine matter") . . . [Later] he has come outside. His forehead is an ambiguous sienna color . . . it is impossible to be sure that he received ashes. When he gets in his Mercury, he does not leave immediately but sits looking down at something on the seat beside him. A sample case? An insurance manual? I watch him closely in the rearview mirror. It is impossible to say why he is here. Is it part and parcel of the complex business of coming up in the world? Or is it because he believes that God himself is present here at the corner of Elysian Fields and Bons Enfants? Or is he here for both reasons: through some dim, dazzling trick of grace, coming for one and receiving the other as God's own importunate bonus? It is impossible to say.*

"We shall not cease from exploration," T. S. Eliot mused, "and the end of all our exploring will be to arrive where we started and know the place for the first time."

When an adopted person is permitted and encouraged to search for his genetic connections, for his origins, a paradox occurs: he may well end up realizing that he rightfully belongs in two places, that he does indeed have two sets of parents.

I began this presentation with a simple cinematic image. Permit me to end with another from the film Empire of the Sun. *It's about a British boy who is living in Shanghai with his parents when the Japanese are about to invade. In the mass confusion of the Europeans' exodus, the boy is separated from his parents and spends his adolescence in a prisoner-of-war camp. It is the last scene of the movie which strikes a deep resonance within me. The war is over and parents of lost children have come to the Red Cross camp in the hope of finding their lost children. We see a group of youngsters huddled in a circle, adults moving slowly through them, desperate to find their missing children. The boy's father passes without recognizing him. His mother does the same, but then returns and studies the boy's haggard, weary face, and then she calls his name. The camera first focuses on the boy's face, then fixes solely on his eyes. The boy is so tired, he cannot even blink. He seems catatonic, his glassy eyes the windows to a worn and weary soul. The boy's mother embraces him. Then, and only then, the creased wrinkles around those eyes begin to relax and the boy finally, gratefully, slowly closes his eyes. The wandering, the worrying, the searching, is at an end. I wonder if this is what St. Augustine meant when he said, "our hearts are restless until they rest in Thee." I wonder if this is what that ancient prayer for the dead is meant to convey when we pray at burial: "Eternal rest grant unto them O Lord. . . ."*

And so permit me to conclude with a prayerful invocation of sorts, a plea to the patron saint of this beautiful city, St. Anthony of Padua. By what trick of grace are we all here today, I wonder, because you know St. Anthony is the patron saint of both the barren and the pregnant. Strengthening adoptive families is about acknowledging the permanence of infertility and the responsibility of an unwanted pregnancy.

And St. Anthony is, as all Catholics know, the founder of things lost. My father is sadly now in the beginning stages of Alzheimer's, and I try to sleep at their house often. The other night I got up early to leave and discovered my car keys missing. I realized that my father had taken them and would not remember where he put them. My mother said: "Say a quick prayer to St. Anthony," which I did just as my father picked up something on the counter, and there the keys were.

Coming to San Antonio has been an especially good experience for me because my cousin and his family live here. My cousin and his wife have been under a great deal of stress these last few days because their teenage daughter ran away. I felt so badly for them, but I really didn't know what to do until I visited the Cathedral of San Fernando yesterday and saw a statue of St. Anthony. I lit a candle and asked St. Anthony to find my cousin's daughter. That very afternoon my cousin called to tell me that they found their daughter at a friend's house, safe and sound. St. Anthony, founder of the lost, can be a powerful ally to those of us who know what it means to lose something or someone. Strengthening adoptive families is about the acknowledgment of loss: the loss of children, the loss of parents, the loss of one's heritage and genetic connection.

St. Anthony is often pictured holding the Christ child in loving adoration. He adores Jesus as both divine and human, holding the tension of Jesus' true identity, his dual nature, without sacrificing the importance of one for the other. St. Anthony does not settle for an either/or solution. Perhaps St. Anthony is after all the best guide we could have to help us reject that dualism which forces us to think of adoption as an either/or dichotomy, having to choose between environment and heredity, and help us to embrace the creative tension found in each adopted person.

For in the adopted person is found a disquieting paradox that reminds all of us we are truly orphans. Adoption plays a mysterious trick on us, but I believe it a trick of grace. In the adopted person one may very well find the ground-of-being where sex and love have intercoursed—the sacrament, if you will, of the fusion of nature and grace.

Thank you for your kind attention.

❖